AF618272

Working Title (Digging) *26*
Works on Paper

*Of the various versions of these works, only one or a selection is listed here. / Diese Arbeiten wurden in verschiedenen Versionen ausgeführt, von denen hier nur eine oder eine Auswahl genannt ist.

CEAL FLOYER
A HANDBOOK

KUNSTMUSEUM BONN
AARGAUER KUNSTHAUS, AARAU

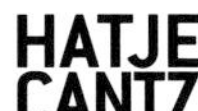

CONTENTS
INHALT

Light Switch
1992

35 mm slide, slide mask, slide projector with 70–120 mm lens / 35-mm-Dia, Diamaske, Diaprojektor mit 70–120-mm-Objektiv
Slide projection, installation / Diaprojektion, Installation
Image dimensions variable / Bildmaße variabel
Several unique country-specific versions / Mehrere länderspezifische Versionen (Unikate)

A projector stationed approximately fifty centimetres from the wall (i.e., at 'arm's length') points to a space where one might expect to find a light switch and projects a slide of a switch—specifically, the kind of switch that would be found in the country where the work is shown. The light switch is depicted in its 'on' position.

Montage of a selection of *Light Switch* versions:
Light Switch –
British – Japanese – German
American – Irish – French
Italian – Turkish

Ein Projektor ist in einer Entfernung von ca. 50 Zentimetern (eine Armlänge) auf einen Wandbereich gerichtet, wo man einen Lichtschalter erwarten kann, und projiziert das Dia eines Lichtschalters auf die Wand. Es handelt sich dabei immer um einen Schalter, der für das Land typisch ist, in dem die Arbeit gezeigt wird. Der Lichtschalter wird in der »An«-Position gezeigt.

Montage einer Auswahl verschiedener *Light Switch* Versionen:
Light Switch –
British – Japanese – German
American – Irish – French
Italian – Turkish

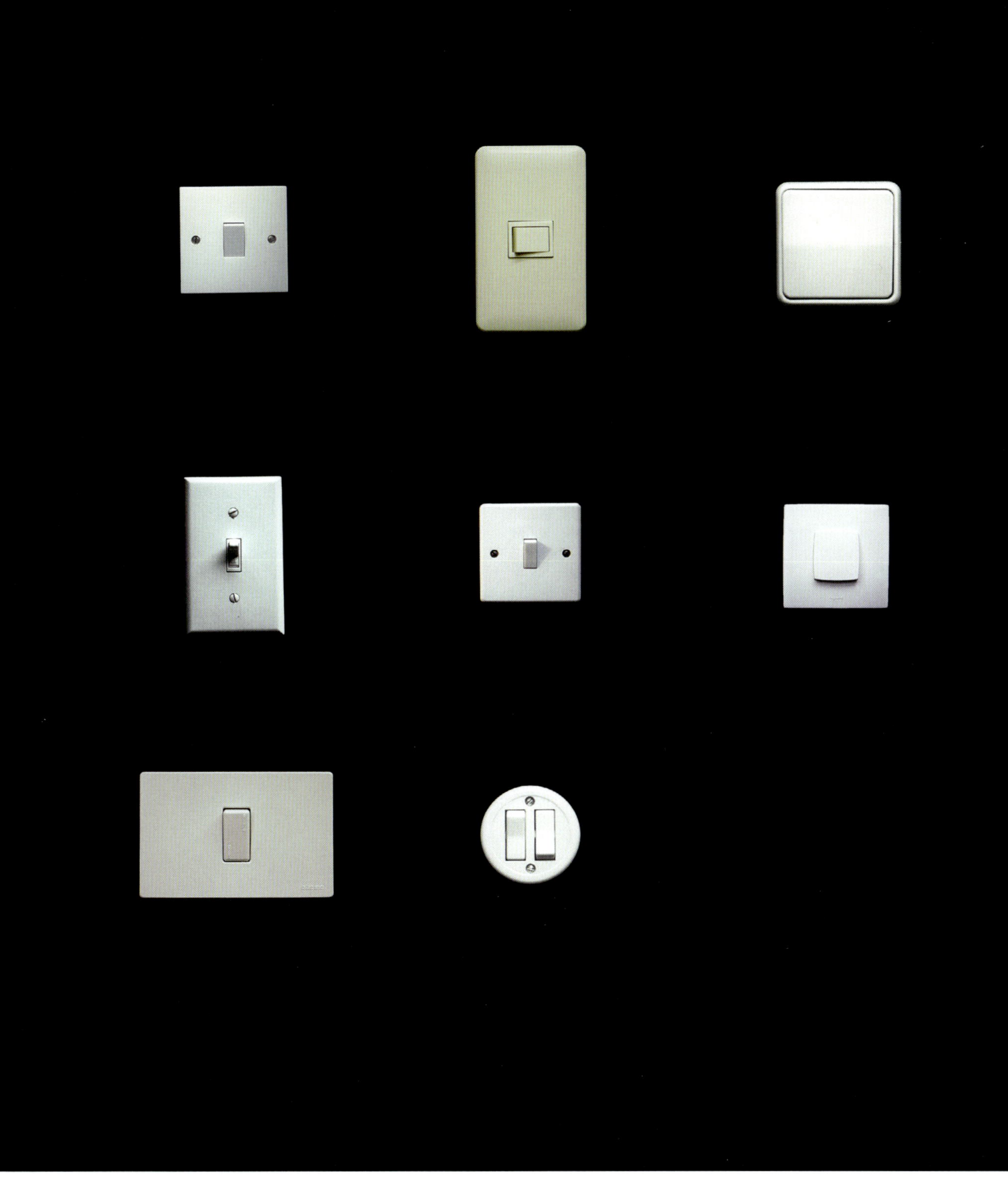

Long Distance (Diptych)
1993

2 slide masks, 2 slide projectors, double projector table / 2 Diamasken, 2 Diaprojektoren, Projektortisch für 2 Projektoren
Light projection / Lichtprojektion
Dimensions variable / Maße variabel
3 + 2 AP

Two slightly touching circles of light, mimicking a binocular viewfinder, are created by two slide projectors placed adjacent on a double projector table at some distance from the wall.

Installation views: Museion, Bolzano, 2014

Zwei nebeneinander auf einem Projektortisch positionierte Diaprojektoren stehen relativ weit von der Wand entfernt, auf die sie zwei kleine, sich leicht berührende Lichtkreise werfen.
Die Lichtprojektion imitiert den klassischen durch Ferngläser gesehenen Bildausschnitt.

Installationsansichten: Museion, Bozen, 2014

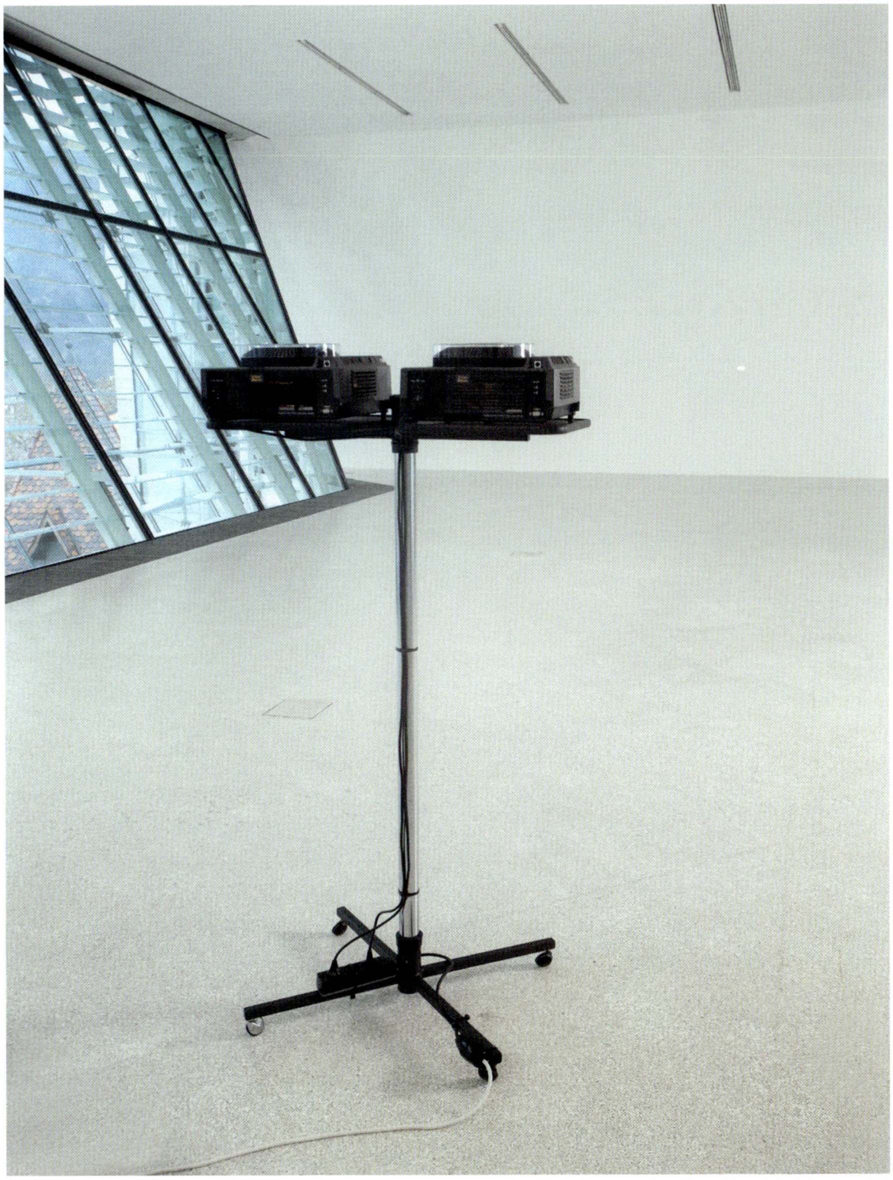

Untitled Installation (Dotted Line)
1993

Slide, slide viewer, plinth, transfer foil /
Dia, Diabetrachter, Sockel, Transferfolie
Installation
Dimensions variable / Maße variabel
3 + 2 AP

A space is edged discreetly with a continuous dotted line. A slide viewer showing a slide of scissors is placed on a plinth. Through the positioning of the work's components in the space, the line registers only retrospectively.

Installation views: Hamburger Bahnhof – Museum für Gegenwart, Berlin, 2013;
KW Institute for Contemporary Art, Berlin, 2009 (Detail lower right)

Alle Wände eines Raumes sind von einer feinen, gestrichelten Linie unmittelbar entlang der Raumecken und -kanten eingefasst. Ein Diabetrachter auf einem Sockel zeigt das Dia einer Schere. Durch die Anordnung der einzelnen Elemente des Werks im Raum registriert man die Linie erst im Nachhinein.

Installationsansichten: Hamburger Bahnhof – Museum für Gegenwart, Berlin, 2013;
KW Institute for Contemporary Art, Berlin, 2009 (Detail rechts unten)

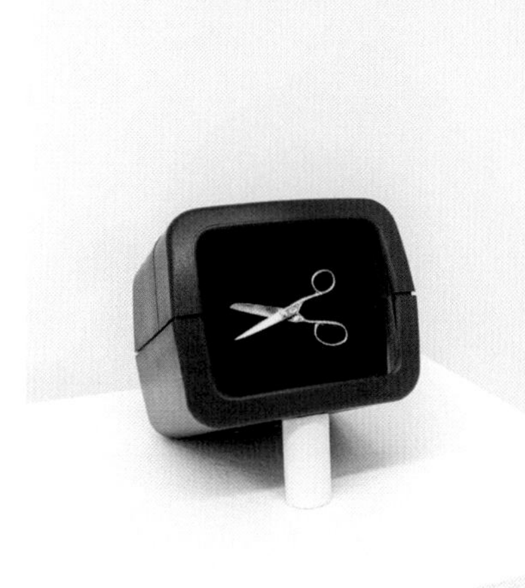

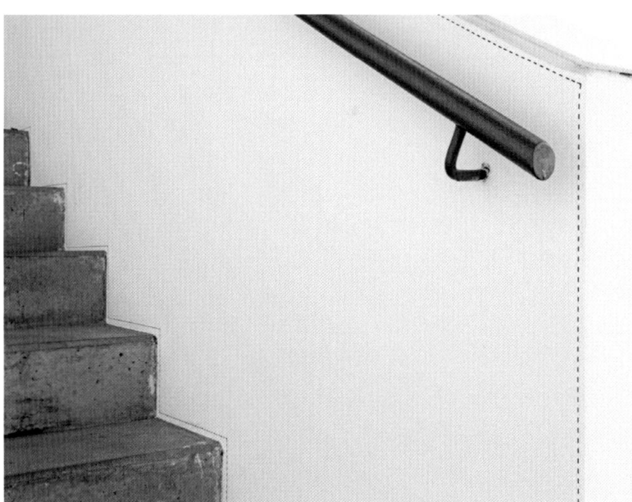

Light
1994

Light bulb, matte white paint, disconnected cord, 4 slide projectors, 4 metal slide masks / Glühbirne, matt weiße Farbe, abgetrenntes Kabel, 4 Diaprojektoren, 4 Metall-Diamasken
Installation
Dimensions variable / Maße variabel

A light bulb is lit from four sides by slide projectors with slide masks cut with a light bulb shape. The cord is visibly cut off.

Installation views: Museion, Bolzano, 2014

Eine Glühbirne wird von vier Seiten von Diaprojektoren mit Diamasken beleuchtet, die auf die Form der Glühbirnen zugeschnitten sind. Das Kabel der Glühbirne ist deutlich sichtbar abgetrennt.

Installationsansichten: Museion, Bozen, 2014

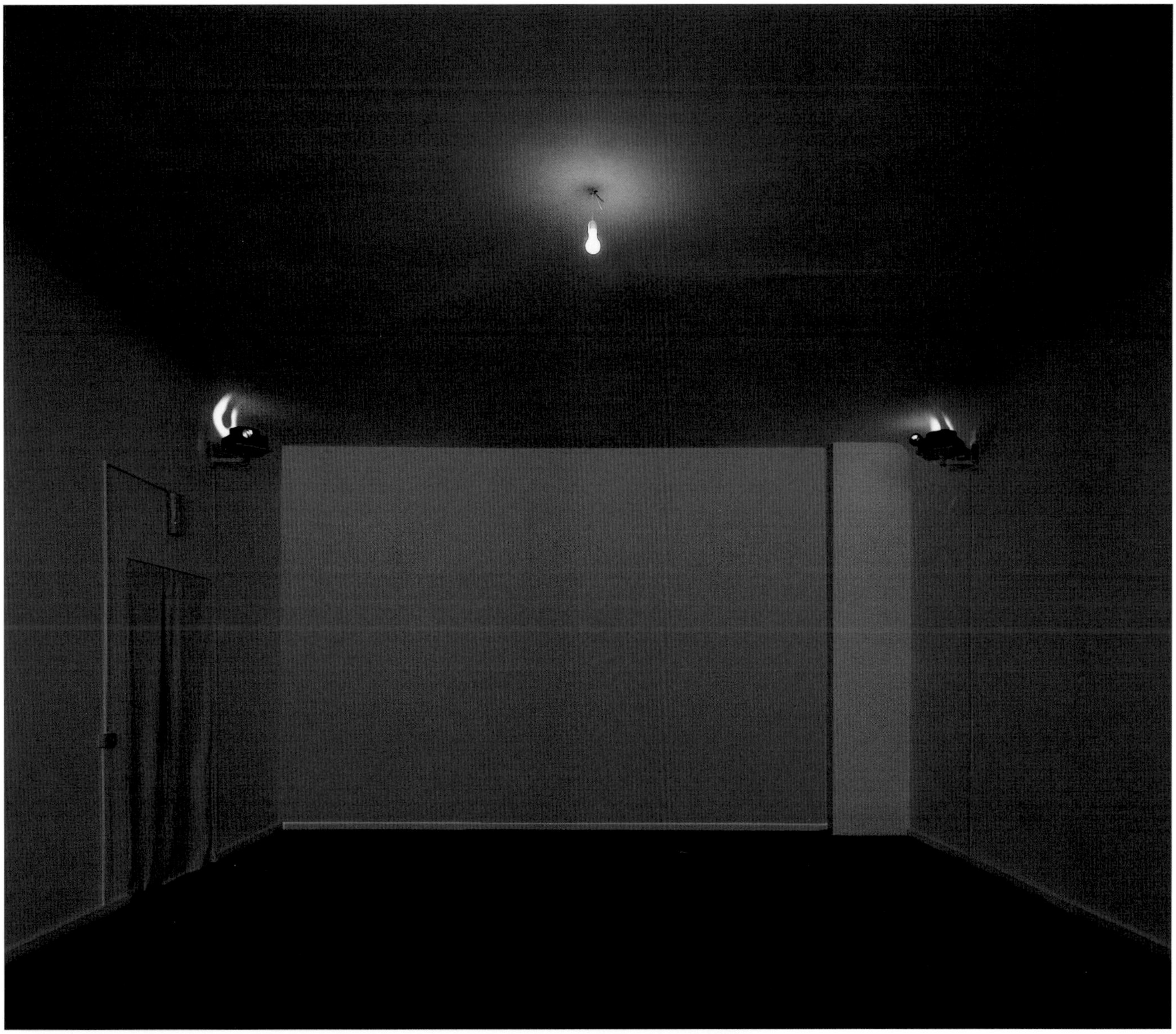

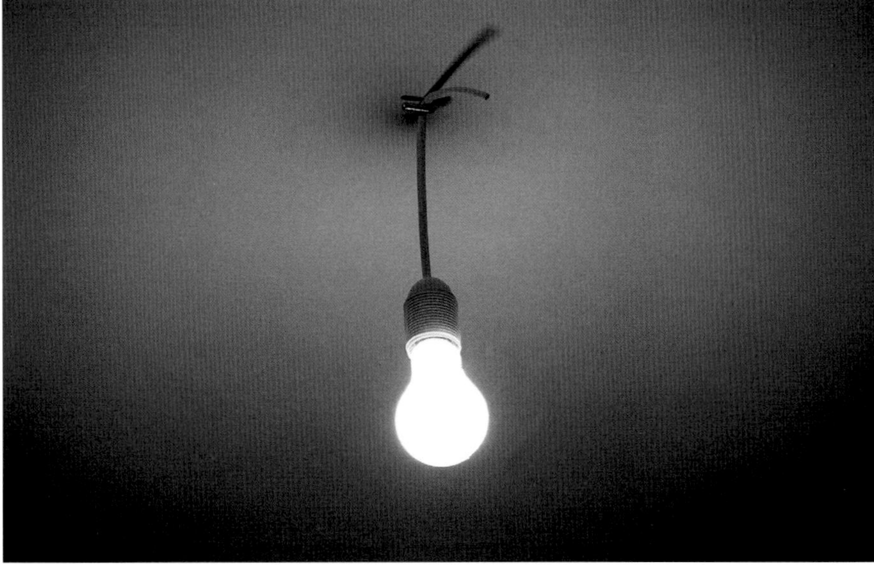

Pushed / Pulled
1994

Door plates / Türschilder
Installation, intervention / Installation, Intervention
Dimensions variable / Maße variabel
Unique object / Unikat

The 'push / pull' plates on a door (or double doors) are replaced by modified plates reading 'pushed / pulled'.

Installation view: Goldsmiths, University of London, 1994

Die Schilder »push« / »pull«, – »Drücken« / »Ziehen« – an einer Tür oder Flügeltür sind auf beiden Seiten der Tür durch modifizierte Schilder mit der Aufschrift »pushed« / »pulled« ersetzt.

Installationsansicht: Goldsmiths, University of London, 1994

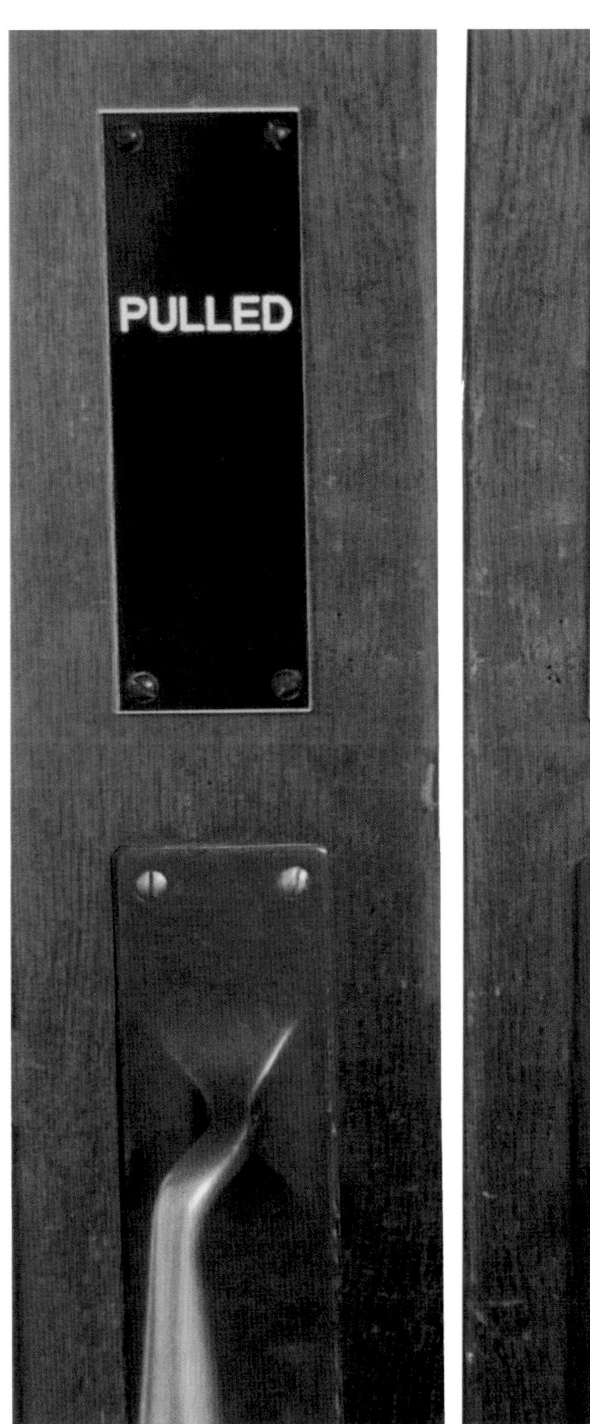
PULLED
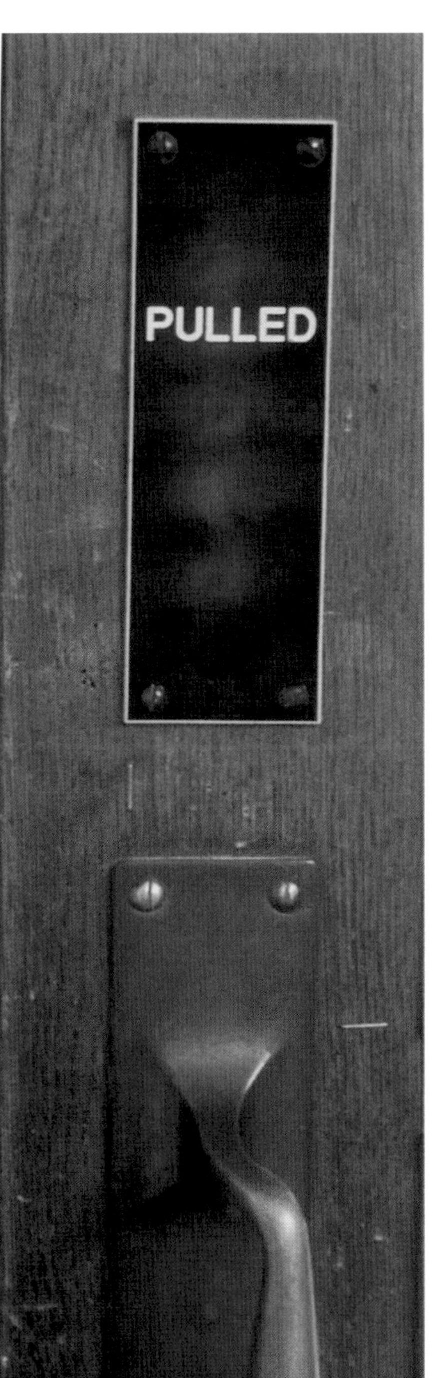
PULLED

Door
1995

35 mm metal slide mask, slide projector with 70–120 mm lens / 35-mm Metall-Diamaske, Diaprojektor mit 70–120 mm Objektiv
Projection / Projektion
Dimensions variable / Maße variabel
5 + 2 AP

A fine horizontal strip of light is projected onto the bottom of a door. The projector is on the floor, approximately two metres away.

Installation view: Kunstmuseum Basel – Museum für Gegenwartskunst, 2008

Ein feiner horizontaler Streifen Licht wird auf die untere Kante einer Tür projiziert. Der Projektor steht ca. 2 Meter entfernt auf dem Boden.

Installationsansicht: Kunstmuseum Basel – Museum für Gegenwartskunst, 2008

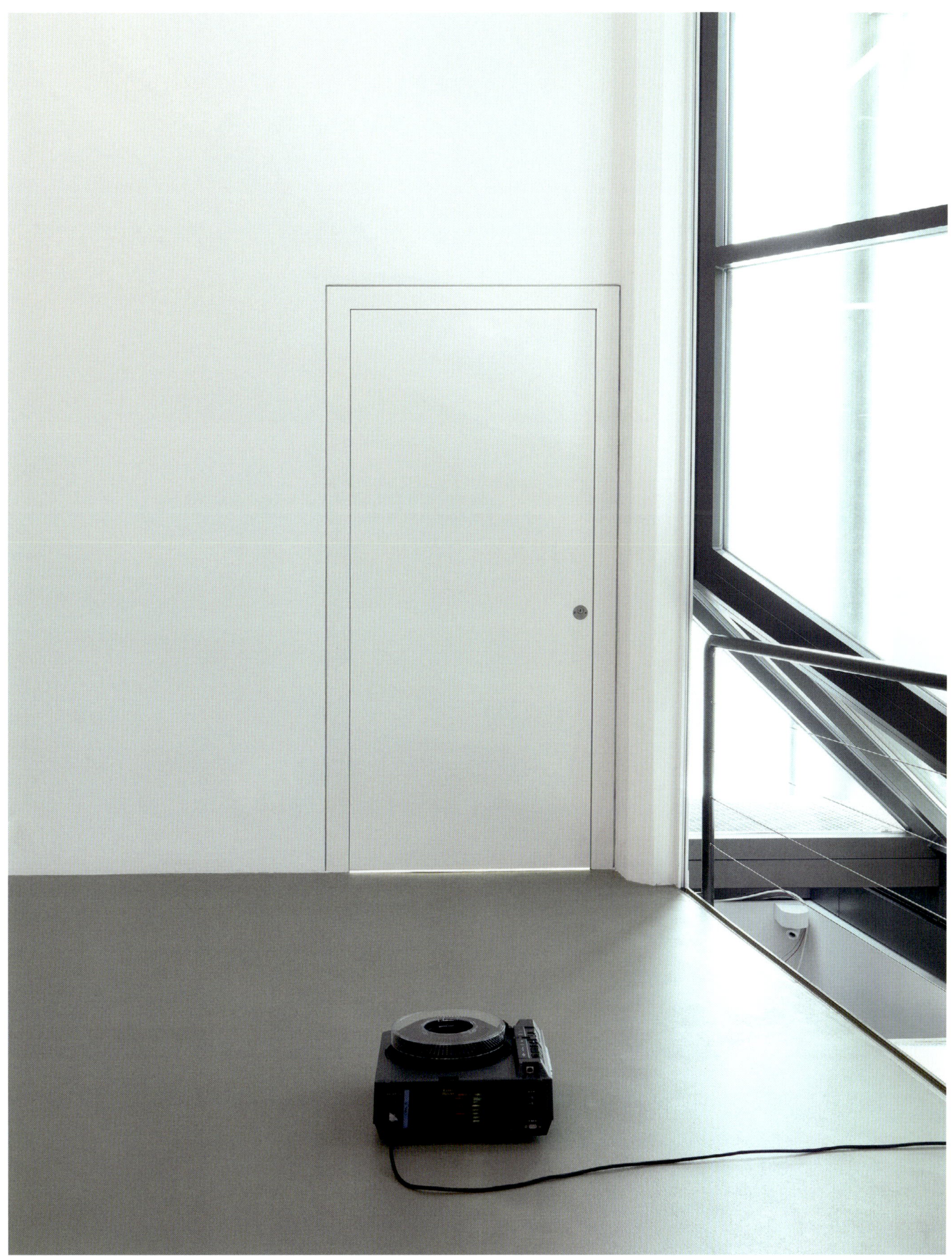

Unfinished
1995

DVD, DVD player, projector /
DVD, DVD-Spieler, Projektor
Projection loop, without sound /
Projektionsschleife ohne Ton
5 + 2 AP

A silent film loop showing two twiddling thumbs is projected onto a ninety-degree corner. The work is installed on the threshold of an entrance hall, foyer, or other space intended primarily for waiting or passing through.

Installation view: Kunsthalle Bern, 1999

Auf die Ecke einer niedrigen Wand ist eine Stummfilmschleife projiziert, die zwei sich umeinander drehende Daumen zeigt. Die Arbeit wird in einer Eingangshalle, einem Foyer oder in einem Warteraum oder Durchgangsbereich gezeigt.

Installationsansicht: Kunsthalle Bern, 1999

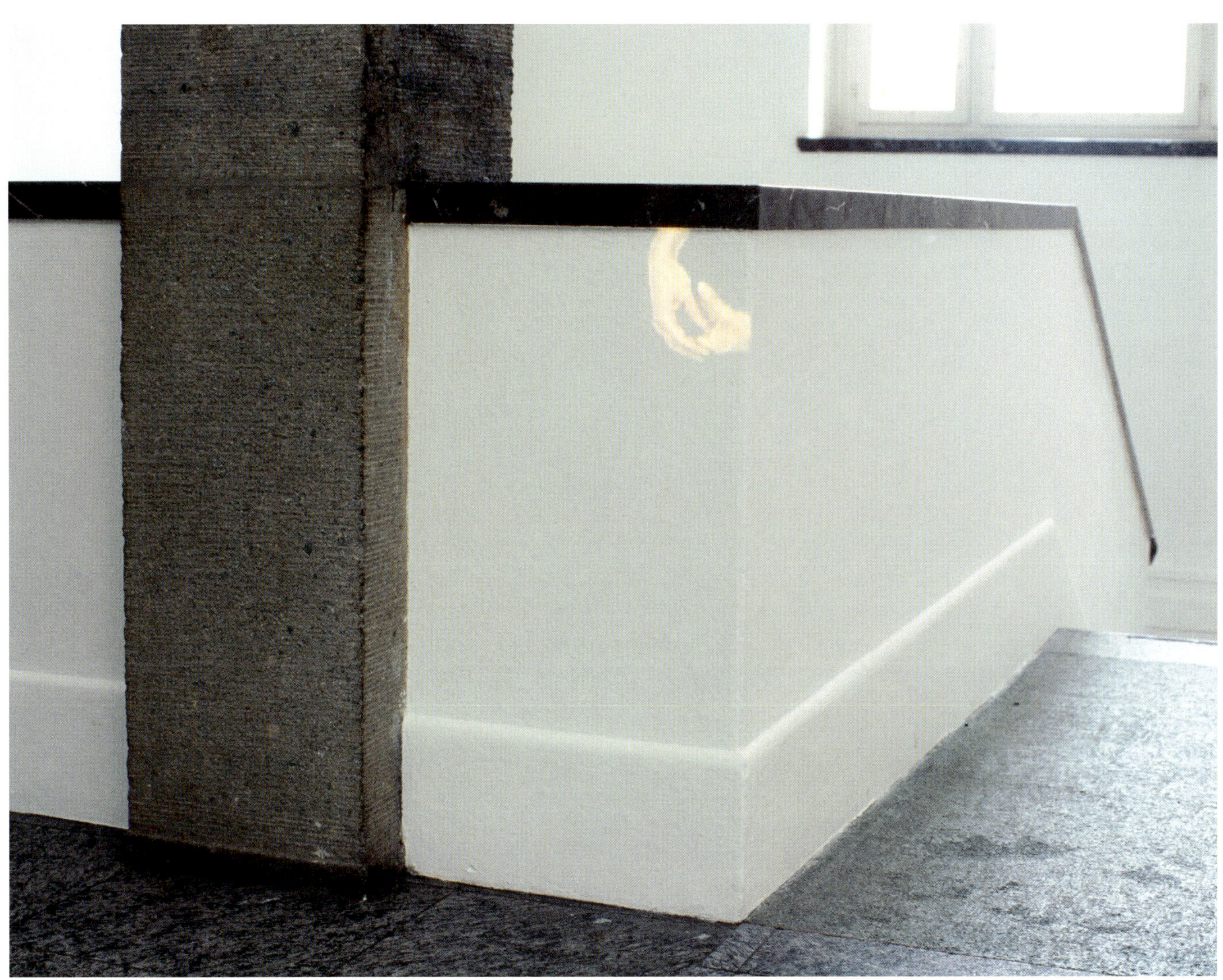

Working Title (Digging)
1995

CD, CD player, amplifier, 2 speakers, black cables / CD, CD-Spieler, Verstärker, 2 Lautsprecher, schwarze Kabel
Audio sculpture, installation / Audioskulptur, Installation
Dimensions variable / Maße variabel
5 + 2 AP

In this audio installation, one speaker emits the sound of a shovel digging and the other the sound of earth hitting the ground. Both speakers are placed face up on the floor on different sides of the room. The distance between the speakers is defined by the audio trajectory of the perceived action.

Installation view: Cristina Guerra Contemporary Art, Lisbon, 2004

Aus einem der Lautsprecher hört man das Geräusch einer grabenden Schaufel und aus dem anderen das Geräusch von Erde, die auf den Boden fällt. Beide Lautsprecher stehen auf dem Boden und sind zur Decke ausgerichtet. Sie sind in einiger Entfernung voneinander platziert, wobei der Abstand zwischen ihnen durch die Flugbahn der akustisch wahrgenommenen Aktion definiert ist.

Installationsansicht: Cristina Guerra Contemporary Art, Lissabon, 2004

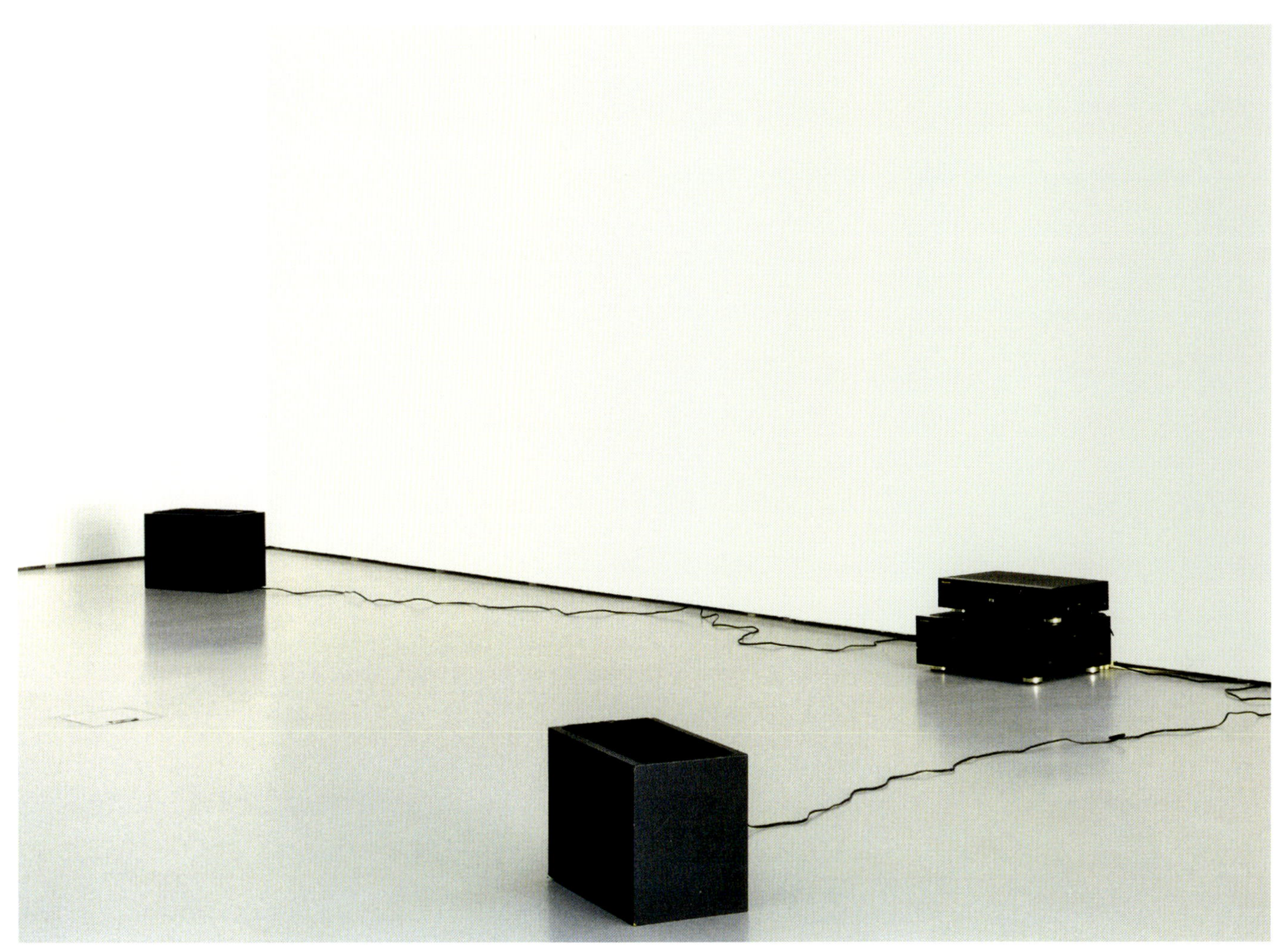

Garbage Bag
1996

Black plastic garbage bag, air, twist tie /
Schwarzer Plastik-Müllsack, Luft, Bindedraht
Installation
Dimensions variable / Maße variabel
5 + 2 AP

Tied shut and apparently full, a garbage bag is placed close to a doorway. It is filled with air.

Installation view: Lisson Gallery, London, 1997

Ein scheinbar gefüllter, zugeschnürter Müllsack steht in der Nähe einer Tür. Darin ist Luft.

Installationsansicht: Lisson Gallery, London, 1997

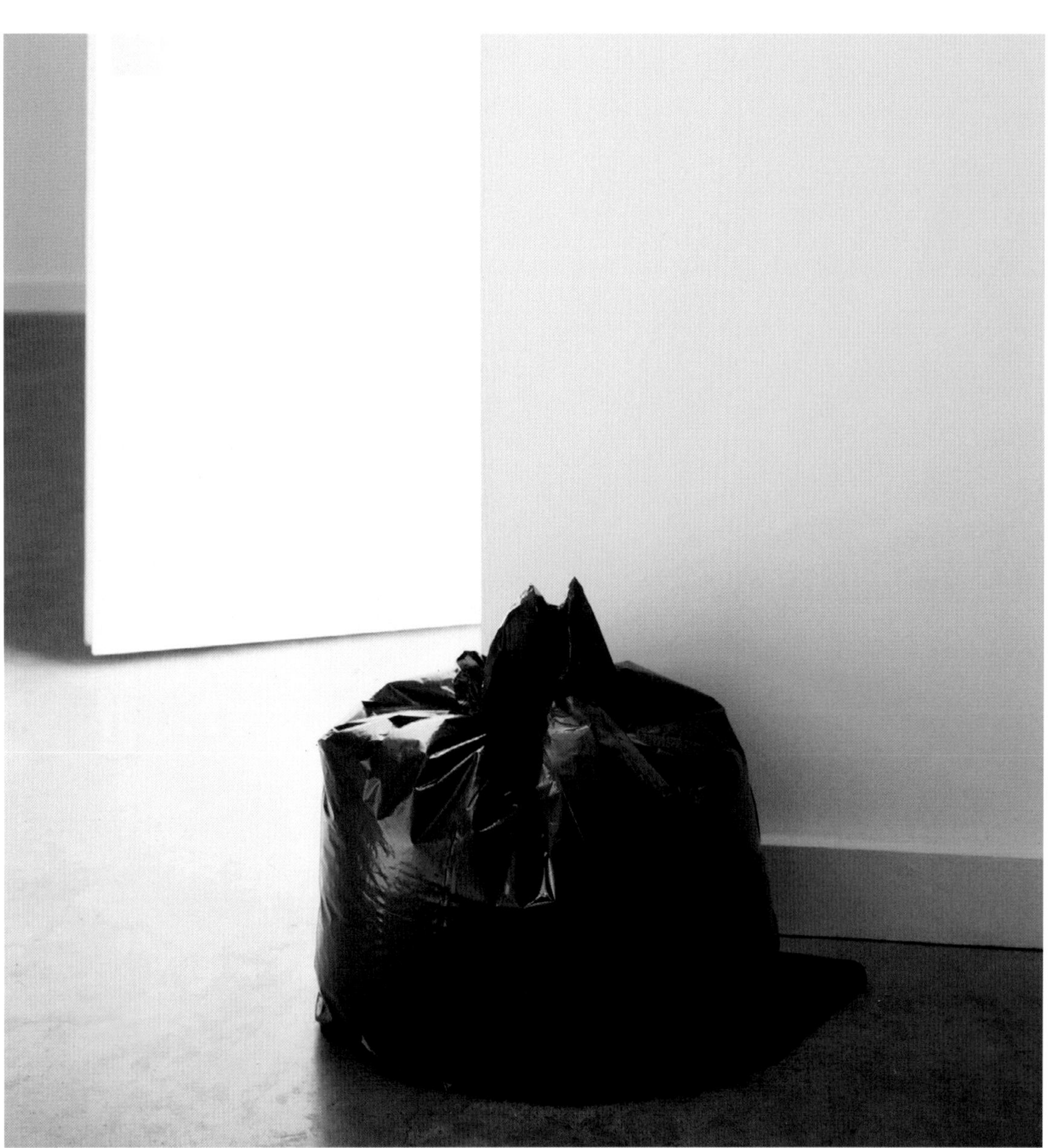

Sold
1996

Cadmium red oil paint in drilled hole /
Cadmiumrote Ölfarbe in gebohrtem Loch
Wall-based work / Wandarbeit
Diameter / Durchmesser: 7 mm
5 + 2 AP

A hole in the wall is filled with cadmium red oil paint. The hole is the size of the iconic red sticker indicating that a work of art has been sold. It is positioned beside the bottom right corner of a painting.

Installation view: Museum für Moderne Kunst, Frankfurt am Main, 2005

Das mit cadmiumroter Ölfarbe gefüllte Loch in der Wand hat die Größe der Aufkleber, mit denen angezeigt wird, dass ein Werk verkauft ist. Es ist neben die rechte untere Ecke eines Bildes platziert.

Installationsansicht: Museum für Moderne Kunst, Frankfurt am Main, 2005

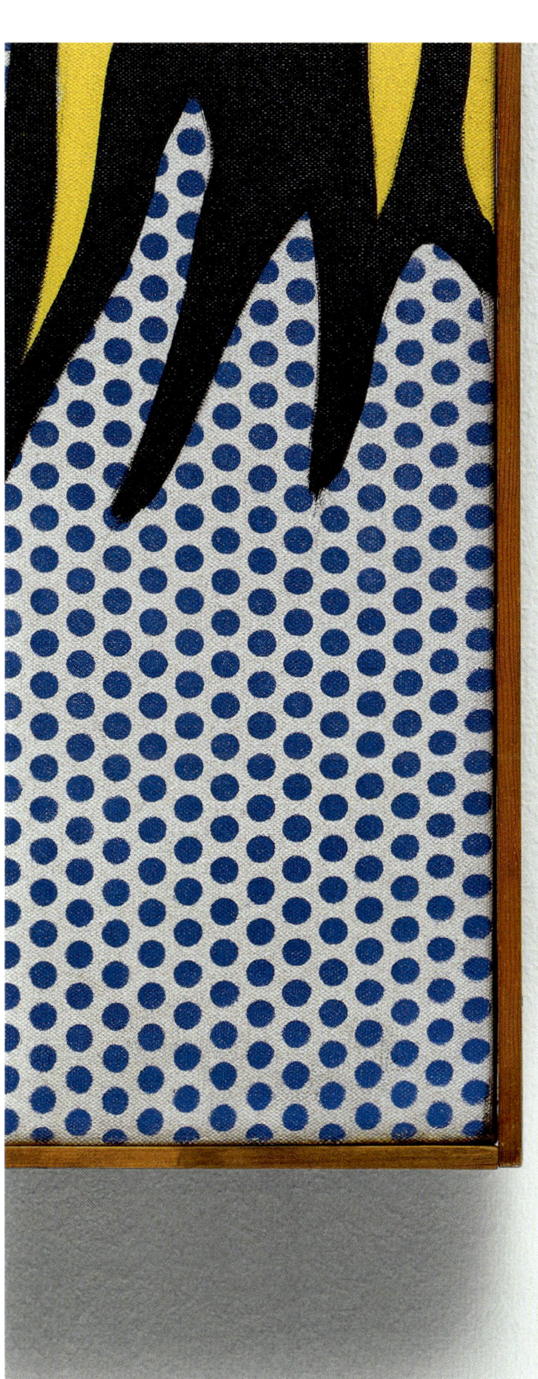

Blind
1997

Video monitor, video player, video /
Video-Bildschirm, Video-Spieler, Video
Video on monitor, loop without sound /
Video auf Bildschirm, Projektionsschleife ohne Ton
Duration / Dauer: 30´
3 + 2 AP

The thirty-minute video, presented on a monitor, depicts a static shot of an open white Venetian blind. The blind sways so that one can sometimes see the black window frame behind it. It becomes obvious that the window is open and that the blind is moving because of the draft.

Installation view: Madre · Museo d'arte contemporanea Donnaregina, Naples, 2008

Das englische Wort »blind« bedeutet sowohl »blind« als auch »Blende« oder »Jalousie«. Das 30-minütige Video, das auf einem Monitor präsentiert wird, zeigt die statische Einstellung einer weißen, lichtdurchlässigen Jalousie. Die Jalousie schwingt, sodass sich manchmal der Fensterrahmen als schwarze Kontur abzeichnet. Man erkennt, dass das Fenster offen steht und die Jalousie durch den Luftzug bewegt wird.

Installationsansicht: Madre · Museo d'arte contemporanea Donnaregina, Neapel, 2008

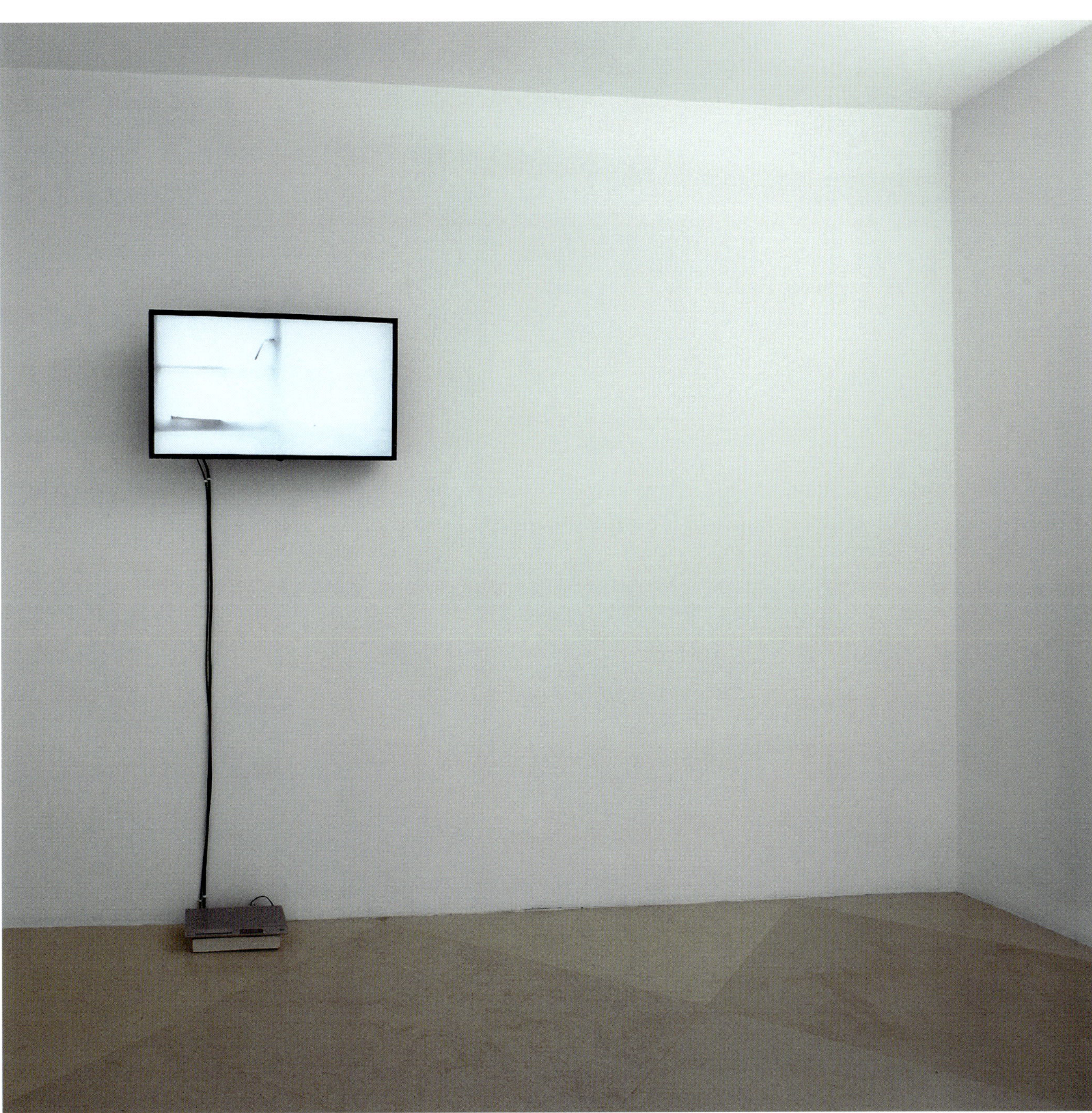

Monochrome Till Receipt (White)
1998

Ink on paper, 3M spray mount /
Tinte auf Papier, 3M-Sprühkleber
Work on paper / Arbeit auf Papier
Dimensions variable / Maße variabel
10 unique country-specific versions /
10 länderspezifische Versionen (Unikate)

A supermarket receipt is attached to the centre of a white wall: a document of the exclusively white products purchased locally by the artist shortly before the presentation of the work.

A selection of *Monochrome Till Receipt (White)* versions:
Monochrome Till Receipt (White) – British – Norwegian – German

Ein Supermarkt-Kassenzettel, mittig auf einer weißen Wand fixiert, ist ein Dokument der ausschließlich weißen Produkte, die die Künstlerin unmittelbar vor der Präsentation vor Ort gekauft hat.

Eine Auswahl verschiedener *Monochrome Till Receipt (White)*-Versionen:
Monochrome Till Receipt (White) – British – Norwegian – German

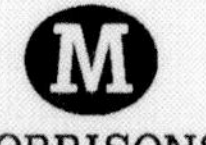

MORRISONS

Fresh choice for you

Wm MORRISON
Supermarkets plc BD3 7DL
Camden
Manager : Jim Donovan
Telephone : 0207 4280405
Vat No : 343475355

Today
Don't forget your
reusable bags

DATE: 09/06/2009 TIME: 17:53
TILL: 0011 NO: 01198386
You were served by: NAEEM

DESCRIPTION	£	
ALLINSON FLOUR	1.52	D
KRAFT PHILADELPHIA	1.33	D
'M'HADDOCK PORTIONS	3.99	D
ORGANIC CHOCOLATE	1.75	A
WHITE KIDNEY BEANS	1.19	D
PICKLED EGGS	1.15	D
NIVEA SHOWER	1.89	A
CAULDRON TOFU	1.09	D
PURA VEGETABLE OIL	0.70	D
CAREX	1.35	A
BOIL IN THE BAG RICE	1.77	D
DENTEK FLOSSERS	2.93	A
KORBOND WHITE THREAD	0.79	A
NIVEA HAND CREAM	2.17	A
'M'F/H CUTLERY SET	0.87	A
'M' ORGANIC MILK	0.53	D
ALKA SELTZER	2.50	A
'M'TISSUES	1.93	A
JOHNSONS BABY POWDER	0.94	A
NIVEA FOR MEN	1.94	A
SIMPLE SOAP	0.90	A
LONGLEY FARM YOGURT	0.75	D
LILLETS COMPACT	1.88	B
GALBANI MOZZARELLA	1.49	D
'M'VALUE CLOTHS	0.45	A
'M'CREME FRAICHE	0.98	D
'M'30 PAPER DOYLEYS	0.87	A
*Tableware Offer	-0.24	
'M'SWING BIN LINERS	1.69	A
SENSODYNE PASTE	2.40	A
SEA SALT	2.09	D
'M'POCKET TISSUES	0.93	A
'M' MOZZARELLA BLOCK	2.38	D
AUSSIE SHAMPOO	3.40	A
'M'GRANULATED SUGAR	0.51	D
GLOWHITE	1.82	A
'M'VALUE T/BRUSHES	0.20	A
WRIGLEYS GUM	2.09	A
COMFORT NATURALS	1.45	A
'M'COTTON WOOL PADS	0.54	A
'M'PLASTIC PLATES	0.87	A
MINT IMPERIALS	0.83	A
POLYESTER ELASTIC	0.97	A
'M'SILVERSKIN ONIONS	0.89	D
NIVEA SHOWER	1.89	A
'M' FACE CLOTHS	0.97	A
KORBOND HOOK & LOOP	1.75	A
'M'COTTON WOOL BUDS	0.38	A
SAVLON CREAM	1.61	A
ANDREX 2 ROLL	1.25	A

Items Sold: 49 TOTAL £70.32

CASH £80.00

Change £9.68

VAT A 15.0%	(£46.08):	£6.01
VAT B 5.0%	(£1.88):	£0.09
VAT D 0.0%	(£22.36):	£0.00
VAT Total		£6.10

MULTISAVE
£0.24
SAVINGS
AT MORRISONS

Thank you for shopping at Morrisons
Please call again

ICA Aker Brygge
Holmensgt 7
TLF. 22 01 78 60
ORG.NR. NO 931186744 MVA

Operatør nr. 9. Aria
Kvitt. 1024. 20.05.15 12.25 Kasse 4

MAKE UP PADS 80STK	6.90	N
KONVOLUTT C5	14.90	N
STEINBITFILET OPPTINT	97.51	M
TOALETTPAPIR 16RL	69.90	N
JASMINRIS 1KG	30.90	M
DOVE KREMSÅPE	18.90	N
TAMPAX REGULAR	29.90	N
NEUTRAL MASK.VASK	54.90	N
BOMULLSPINNER J&J	23.90	N
KLEENEX BALM MINI	26.90	N
AVFALLSPOSE	10.90	N
ZENDIUM FRESH+ WH	36.90	N
GARDSEGG L/M 6STK	26.90	M
OPPVASKBØRSTE ICA	14.50	N
BLOMKAL STK	19.90	M
CHAMPIGNON HEL PK	6.90	M
HVETEMEL	11.90	M
KREMFLØTE 0,75L	49.90	M
MALDON SALT	42.50	M
RISENGRØT VELBEK.	28.90	M
CREME FRAICHE	23.90	M
FISKEPUDDING	10.50	M
STORE HVITE BØNNER 380G ICA	10.50	M
AIOLI 200ML	41.50	M
Q-LETTMELK 1L	16.50	M
SETERRØMME	26.50	M
YOGHURT NATURELL	37.50	M
HVITLØK 20*100 GR	9.90	M
SUPERBRA RISOTTO	49.90	M
PHILADELPHIA OST	32.90	M
PETROU 250G	62.90	M
GRESK FETA	40.90	M
BÆREPOSE PLAST	0.99	N
BÆREPOSE PLAST	0.99	N

TOTAL 989.19
Term:982-008009
SWE:2755999
Eurocard
************7886
20/05/2015 12:25
AID:A0000000041010
TVR:0000008000
TSI:E800
REF:217234540883 686
RESP:00 497510 Ca1 7
Personlig kode

VAREKJØP 989,19
TOTAL NOK 989,19

GODKJENT
BEHOLD KVITTERINGEN

MASTERCARD, TERM. 989.19
Tilbake 0.00

Type	Brutto	Mva-%	Mva	Netto
N	310.48	25.00	62.10	248.38
M	678.71	15.00	88.53	590.18

---

* Ha en fin dag *
Takk for handelen!
Velkommen igjen.

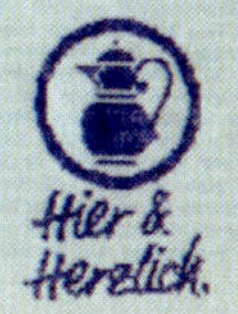

Hier & Herzlich.

ANNENSTR. 4a
10179 BERLIN
TEL.: 030 / 2756000
www.kaisers.de

		EUR
PILZE	2	1,99
BIO FENCHEL	2	3,49
RETTICH W.	2	0,99
SILBERZWIEB.	2	0,69
MIRACEL WHIP	2	1,29
WEISS.BOHNEN	2	2,49
TOFU NATUR	2	2,49
HUETTENKAESE	2	1,09
ZAZIKI 250G	2	0,89
MOZZARELLA	2	0,99
PHILADELPHIA	2	1,39
EIER 10ER	2	1,09
KABELJAUFIL.	2	4,49
FR.ALP.MILCH	2	1,09
KNOBLAUCH	2	1,29
GAENSESCHMAL	2	0,99
JOGHURT	2	0,69
CREME FRAICH	2	0,75
SPEISESALZ	2	0,59
UNCLE BENS	2	2,59
SAMMYS TOAST	2	1,69
TELLER	1	1,49
TEIGSCHABER	1	1,79
BACKFOERMCH.	1	1,99
HAUSH.KERZEN	1	1,79
STARK.LYCHEE	2	0,99
TORTENSPITZE	1	1,49
TISCHDECKE	1	8,99
OB NORM 16ER	1	1,99
LUX SEIFE	1	0,49
SERVIETTEN	1	1,19
DOVE LOTION	1	3,99
NORMALLAMPEN	1	1,79
SENSODYNE ZC	1	3,49
UNTERWAESCHE	1	8,99
UNTERWAESCHE	1	8,99
BAUMW.SOCKE	1	2,49
WAESCHEWEISS	1	1,29
DEMAK UP 70	1	1,59
RASIERSCHAUM	1	2,59
TIC TAC	2	0,49
UMSCHLAEGE	1	2,69
MUELLBEUTEL	1	0,69
BRIEFBLOCK	1	1,99
PRITT CORR.	1	2,39
RC TOIPA	1	0,79
WC-BUERSTE	1	2,89
Summe	EUR	102,39
EURO		102,40
Rueckgeld	EUR	0,01

1 MwSt 19% von	67,86	10,83
2 MwSt 7% von	34,53	2,26
NETTO-UMSATZ		89,30

Durch Einsatz Ihrer Bonuskarte
. hätten Sie 51 Digits
erhalten.

Kas: 004/0057 Bon0444 PC01 P
Dat.02.04.2008 Zeit17:46:58 47

STEUER-NR.: 5120/5820/0012

Mo-SA sind wir täglich
bis 24:00 Uhr für Sie da !
Danke für Ihren Einkauf !

Bucket
1999

CD, portable CD player with audio speaker, black plastic bucket, white cable /
CD, tragbarer CD-Spieler mit Lautsprecher, schwarzer Plastikeimer, weißes Kabel
Audioskulptur, Installation / Audio sculpture, installation
Dimensions variable / Maße variabel
3 + 2 AP

A common black bucket is placed on the floor. The CD player and loudspeaker placed inside it are readily apparent, as is the white cable leading to an electric socket. The CD plays a repetitive sound suggestive of dripping water.

Installation view: Kunstmuseum Basel – Museum für Gegenwartskunst, 2008

Ein einfacher schwarzer Eimer steht auf dem Boden. Der CD-Spieler und der Lautsprecher darin sind leicht zu erkennen, ebenso das weiße Kabel, das zu einer Steckdose führt. Der CD-Spieler spielt eine sich wiederholende Tonaufnahme ab, die sich wie das Tropfen von Wasser anhört.

Installationsansicht: Kunstmuseum Basel – Museum für Gegenwartskunst, 2008

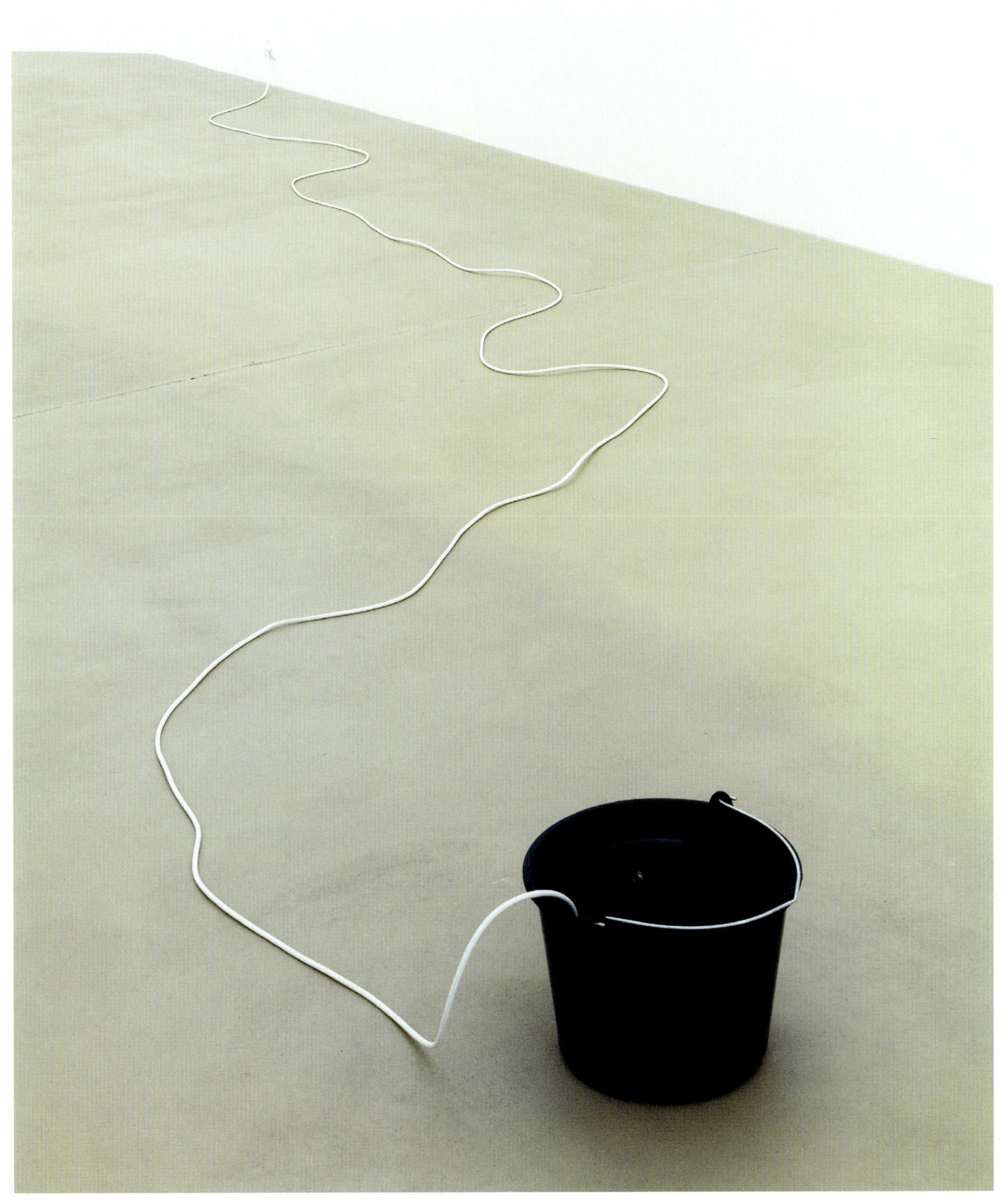

Half Empty
1999

Colour photograph mounted on aluminium / Farbfotografie auf Aluminium
Photograph / Fotografie
Dimensions / Maße: 105 × 105 cm
3 + 2 AP

Half Empty depicts a close-up of a simple glass of water in front of a neutral background. The photograph is a discrete part of the two-part work *Half Empty / Half Full.* The two photographs—always exhibited together in the context of an exhibition—are never seen together. Both photographs are shots of the same glass, one taken shortly after the other.

Installation view: Ikon Gallery, Birmingham, 2001

Half Empty zeigt ein schlichtes Glas mit Wasser in starker Vergrößerung vor hellem Hintergrund. Das Foto ist ein separater Teil der zweiteiligen Arbeit *Half Empty / Half Full*. Die beiden Fotos werden im Rahmen einer Ausstellung immer zusammen gezeigt, sind jedoch nie auf einen Blick zu sehen. Die beiden Bilder sind Abzüge von zwei verschiedenen Negativen, die in kurzem zeitlichen Abstand von demselben Glas gemacht wurden.

Installationsansicht: Ikon Gallery, Birmingham, 2001

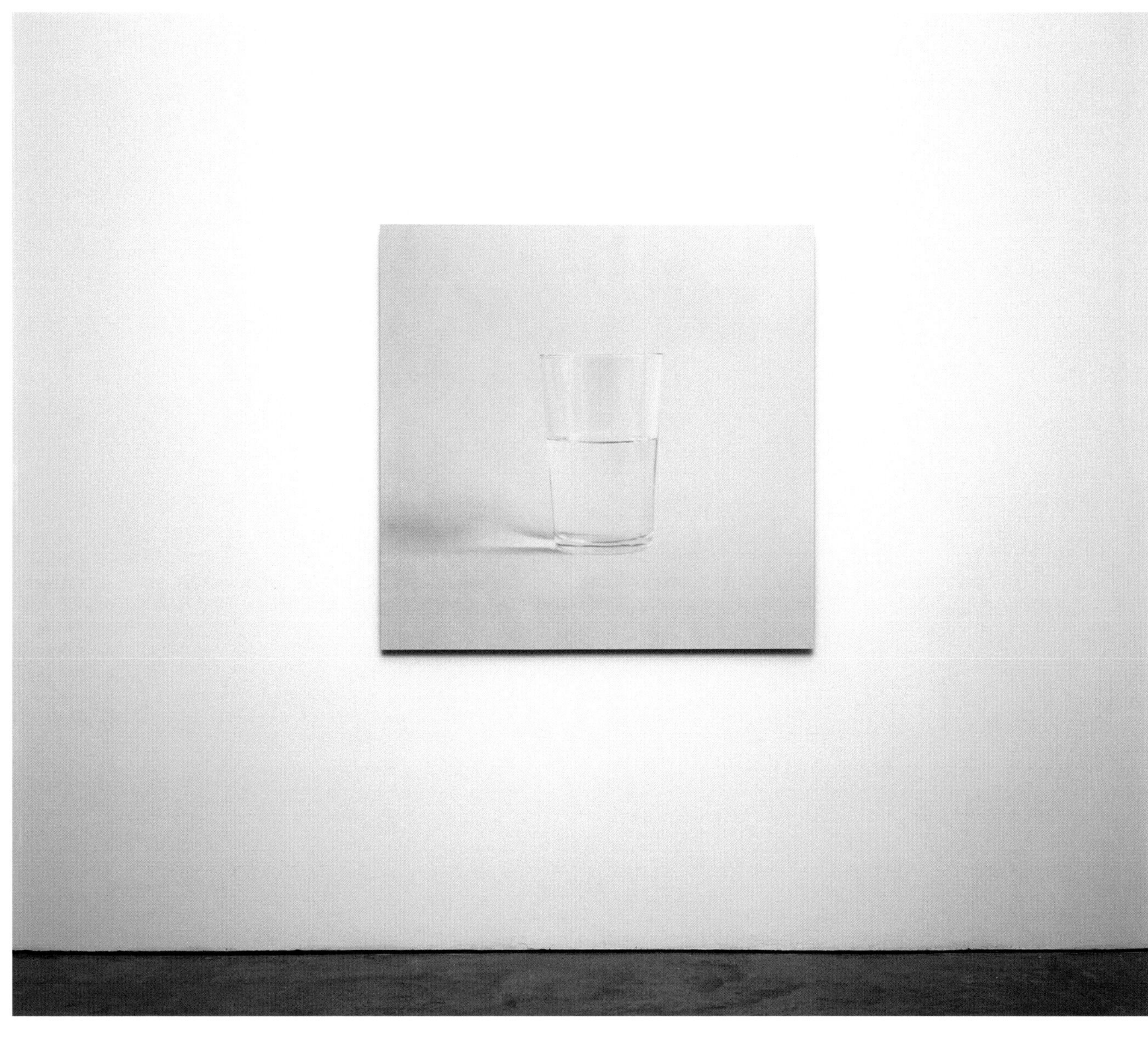

Half Full
1999

Colour photograph mounted on aluminium /
Farbfotografie auf Aluminium
Photograph / Fotografie
Dimensions / Maße: 105 × 105 cm
3 + 2 AP

Half Full depicts a close-up of a simple glass of water in front of a neutral background. The photograph is a discrete part of the two-part work *Half Empty / Half Full*. The two photographs—always exhibited together in the context of an exhibition—are never seen together. Both photographs are shots taken of the same glass, one shortly after the other.

Installation view: Ikon Gallery, Birmingham, 2001

Half Full zeigt ein schlichtes Glas mit Wasser in starker Vergrößerung vor hellem Hintergrund. Das Foto ist ein separater Teil der zweiteiligen Arbeit *Half Empty / Half Full*. Die beiden Fotos werden im Rahmen einer Ausstellung immer zusammen gezeigt, sind jedoch nie auf einen Blick zu sehen. Die beiden Bilder sind Abzüge von zwei verschiedenen Negativen, die in kurzem zeitlichen Abstand von demselben Glas gemacht wurden.

Installationsansicht: Ikon Gallery, Birmingham, 2001

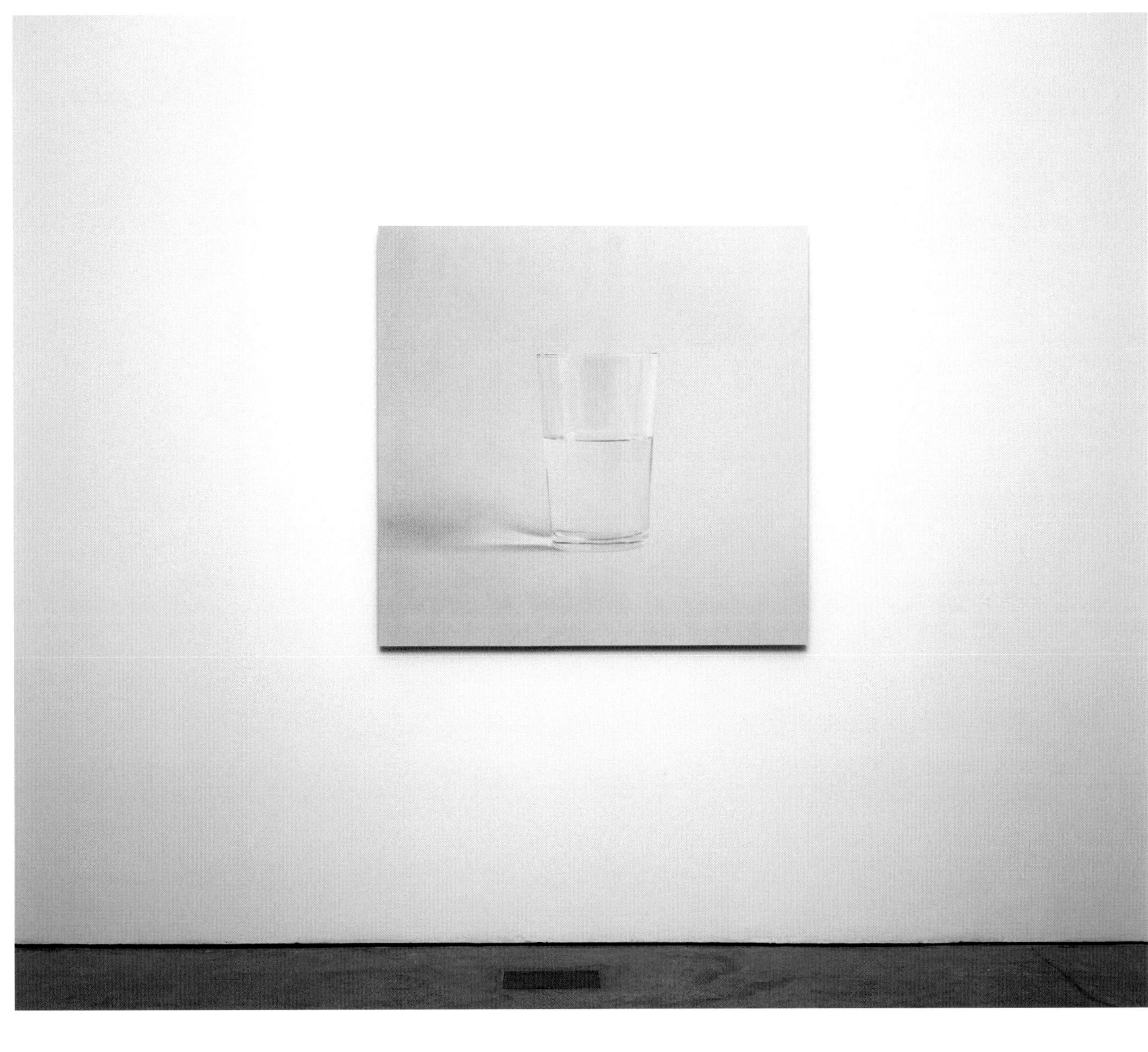

Ink On Paper
1999

Felt-tip pen on blotting paper /
Filzstift auf Löschpapier
Work on paper / Arbeit auf Papier
Dimensions of each sheet variable /
Blattmaße variabel
Versions to date comprise between
6 and 50 sheets / Die bisherigen
Fassungen umfassen 6 bis 50 Blätter

The number of felt-tip pens in the set determines the number of pages belonging to the specific work. The size and range of colours in the set vary according to the company that produced them. Each pen is fixed upright in the middle of a blank sheet of paper and drained until completely empty. The installation of the pages (ideally in a single row) follows the order of colours in the set of markers used.

Installation view: *Ink On Paper (set of 40),* Museum of Contemporary Art North Miami, 2010

Die Anzahl der Blätter, die zum Werk gehören, richtet sich nach der Anzahl der Filzstifte, die im Set angeboten werden. Der Umfang und die Farbauswahl der Filzstiftsets variieren abhängig von der Firma, die sie herstellt. Jeder Filzstift eines Sortiments wird senkrecht in der Mitte des Löschblatts fixiert, bis er vollständig ausgelaufen ist. Bei der Installation des mehrteiligen Werks (idealerweise in einer Reihe) wird die Farbreihenfolge des Filzstiftsortiments übernommen.

Installationsansicht: *Ink On Paper (set of 40),* Museum of Contemporary Art North Miami, 2010

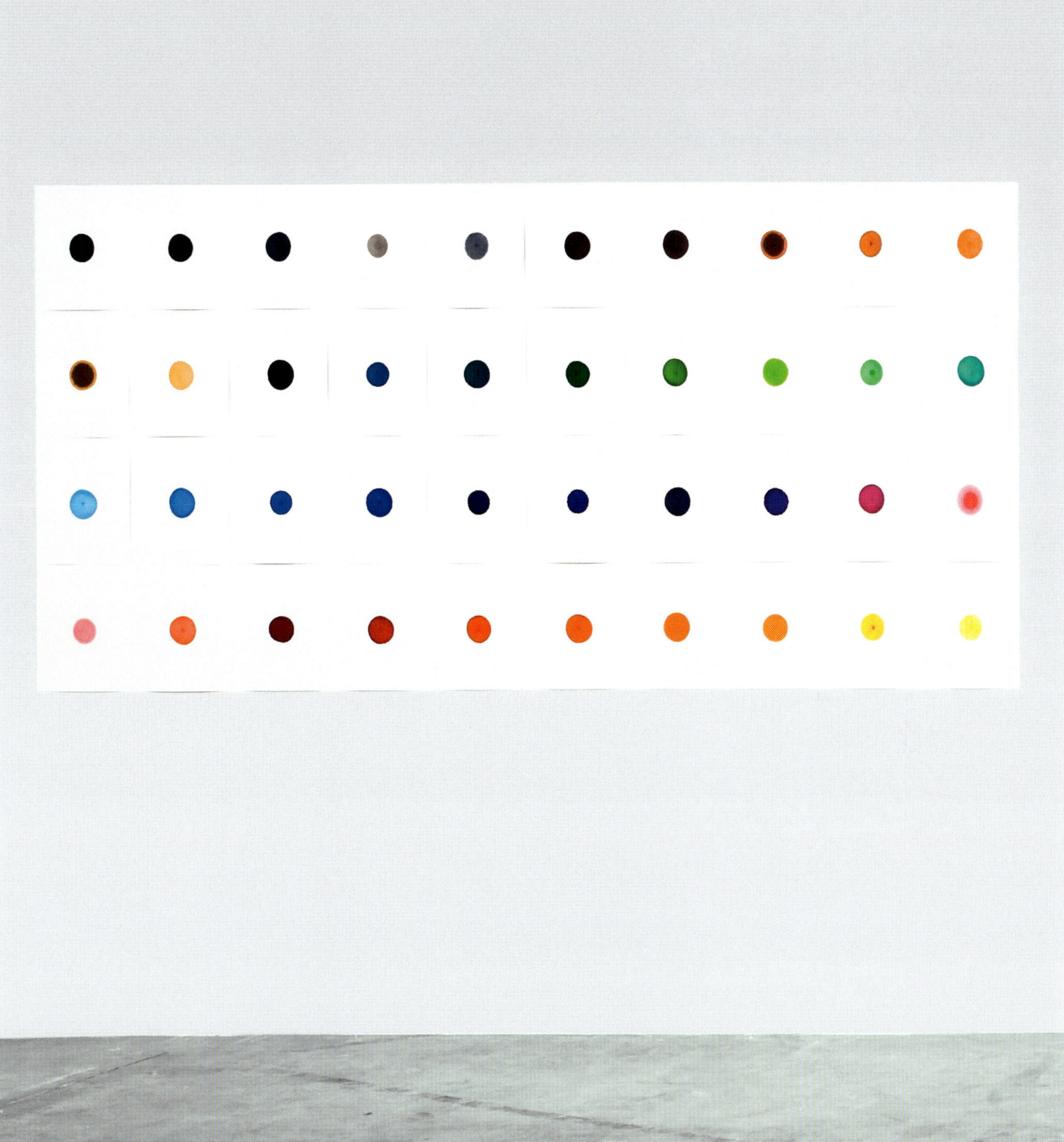

Ink On Paper (Video)
1999

Monitor, DVD, DVD player, plinth / Bildschirm, DVD, DVD-Spieler, Sockel
Video on monitor, silent / Video auf Bildschirm, ohne Ton
Duration / Dauer: 51´ 53´´
3 + 2 AP

The camera is focused on the forearms and hands of the artist motionlessly holding a blue felt-tip pen in the middle of a sheet of blotting paper. The video ends once the ink runs out. *Ink On Paper (Video)* is not to be shown in conjunction with *Ink On Paper*.

Video still

Die Kamera ist auf die Unterarme und Hände der Künstlerin gerichtet. Bewegungslos hält sie einen blauen Filzstift in die Mitte eines Löschpapiers. Das Video endet, wenn der Filzstift ausgelaufen ist. *Ink on Paper (Video)* wird nicht gleichzeitig in einer Ausstellung mit *Ink on Paper* gezeigt.

Videostill

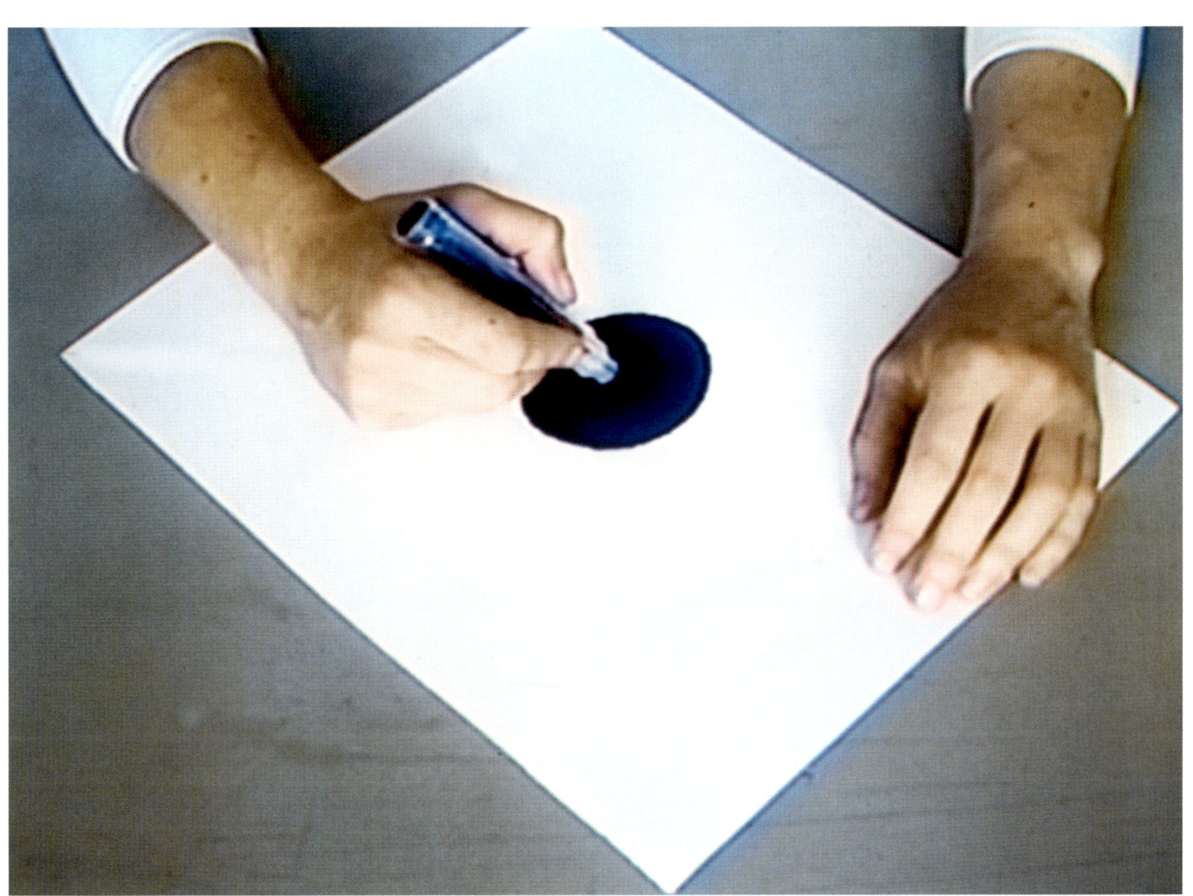

Title Variable (. . .)
2001

Five-ply black elastic, 2 steel pin tacks, wall /
Fünflagiges schwarzes Gummiband,
2 Stahlheftzwecken, Wand
Sculpture, installation / Skulptur, Installation
Dimensions variable / Maße variabel
5 + 2 AP

A standard, five-ply black elastic is fixed along the entire length of a wall at a height of 120 centimetres. The elastic is stretched to its maximum length, its ends fixed with two steel tacks. The length of un-stretched elastic required to stretch the entire length of the wall gives the work its title. At each showing, a label denoting that title is fixed nearby on the wall. The 'title' is 'variable'.

Installation view: *Title Variable (1 m 45 cm),*
Madre · Museo d'arte contemporanea
Donnaregina, Naples, 2008

Ein fünflagiges, handelsübliches schwarzes Gummiband ist auf einer Höhe von 1,2 Metern von Ecke zu Ecke eine Wand entlang gespannt. Das Gummi wurde so weit wie möglich gedehnt und mit Stahlheftzwecken in den Ecken befestigt. Die Länge des ungespannten Gummibandes, das dafür nötig ist, wird zum Titel der installierten Arbeit. Ein Label mit dem Titel der jeweiligen Ausführung hängt in unmittelbarer Nähe der Arbeit auf der Wand.
Der Titel ist variabel.

Installationsansicht: *Title Variable (1 m 45 cm),*
Madre · Museo d'arte contemporanea
Donnaregina, Neapel, 2008

Helix
2001

Shelf, Helix template, 32 assorted objects / Regalbrett, Helix-Schablone, Sortiment aus 32 Objekten
Sculpture / Skulptur
Dimensions variable / Maße variabel
Several versions / Mehrere Versionen (Unikate)

51
Helix, 2001
12.5 × 20 × 16 cm

52
Helix, 2003
12 × 20 × 16 cm

53
Helix, 2012
45 × 20 × 16 cm

The first manifestation of *Helix* originated in 2001. There are several unique variations of this work. The idea is based on the product name of a drawing template produced in England, called Helix. There are thirty-two circular cut-outs on the stencil, the smallest having a diameter of three millimetres. The circles increase in size by increments of one millimetre, with the largest having a diameter of thirty-four millimetres. The stencil serves as a holder for thirty-two found objects that fit exactly into the circular cut-outs, be it a cigarette lighter, a tube of toothpaste, a pill, or a tube of Smarties. The two-dimensional stencil serves to order a series of three-dimensional objects. The work is installed on a shelf on a wall.

Eine erste Arbeit mit dem Titel *Helix* entstand 2001. Es gibt verschiedene Variationen dieses Werks, bei denen es sich jeweils um Unikate handelt. Die Idee geht auf den Produktnamen Helix einer in England produzierten Zeichenschablone für Kreise zurück. Auf der Schablone sind 32 ausgeschnittene Kreise angeordnet, der kleinste hat einen Durchmesser von 3 Millimetern. In 1-Millimeter-Schritten werden die Kreise größer, bis zum größten Kreis mit dem Durchmesser von 34 Millimetern. Diese Schablone dient als Halterung für 32 gefundene Gegenstände, die rund sind beziehungsweise einen runden Deckel oder Boden haben und genau in die Kreisausschnitte passen, wie beispielsweise ein Feuerzeug, eine Tube Zahnpasta, eine Tablette oder eine Smarties-Schachtel. Die zweidimensionale Zeichenschablone dient dazu, eine Reihe von dreidimensionalen Objekten zu ordnen. Die Arbeit ist auf einem Regal an der Wand installiert.

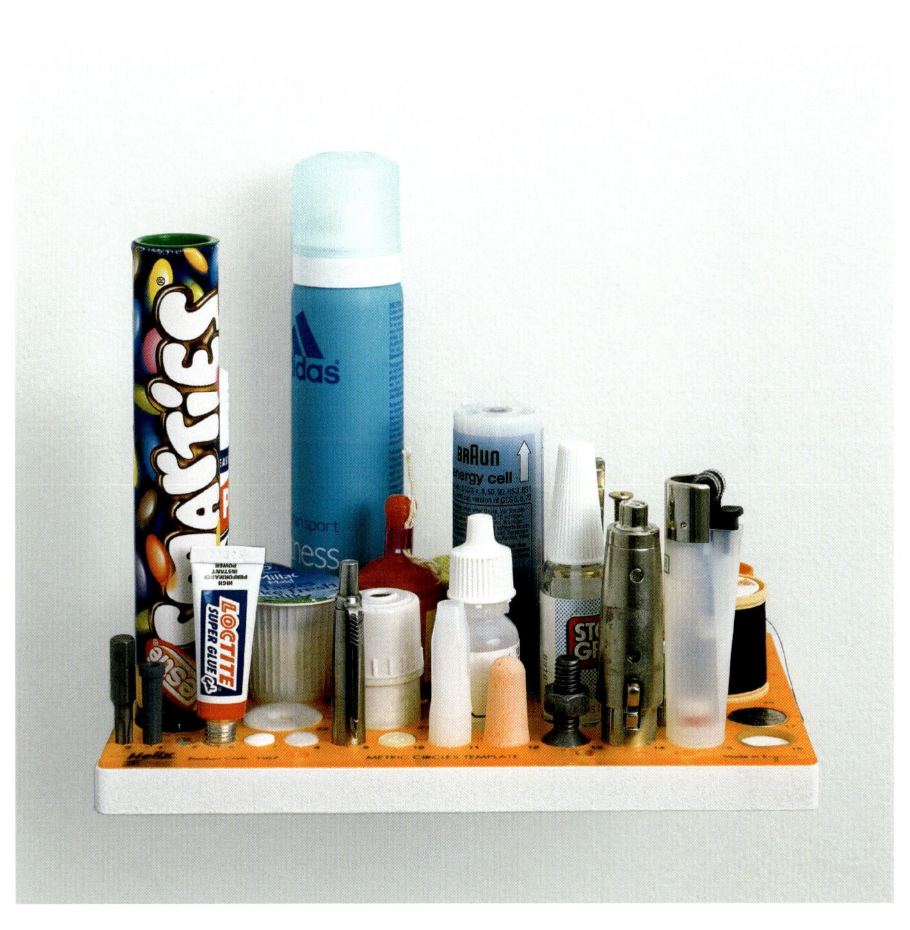
LOCTITE
SUPER GLUE
BRAUN

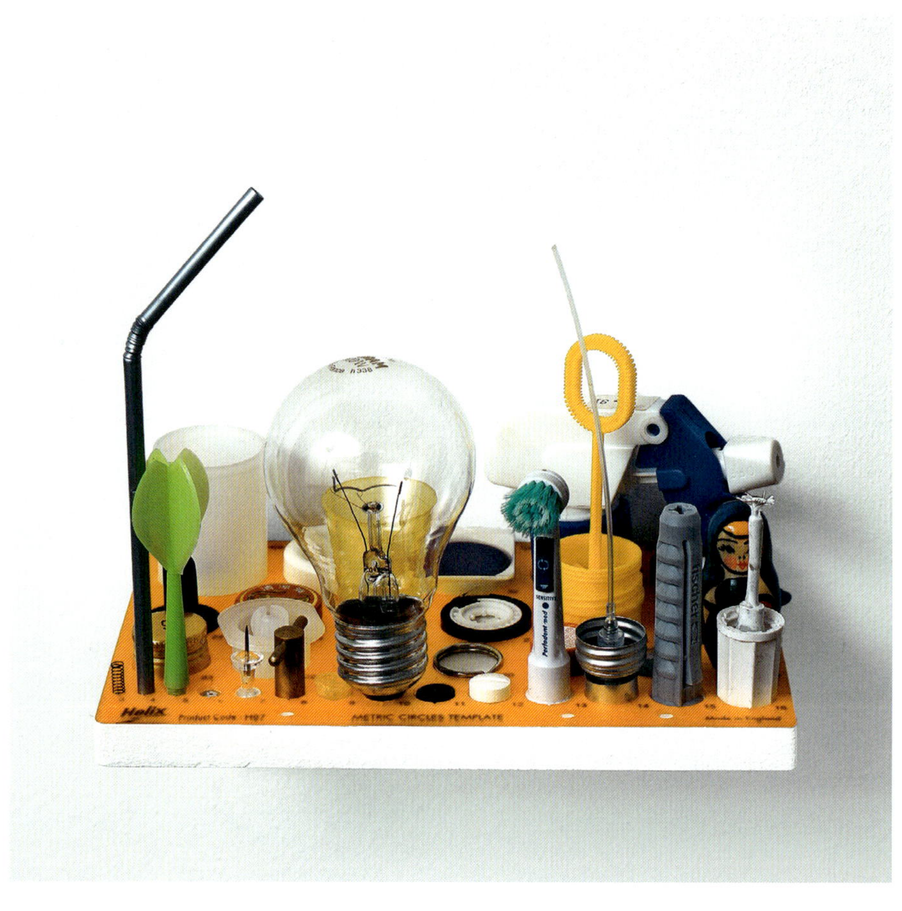
Helix
METRIC CIRCLES TEMPLATE
SENSITIVE
Perfodent med

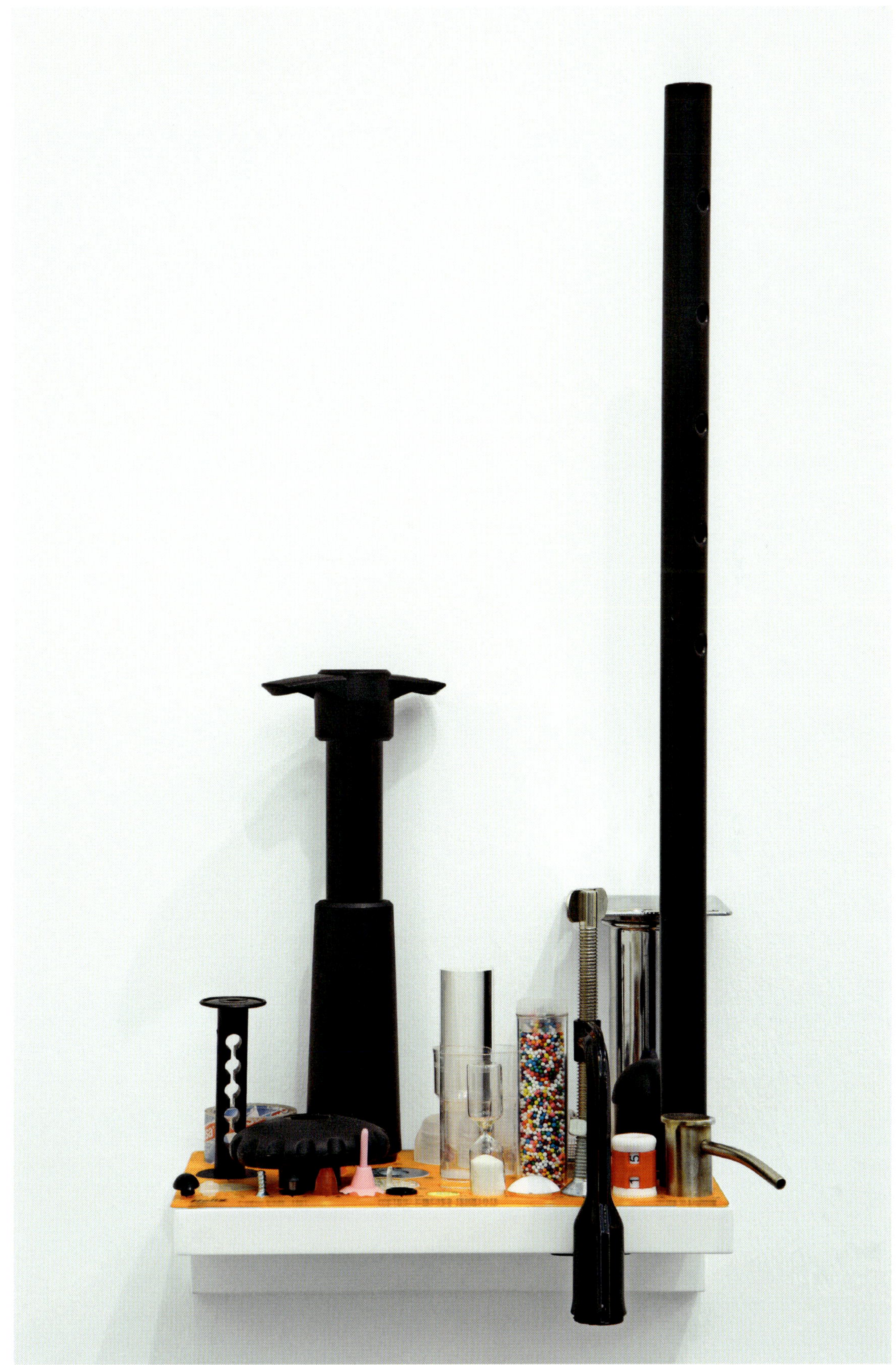

Nail Biting Performance
2001

Performance
Duration variable / Dauer variabel

Nail Biting Performance is performed by Floyer herself. It takes place before or between acts in an auditorium of spectators who have come to see the performance that was actually billed. She enters the empty stage, approaches a microphone and commences biting the nails of each hand. The sound is conveyed over the auditorium loudspeakers. When all fingernails have been bitten, Floyer exits the stage.
The performance first took place on February 7, 2001, at the Symphony Hall of Birmingham, where the orchestra performed Beethoven's Leonore Overture no. 2. Floyer's *Nail Biting Performance* took place during intermission and was followed by the orchestra's performance of Stravinsky's *Rite of Spring*.

Press conference, documenta 13, Kassel, June 6, 2012

Die englische Redewendung »nail biting performance« bezeichnet eine besonders aufregende und mitreißende Veranstaltung. Floyer führt ihre *Nail Biting Performance* immer selbst auf. Sie findet vor einem Auditorium, vor oder zwischen Teilen der Veranstaltung statt, zu der das Publikum erschienen ist und für die es bezahlt hat. Die Künstlerin tritt auf der leeren Bühne an ein Mikrofon und beginnt damit, nacheinander die Fingernägel beider Hände abzubeißen. Das Geräusch wird über die Lautsprecheranlage in den Saal übertragen. Wenn alle Fingernägel abgebissen sind, verlässt Floyer die Bühne.
Diese Performance fand erstmals am 7. Februar 2001 in der Symphony Hall of Birmingham statt, wo das Orchester an dem Abend Beethovens Leonoren-Ouvertüre Nr. 2 aufführte. In der Pause folgte die *Nail Biting Performance*, und im Anschluss daran spielte das Orchester Strawinskys *Sacre du printemps*.

Pressekonferenz documenta 13, Kassel, 6. Juni 2012

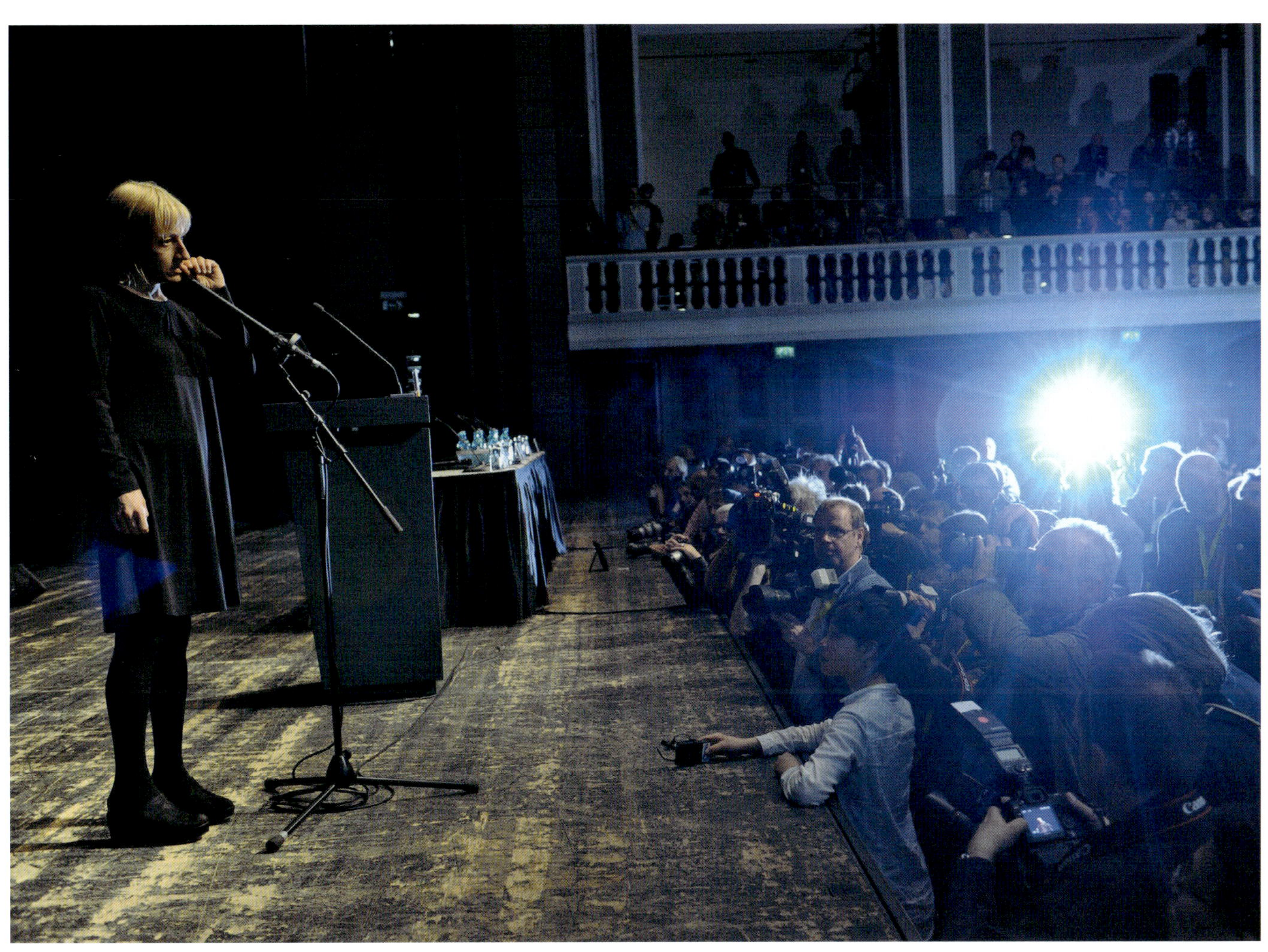

Ongoing Projection
2001

DVD, DVD player, projector /
DVD, DVD-Spieler, Projektor
Projection loop, without sound /
Projektionsschleife ohne Ton
Dimensions variable / Maße variabel
3 + 2 AP

The looped footage shows the turning pages of a blank, ring-bound notebook projected so that the notebook's spine aligns with the corner of a wall.

Installation view: Center for Contemporary Art, Tel Aviv, 2011

Die geloopte Filmaufnahme zeigt das Blättern von Seiten in einem ringgebundenen Notizbuch. Der Film wird so auf die Wand projiziert, dass die Spiralbindung mit einer Ecke des Raumes zusammenfällt.

Installationsansicht: Center for Contemporary Art, Tel Aviv, 2011

Auto Focus
2002

Slide projector, telescopic tilting stand / Diaprojektor, ausziehbarer Kippständer
Projection / Projektion
Dimensions variable / Maße variabel
5 + 2 AP

An empty slide projector is pointed at a wall. Without images to focus on, the automatic lens oscillates between its two potential focal planes.

Installation view: Esther Schipper, Berlin, 2013

Ein leerer Diaprojektor ist auf eine Wand gerichtet. Aufgrund des fehlenden Motivs bewegt sich das automatische Objektiv permanent zwischen den möglichen Fokalebenen.

Installationsansicht: Esther Schipper, Berlin, 2013

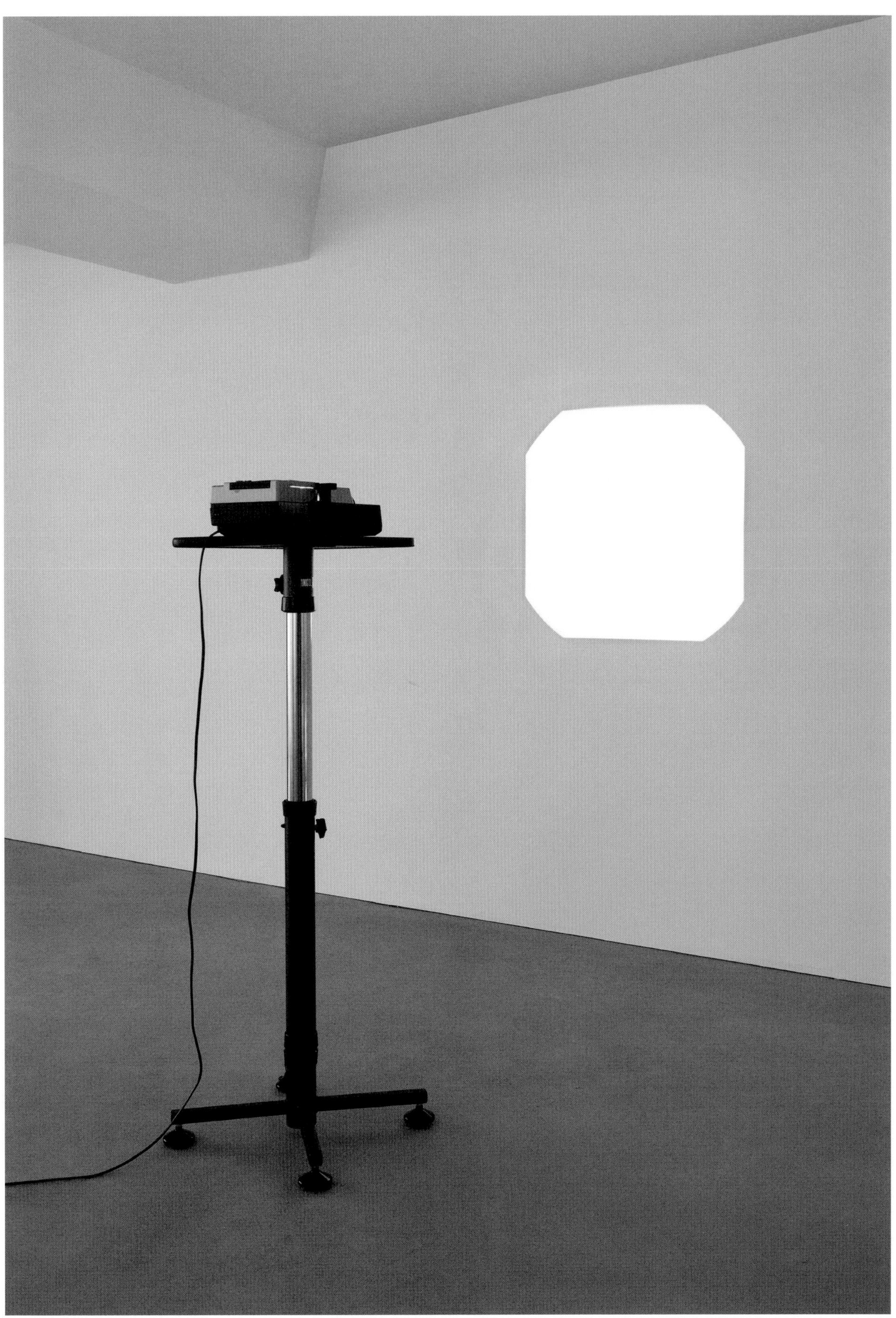

Wall
2002

Adhesive tape on wall / Klebeband auf Wand
Wall-based work / Wandarbeit
Dimensions variable / Maße variabel
3 + 2 AP

A wall is covered with bands of yellow-and-black striped warning tape placed diagonally so that the otherwise diagonal stripes become horizontal.

Installation views: Lisson Gallery, London, 2009

Handelsübliches, gelb-schwarzes Warnband ist diagonal auf einer Wand installiert, sodass das diagonal gestreifte Klebeband die Wand mit horizontalen Streifen überzieht.

Installationsansichten: Lisson Gallery, London, 2009

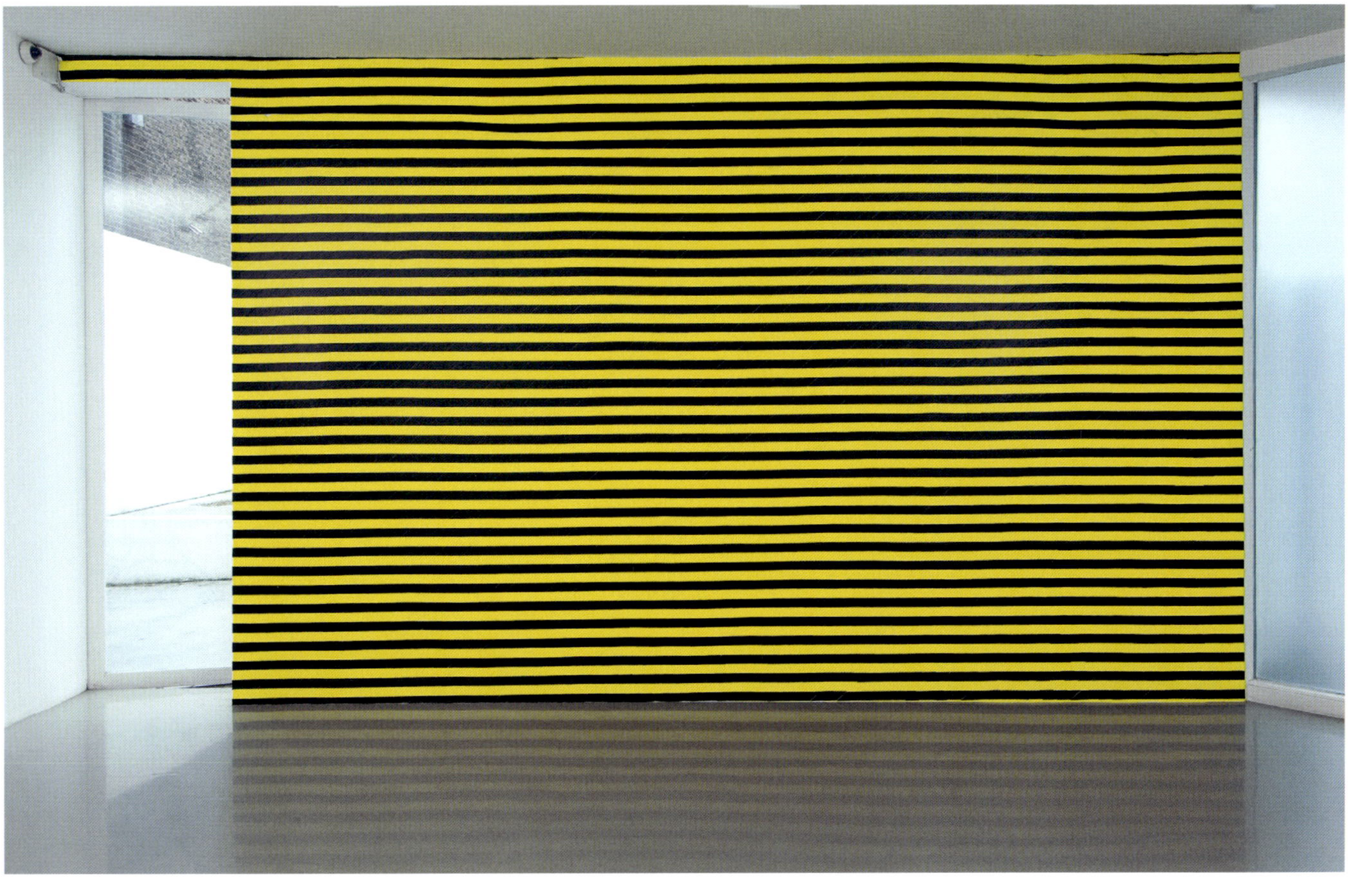

Warning Birds
2002

Self-adhesive 'warning bird' stickers on window / Selbstklebende Vogel-Warnaufkleber auf Fensterscheibe
Installation
Dimensions variable / Maße variabel
3 + 2 AP

Installation views: Kölnischer Kunstverein, 2013

Installationsansichten: Kölnischer Kunstverein, 2013

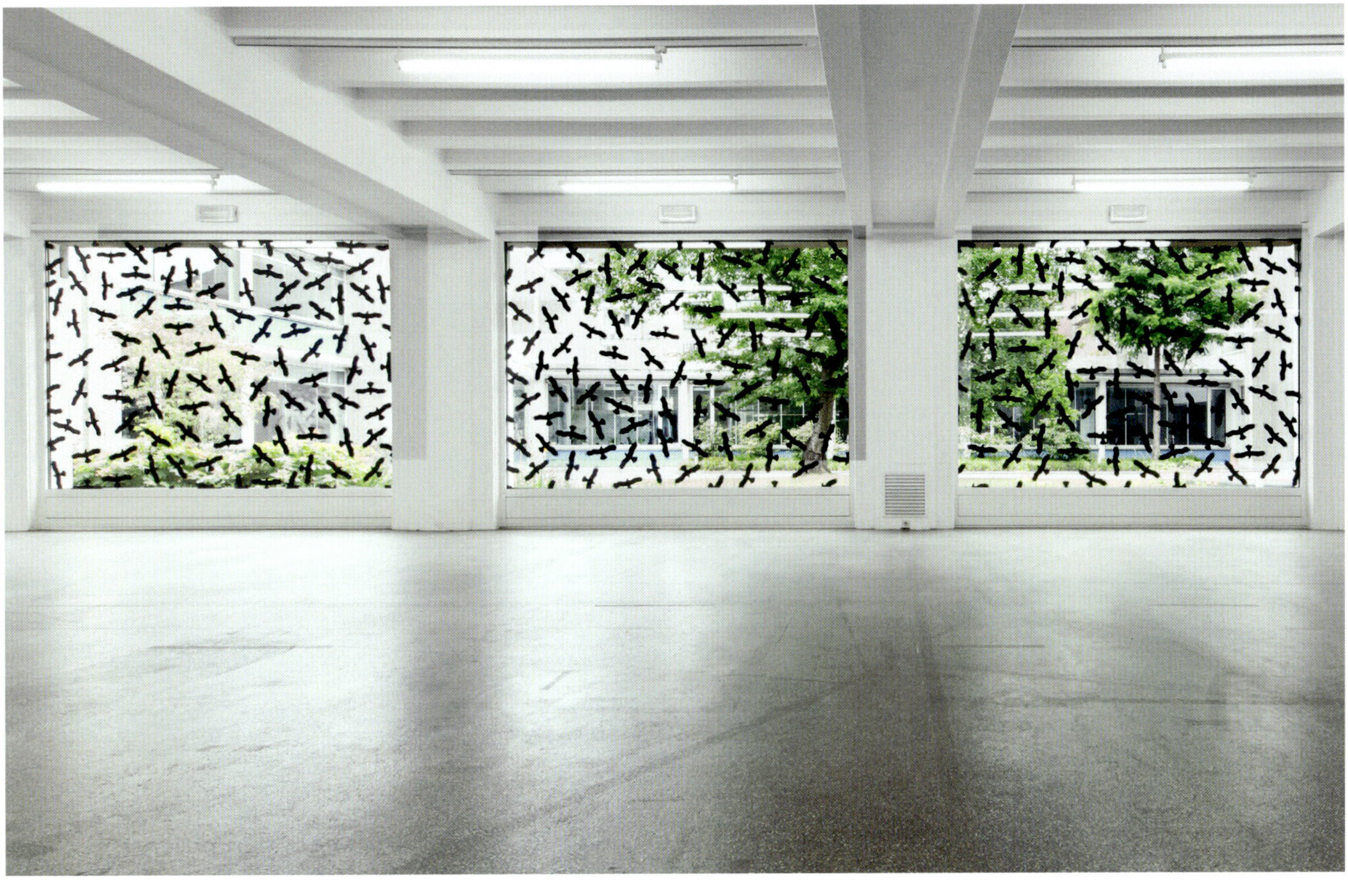

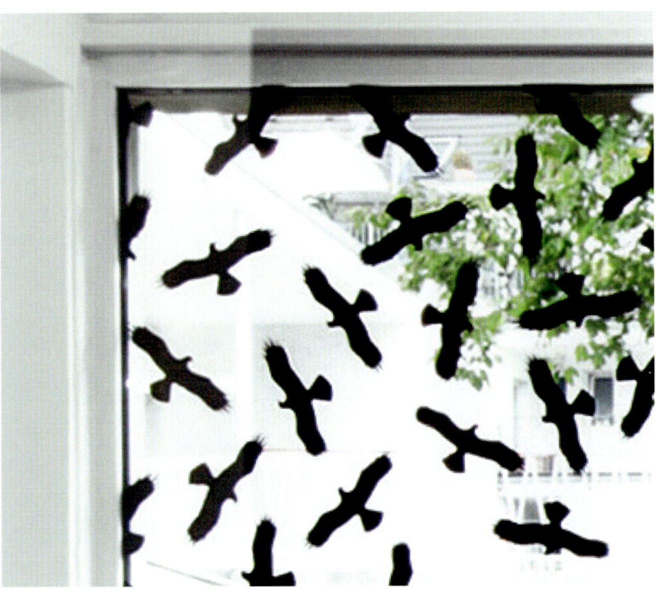

Waterline
2002

DVD, DVD player / DVD, DVD-Spieler
Projection loop without sound /
Projektionsschleife ohne Ton
Duration / Dauer: 1´ 54´´
3 + 2 AP

The projection, which fills an entire wall, shows the front of an aquarium that is slowly being filled with water. Eventually, the waterline itself becomes visible in the foreground. The transitory states are ambiguous; there is no telling whether the screen is showing water or its absence.

Installation view: Index, Stockholm, 2002, and 3 video stills

Die wandfüllende Projektion zeigt den frontalen Blick auf ein Aquarium, das langsam mit Wasser gefüllt wird. Die Wasserlinie wird schließlich im Vordergrund sichtbar. Die Übergangszustände sind widersprüchlich, sodass man nicht sagen kann, wo Wasser und wo kein Wasser zu sehen ist.

Installationsansicht: Index, Stockholm, 2002 und 3 Videostills

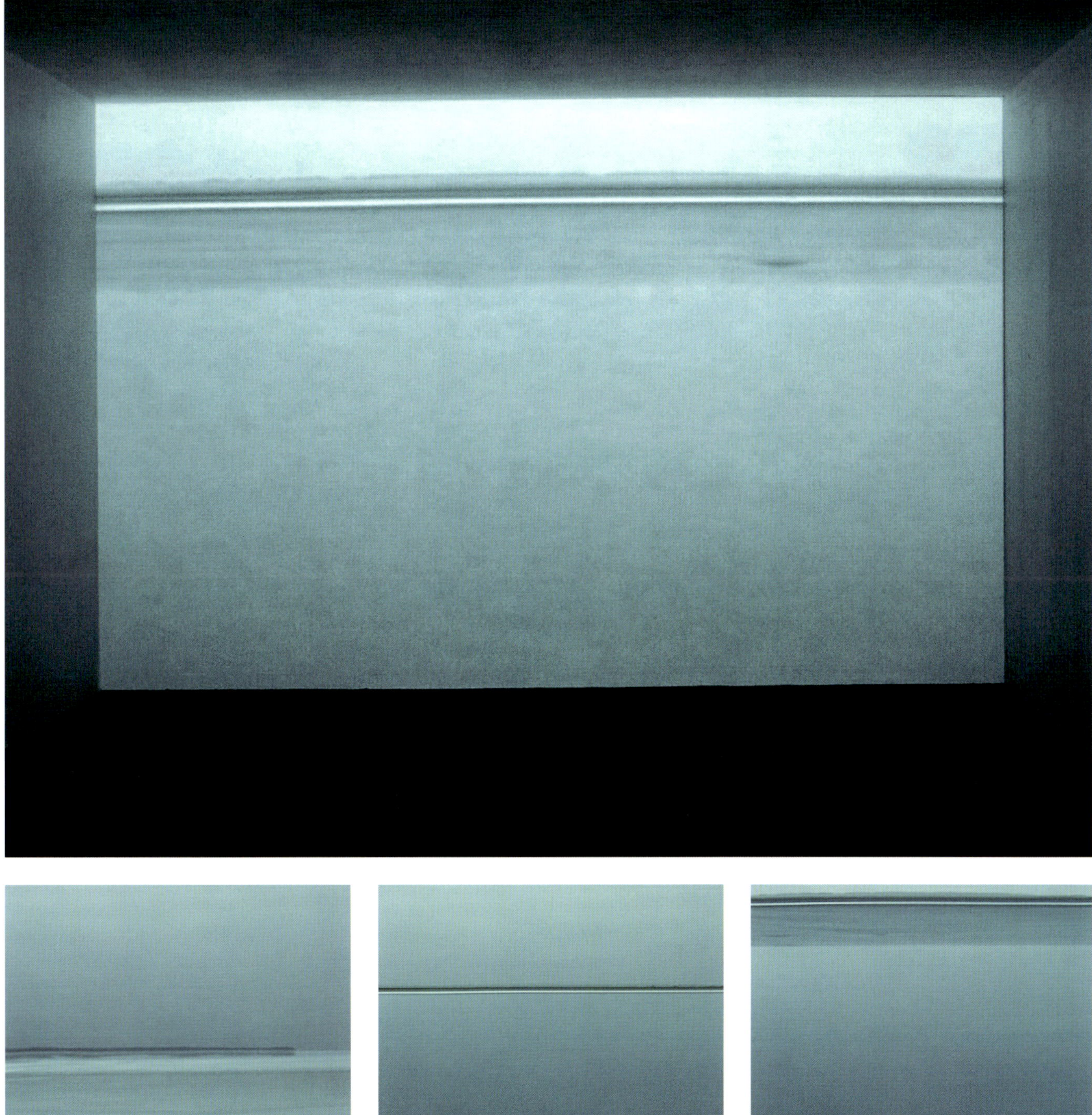

1–25
2003

DVD, DVD player, projector /
DVD, DVD-Spieler, Projektor
Video projection, silent /
Videoprojektion ohne Ton
Duration / Dauer: 325´´
Several unique language-specific versions;
to date: English, French, German, Italian /
Mehrere Versionen (Unikate) in verschiedenen
Sprachen; bisher: Englisch, Französisch,
Deutsch, Italienisch

1–24
2003

Duration / Dauer: 300´´
Several unique language-specific versions;
to date: Canadian French / Mehrere Versionen
(Unikate) in verschiedenen Sprachen; bisher:
Kanadisches Französisch

1–30
2003

Duration / Dauer: 465´´
Several unique language-specific versions;
to date: Korean / Mehrere Versionen (Unikate)
in verschiedenen Sprachen; bisher: Koreanisch

The numbers one to twenty-five, spelled out in white on a dark background, are projected onto the middle of a wall. Each number dictates how long it will be shown on screen (i.e., 'five' is shown for five seconds). The number is written in the language of the country in which the work is exhibited. The *1–25* version is shown in countries that use the NTSC video format. In countries that use PAL, the *1–24* version is shown, and where SECAM is used, the *1–30*.

Installation view: DHC / ART Foundation for Contemporary Art, Montreal, 2011

Die ausgeschriebenen Zahlen 1 bis 25 werden in Weiß auf dunklem Grund mittig auf eine Wand projiziert. Die jeweilige Zahl gibt gleichzeitig an, wie viele Sekunden sie im Video zu sehen ist (das heißt die Zahl »fünf« für 5 Sekunden). Die Zahl ist in der Sprache des Landes geschrieben, in dem die Arbeit gezeigt wird. Die Version *1–25* wird nur in Ländern gezeigt, die das NTSC-Videoformat nutzen. In Ländern, in denen das Videoformat PAL üblich ist, zeigt Floyer *1–24* und *1–30* dort, wo SECAM verwendet wird.

Installationsansicht: DHC / ART Foundation for Contemporary Art, Montreal, 2011

quatorze

Overgrowth
2004

Slide projector (medium format) with 90 mm lens, 6 × 6 cm slide / Diaprojektor (Mittelformat) mit 90-mm-Objektiv, 6 × 6 cm Dia
Projection / Projektion
Dimensions variable / Maße variabel
3 + 2 AP

An image of a bonsai tree is projected on a wall large enough to appear 'tree-size'. The work requires a long, rectangular space in order to allow the necessary projection distance and sufficient space behind the projector to suggest the scale could be adjusted even further.

Installation view: Museum of Contemporary Art North Miami, 2010

Das Bild eines Bonsais wird auf eine Wand projiziert, die groß genug ist, um ihn in natürlicher Baumgröße darzustellen. Die Arbeit kann nur in einem langgestreckten Raum gezeigt werden, der eine Projektion aus der notwendigen Entfernung erlaubt und auch hinter dem Projektor noch Platz bietet, sodass die Größe weiter verändert werden könnte.

Installationsansicht: Museum of Contemporary Art North Miami, 2010

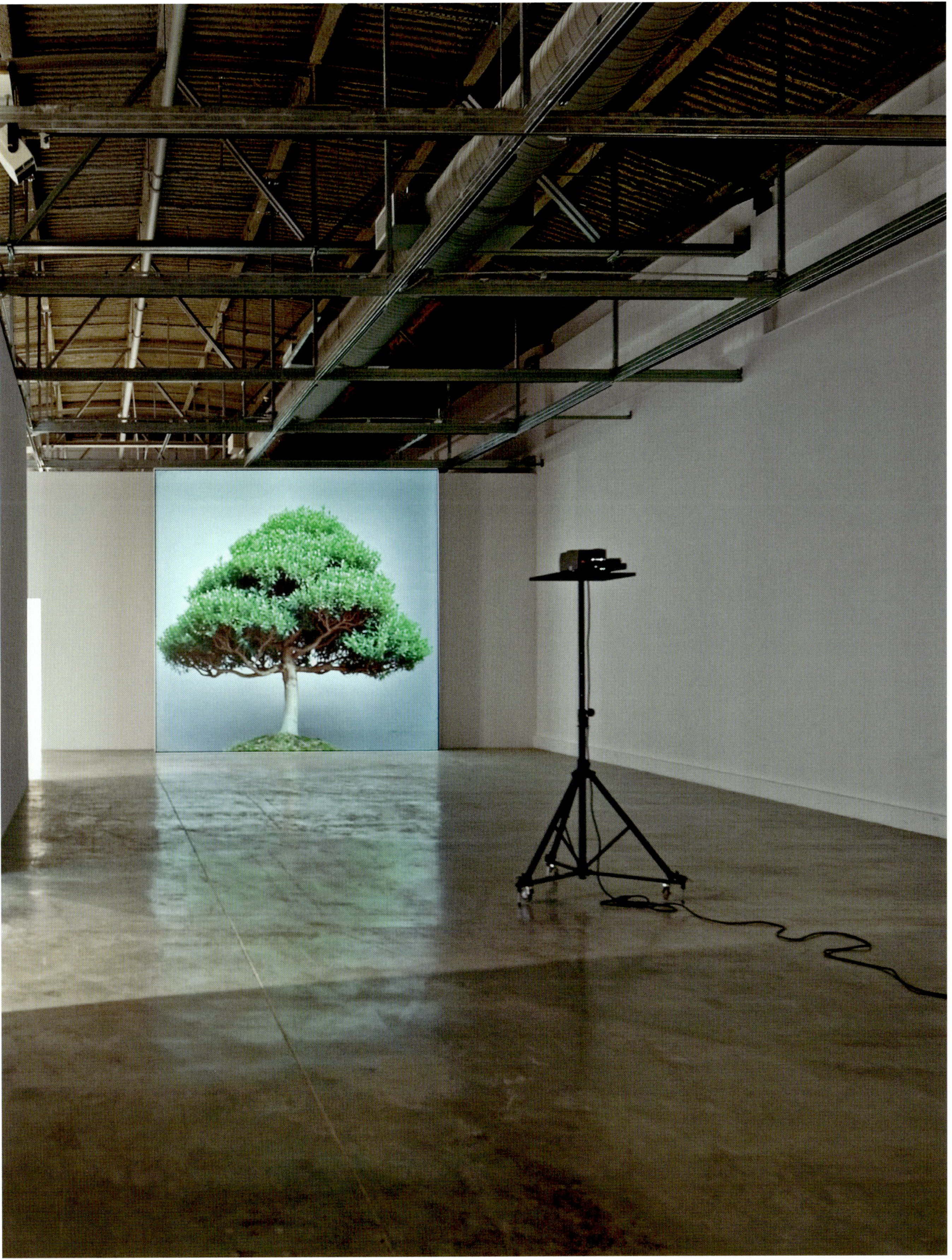

Plumb Line
2004

Plumb bob on string / Senkblei an Schnur
Installation
Dimensions variable / Maße variabel
3 + 2 AP

A plumb bob indicates the dead centre of the architectural footprint of any given site or designated room.

Installation view: Madre · Museo d'arte contemporanea Donnaregina, Naples, 2008

Ein Senkblei markiert die Mitte eines beliebigen Gebäudegrundrisses oder eines bestimmten Raumes.

Installationsansicht: Madre · Museo d'arte contemporanea Donnaregina, Neapel, 2008

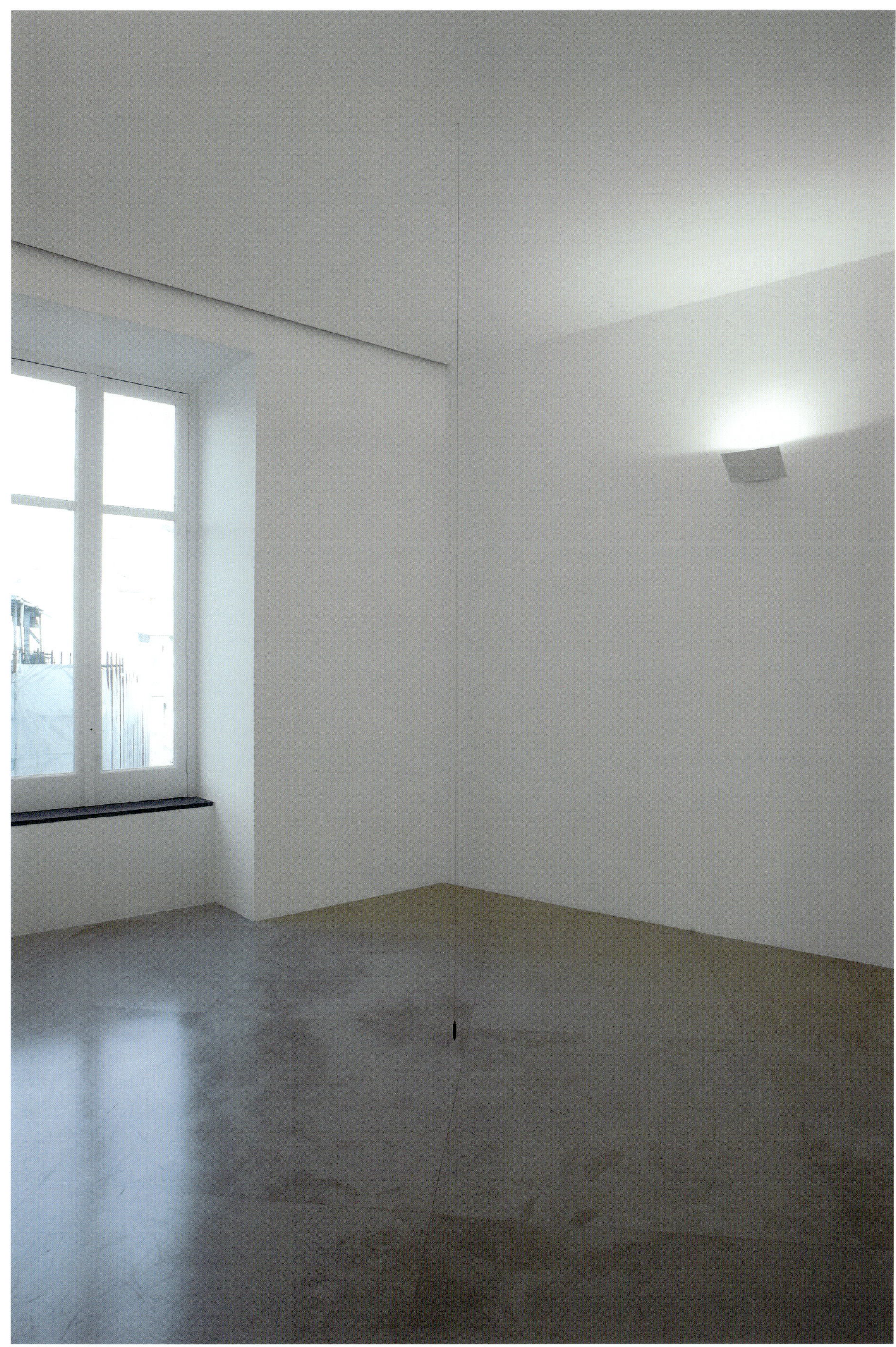

Watercolour
2004

DVD, DVD player, monitor, plinth /
DVD, DVD-Spieler, Monitor, Sockel
Monitor based video with sound /
Video auf Monitor mit Ton
Pedestal / Sockel: 67 × 50 × 121 cm
3 + 2 AP

A monitor, at first white, turns blue, then green, and finally red. Like an aural mnemonic, the subtle 'plink, plink' of the soundtrack gently coaxes along the realisation that what is being shown is a close-up of a glass of water in which a brush is being cleaned. The change of colour is accomplished by adding brush loads of primary pigment (red, yellow, blue) to the glass of water. (The colour palette red, green, and blue, incidentally, corresponds to the chromatic make-up of RGB video technology.)

Installation views: KW Institute for Contemporary Art, Berlin, 2009

Ein Monitor ist zunächst weiß, färbt sich dann blau, grün und schließlich rot. Das verhaltene »pling, pling« der Tonspur führt allmählich zu der Erkenntnis, dass das, was zu sehen ist, die Nahaufnahme eines Wasserglases ist, in dem ein Pinsel gereinigt wird. Der Wechsel der Farben wird durch das Hinzufügen von Pigmenten in den Primärfarben (Rot, Gelb, Blau) mit dem Pinsel erreicht. (Zufällig entspricht die Farbpalette Rot, Grün und Blau dem Farbraum der RGB-Videotechnologie.)

Installationsansichten: KW Institute for Contemporary Art, Berlin, 2009

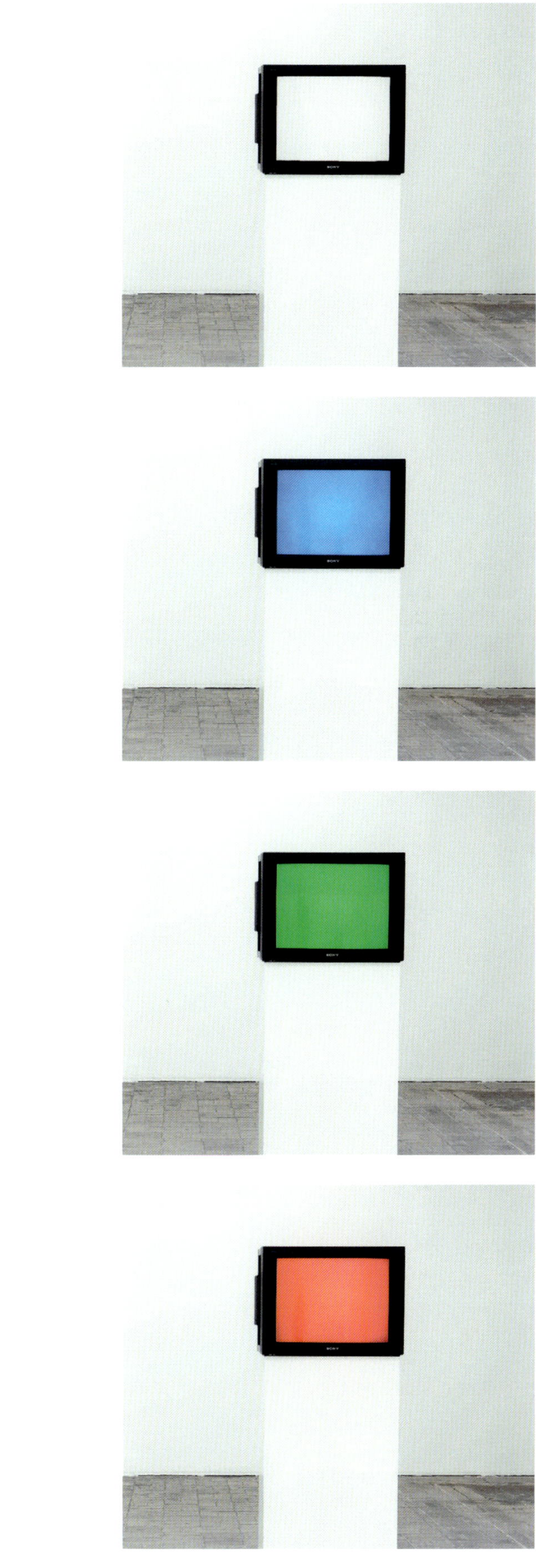

’Til I Get It Right
2005

CD, CD player, 4 speakers, amplifier /
CD, CD-Spieler, 4 Lautsprecher, Verstärker
Audio installation / Audioinstallation
Dimensions variable / Maße variabel
3 + 2 AP

An audio system is installed in an otherwise empty room so that the sound is heard evenly throughout the space. The words ‘falling in love’ have been edited out of country music singer Tammy Wynette’s famous song, rendering it a simple, looped repetition of ‘I’ll just keep on . . . ’til I get it right’.

Installation view: documenta 13, Kassel, 2012

Eine Musikanlage ist so in einem sonst leeren Raum installiert, dass der Ton sich möglichst gleichmäßig verteilt. Die Worte »falling in love« sind aus dem bekannten Lied der Country-Sängerin Tammy Wynette herausgeschnitten, sodass daraus eine ständige Wiederholung von »I’ll just keep on […] ’til I get it right« (ich mache einfach weiter, bis ich es hinbekomme) wird.

Installationsansicht: documenta 13, Kassel, 2012

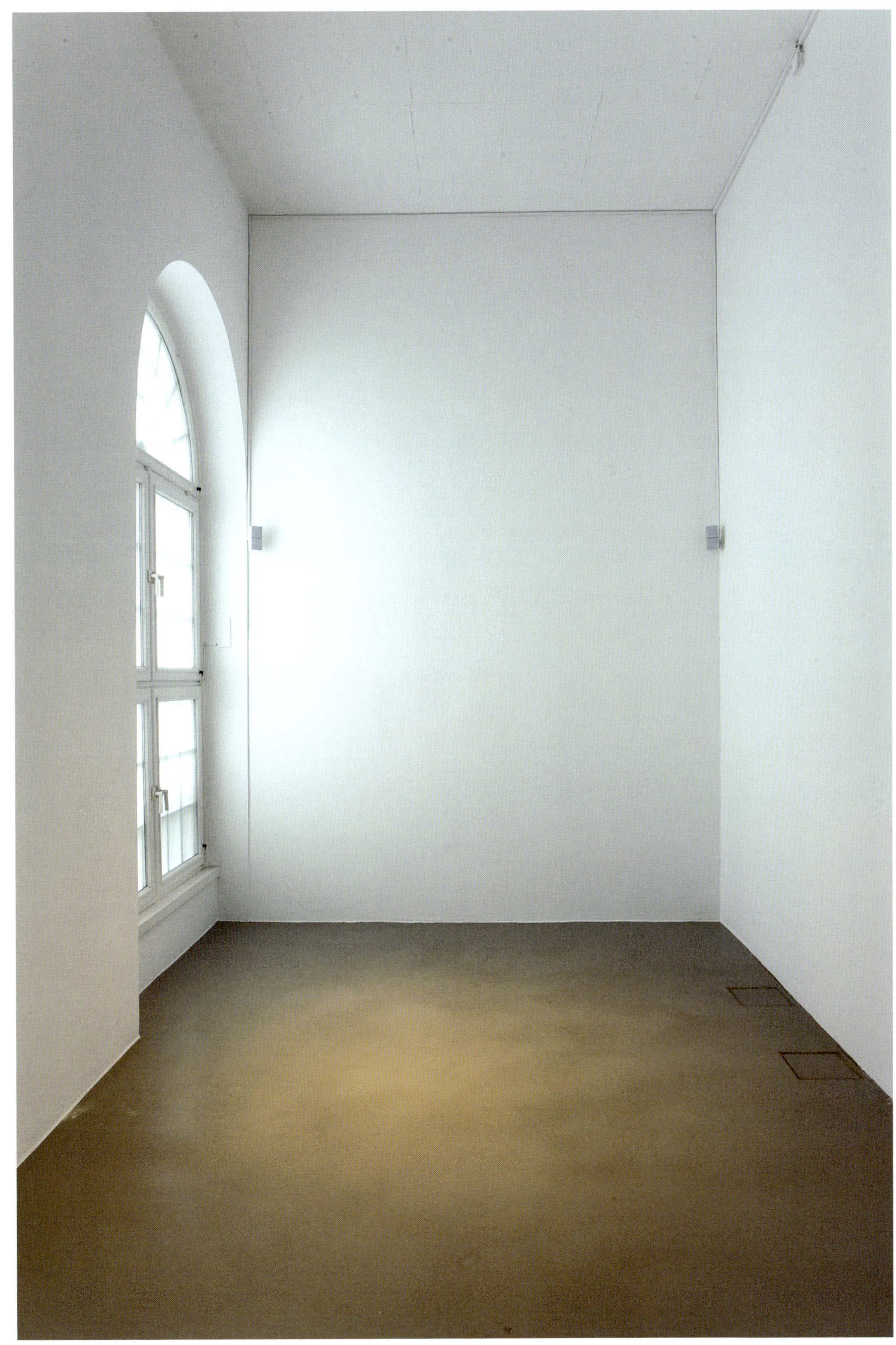

Apollinaris
2005

DVD, DVD player, projector /
DVD, DVD-Spieler, Projektor
Projection, without sound /
Projektion ohne Ton
Duration / Dauer: 10´ 21´´
3 + 2 AP

A projection of white bubbles shooting upwards in front of a black background fills the entire wall. For this work, the camera was set just above the rim of a glass of sparkling water, so only the bubbles are seen, hugely magnified.

Video stills

Eine Projektion von weißen Blasen, die vor schwarzem Hintergrund aufspritzen, füllt die ganze Wand. Für dieses Werk ist die Kamera über dem Rand eines Glases mit Mineralwasser installiert worden, sodass nur die stark vergrößerten Bewegungen der Blasen zu sehen sind.

Videostills

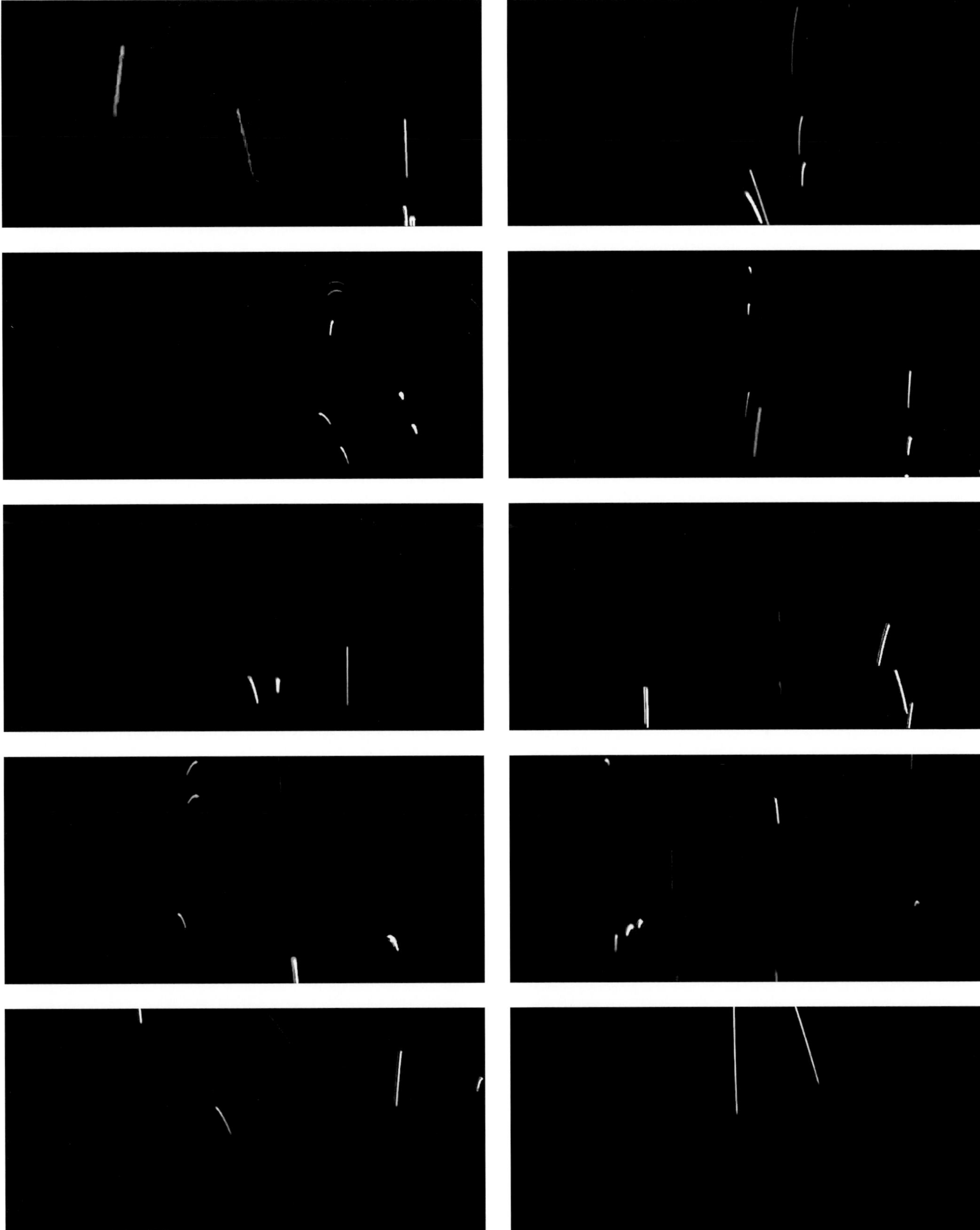

Reversed
2005

C-print mounted on aluminium /
C-Print auf Aluminium
Photograph / Fotografie
Dimensions / Maße: 70 × 100 cm
6 + 2 AP

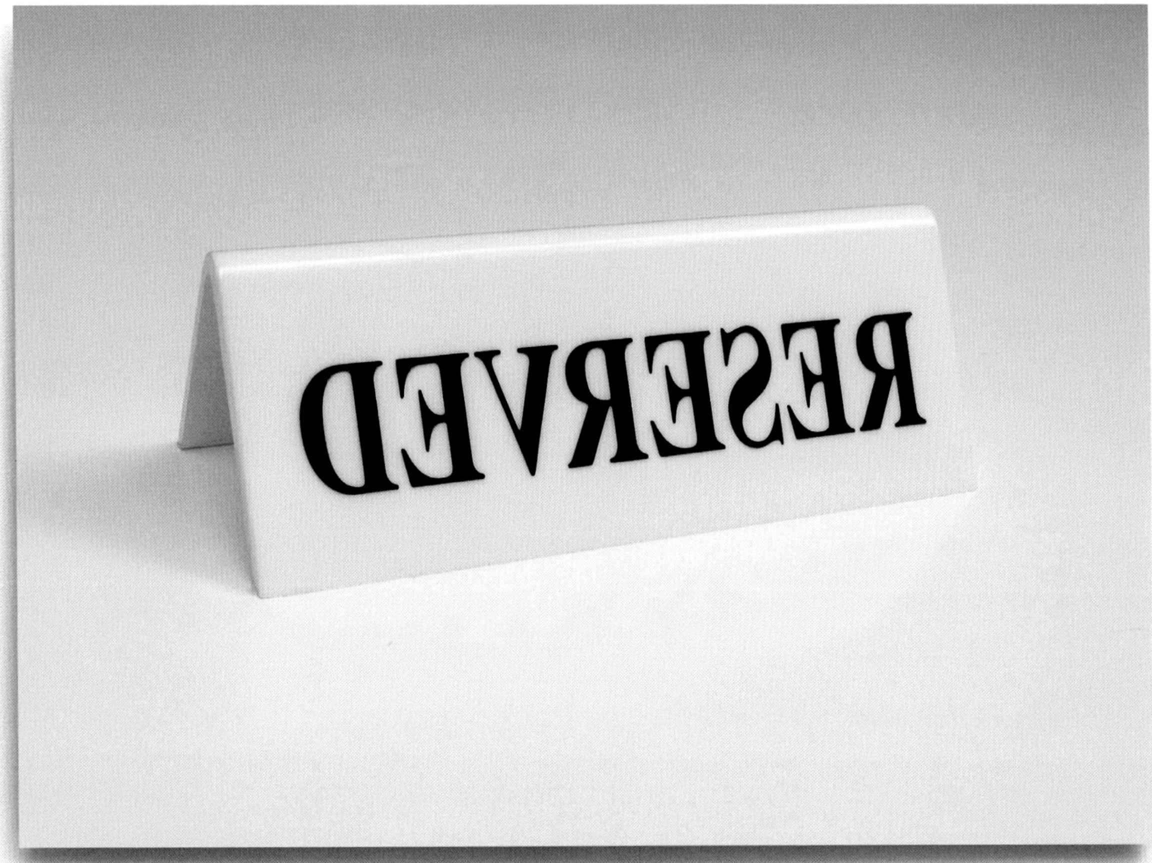

RESERVED

Trash
2005

USB stick, projector /
USB-Speicherstick, Projektor
Projection, installation / Projektion, Installation
Dimensions variable / Maße variabel
3 + 2 AP

An image of a full metal wastepaper basket (the 'trash' icon of a computer desktop) is projected life-size onto the lower-right corner of a (landscape-format) wall.

Installation view: Contemporary Art Gallery, Vancouver, 2005

Das Bild eines vollen Metall-Papierkorbs (das »Abfall«-Symbol auf der Benutzeroberfläche eines Computerbildschirms) wird in der für einen Papierkorb üblichen Größe auf die rechte untere Ecke einer querformatigen Wand projiziert.

Installationsansicht: Contemporary Art Gallery, Vancouver, 2005

Construction
2006

3 ready-made sound effects, 3 CDs, 3 CD players, 3 amplifiers, 3 soundboards, dry wall /
3 vorgefertigte Klangeffekte, 3 CDs,
3 CD-Spieler, 3 Verstärker, 3 Soundboards, Leichtbau-Wand
Audio installation / Audioinstallation
Dimensions variable / Maße variabel
3 + 2 AP

Three soundboards that are centrally embedded into the walls of an otherwise empty space emit the sounds of drilling, hammering, and sanding. The CD players are set on shuffle mode, producing irregular combinations of the three individual sound effects.

Installation view: Art Basel Unlimited, 2006

Drei flache Lautsprecher (Soundboards), die mittig in die Wände eines ansonsten leeren Raumes eingebaut sind, übertragen Bohr-, Hammer- und Schleifgeräusche. Die CD-Spieler sind auf Zufallswiedergabe eingestellt und geben die drei Geräuscheffekte in immer anderen Kombinationen wieder.

Installationsansicht: Art Basel Unlimited, 2006

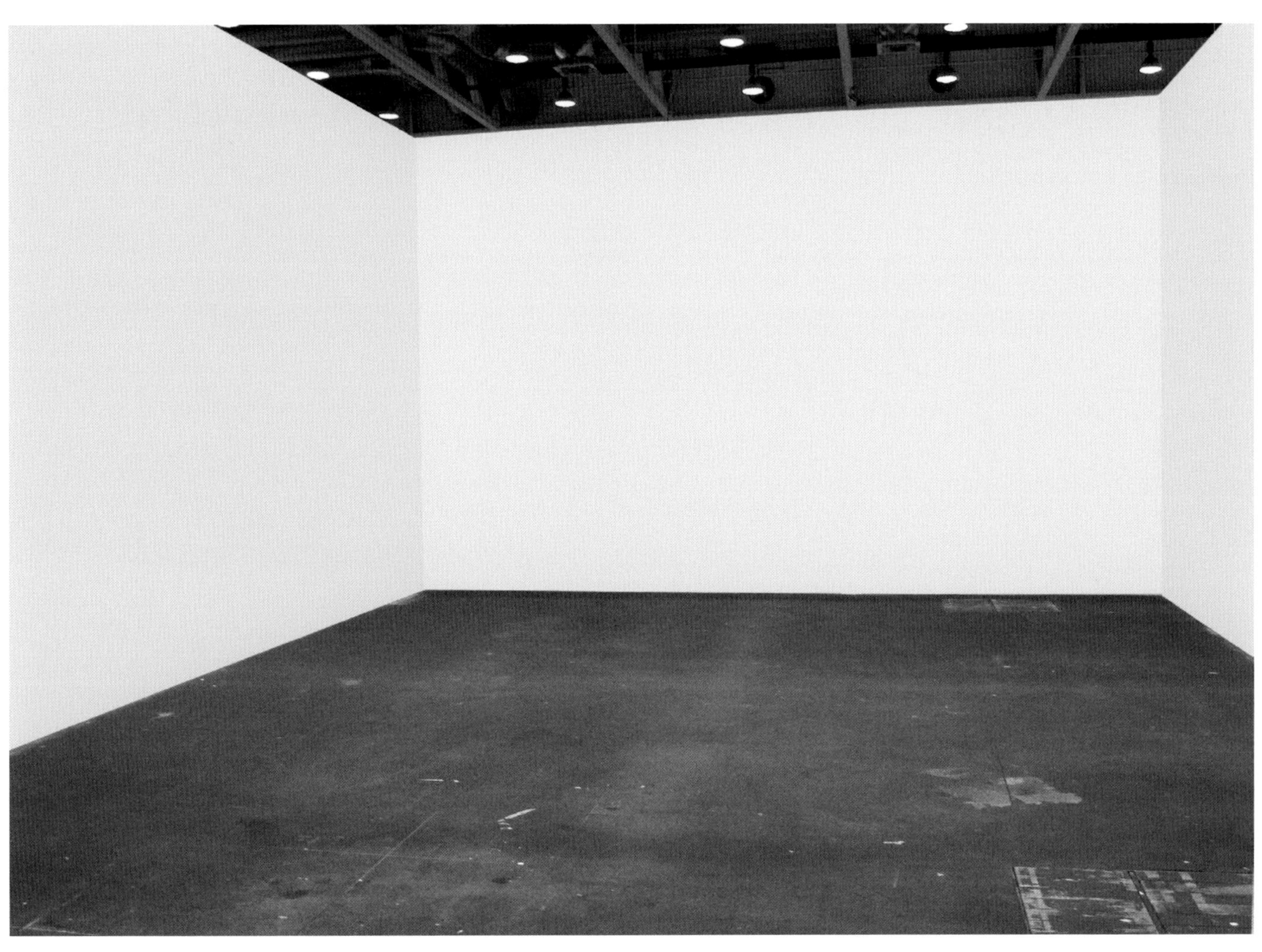

Double Act
2006

Photographic gobo, gobo holder, theatre lamp / Gobo, Gobohalterung, Theaterscheinwerfer
Projection, installation / Projektion, Installation
Dimensions variable / Maße variabel
3 + 2 AP

Double Act suggests a theatre stage by using a spotlight to project the image of a red theatre curtain onto a wall and an ellipse of light onto the floor. While the work plays on the sense of illusion, it is in fact quite structural—a horizontally split image projected into a right angle, with both vertical and horizontal focal planes. The work accentuates the notion of the 'binary', with everything revolving around the idea of two parts, from the title to the elements and media to the distortion of the light itself.

Installation view: Lisson Gallery, London, 2006

Double Act erinnert an eine Theaterbühne: Ein Scheinwerfer projiziert das Bild eines roten Bühnenvorhangs auf die Wand des Ausstellungsraums und zu einer Ellipse gebündeltes Licht auf den Boden. Die Arbeit spielt mit Illusionen, ist aber in Wirklichkeit rein formal – ein horizontal geteiltes Bild wird in eine rechtwinklige Ecke projiziert, mit einer vertikalen und einer horizontalen Brennebene. Das Werk betont die Vorstellung vom »Binären«, alles dreht sich um die Zweiteiligkeit, vom Titel über die Bestandteile und Hilfsmittel bis zur Krümmung des Lichts selbst.

Installationsansicht: Lisson Gallery, London, 2006

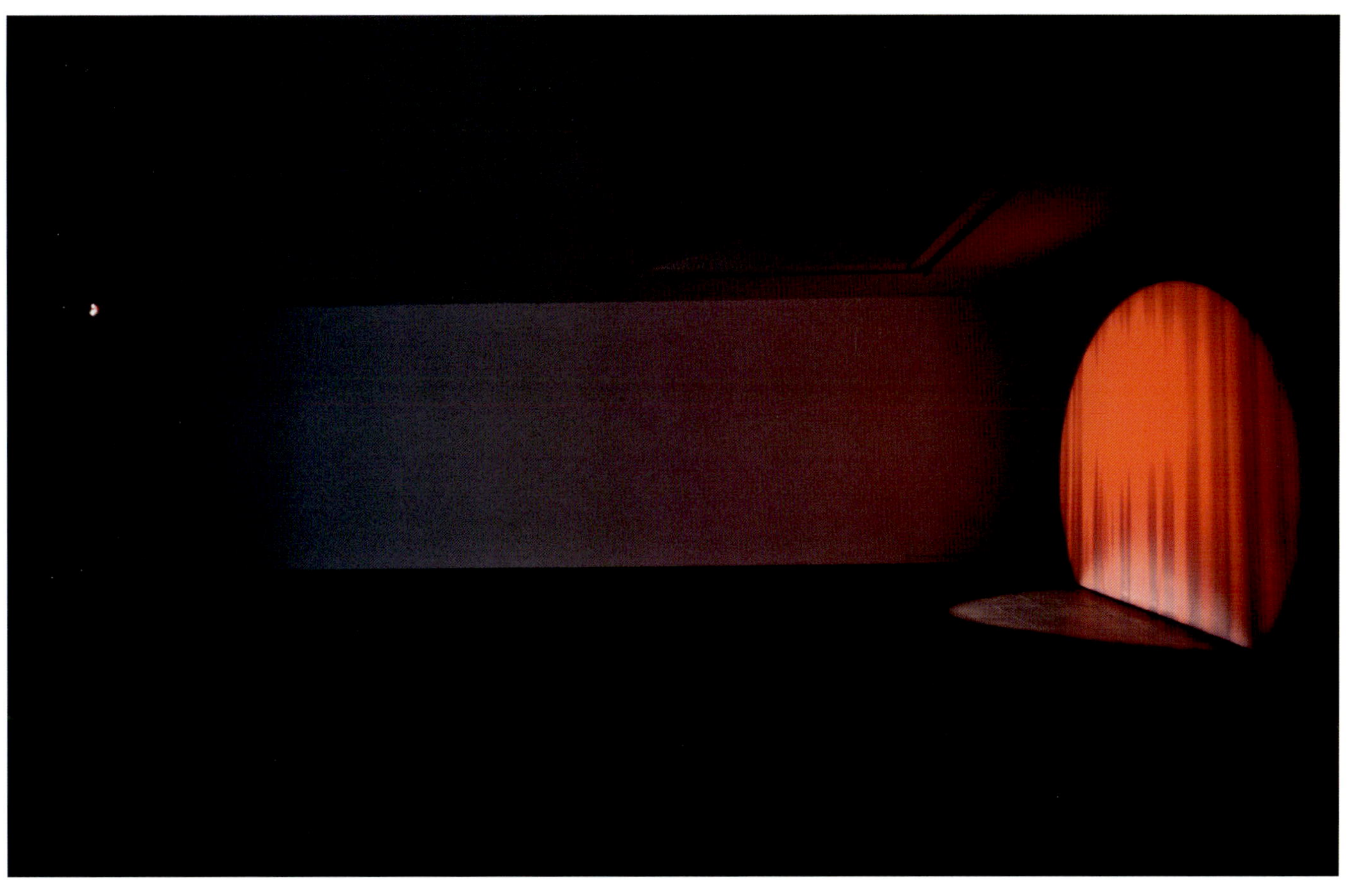

Drill
2006

Drill, drill holes in the wall /
Bohrmaschine, Bohrlöcher in der Wand
Sculpture / Skulptur
Dimensions / Maße: ca. 40 × 26 × 11 cm
3 + 2 AP

Two holes are drilled in a wall at the height of an electric socket, roughly thirty centimetres above the floor. The size of the holes and the distance between them correspond to the contact pins of an electric plug. The plug of the drill is inserted directly into these holes; the drill lies on the floor. The work is presented only in countries that have plugs with round holes.

Das englische Wort »drill« kann sowohl Verb als auch Substantiv sein. Auf der üblichen Steckdosenhöhe von ungefähr 30 Zentimetern über dem Boden sind zwei Löcher in die Wand gebohrt. Die Größe der Bohrlöcher und ihre Anordnung entspricht den Kontaktstäben eines Elektrosteckers. Der Stecker der Bohrmaschine steckt in den Bohrlöchern, die Bohrmaschine liegt auf dem Boden. Präsentiert wird diese Arbeit nur in Ländern, die runde Steckerkontakte haben.

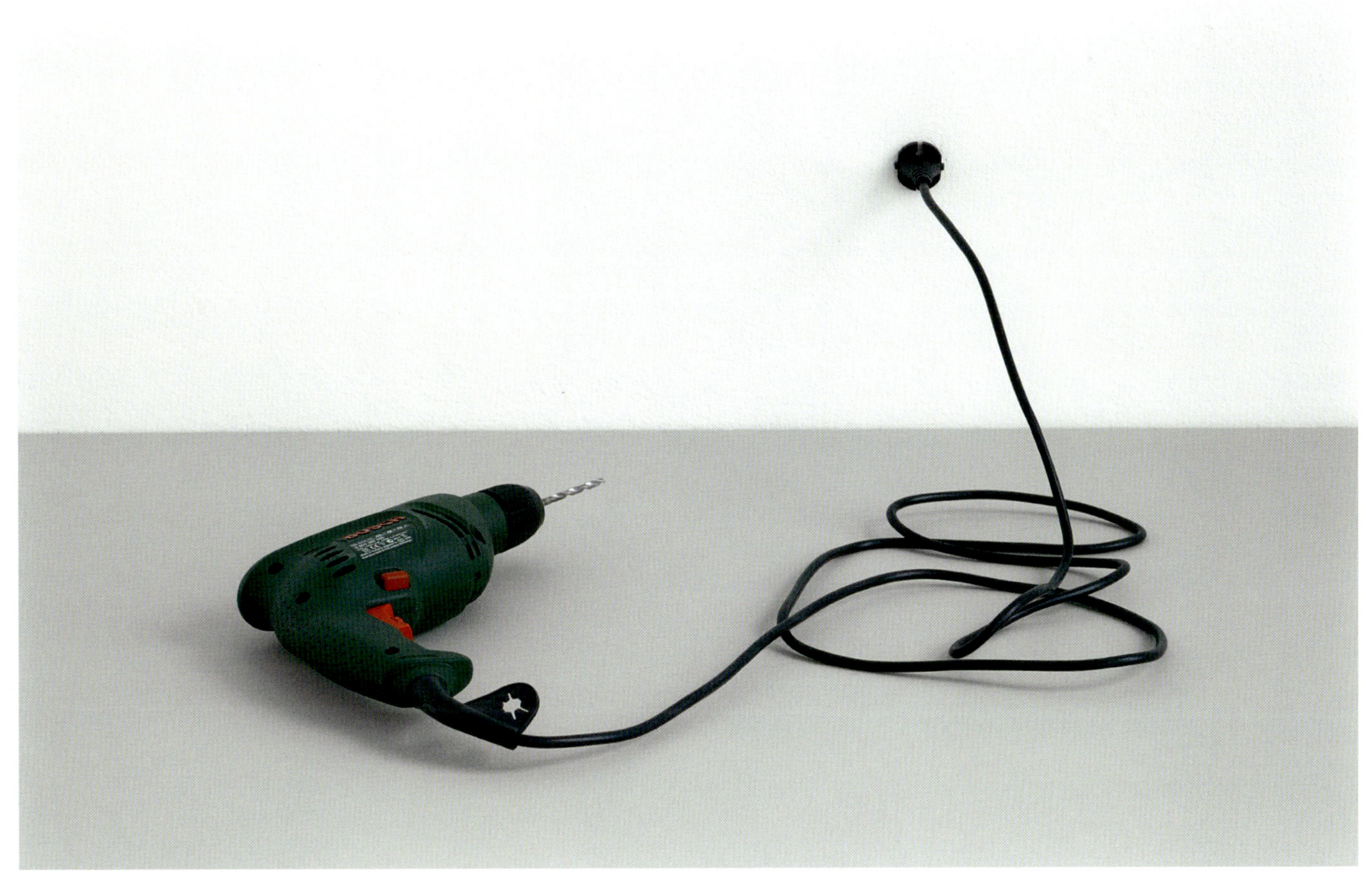

Exit
2006

Amended Emergency exit sign, laser-cut / Abgeändertes Notausgangsschild, lasergeschnitten
Sculpture, intervention / Skulptur, Intervention
Dimensions / Maße: 17.5 × 34 × 0.4 cm
5 + 2 AP

A white pictogram of a running figure on a green background indicates the exit door as in a generic emergency exit sign. The symbolic door itself is cut out. In an exhibition space, the modified exit sign is installed at the same level as any other such generic signage.

Installation views: Museion, Bolzano, 2014

Ein weißes Piktogramm mit einer laufenden Figur auf grünem Grund weist den Weg zum nächsten Notausgang wie auf einem gewöhnlichen Notausgangsschild. Das Symbol der Tür selbst ist ausgeschnitten. Im Ausstellungsraum wird das modifizierte Notausgangsschild auf derselben Höhe wie andere Hinweis- und Signalschilder installiert.

Installationsansichten: Museion, Bozen, 2014

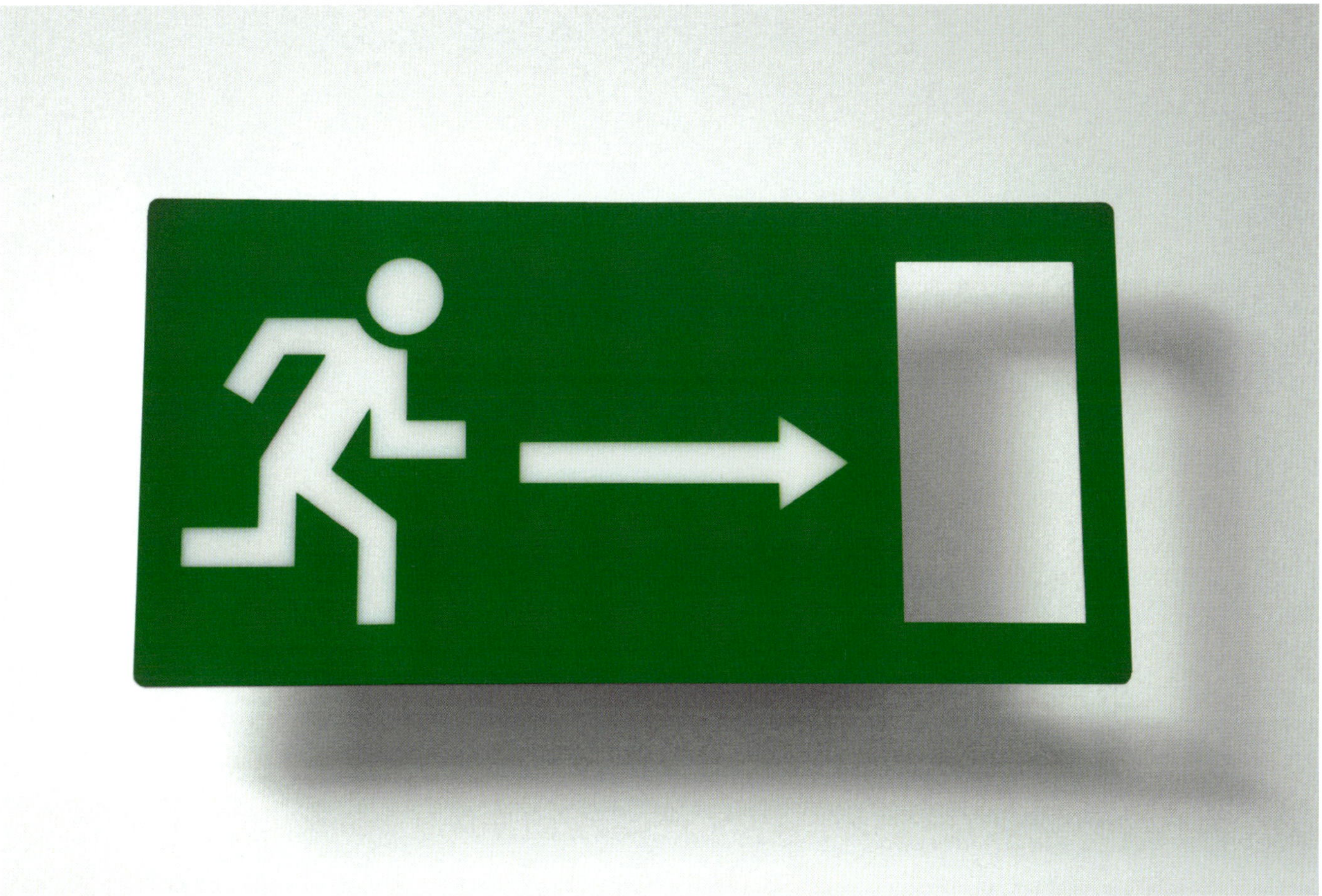

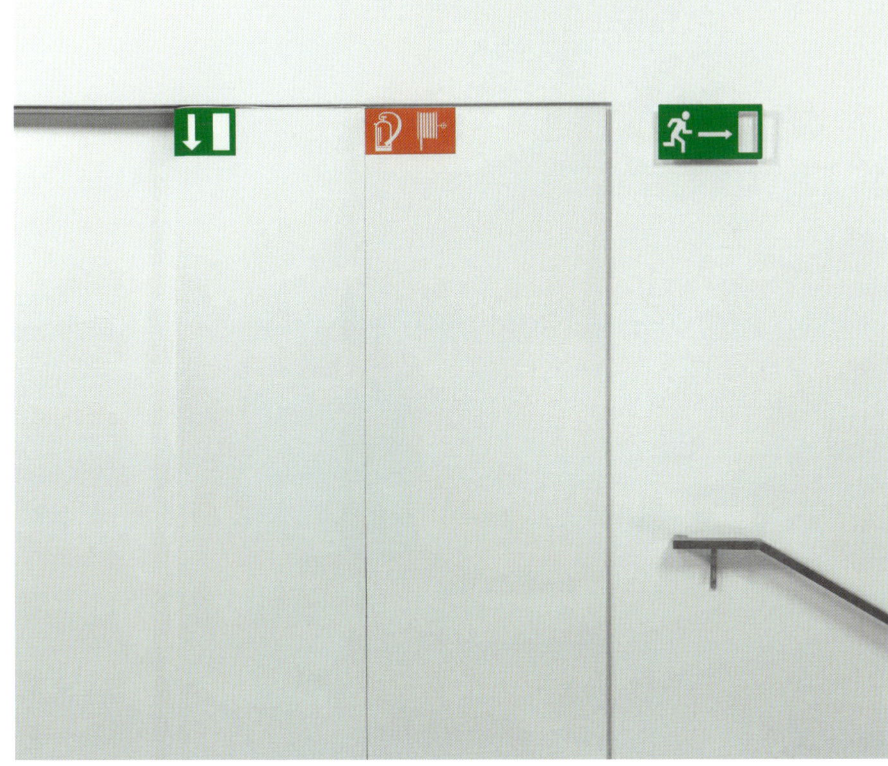

Genuine Reduction
2006

Modified silkscreen paper sign /
Abgeändertes Siebdruck-Papierschild
Wall-based sculpture, installation /
Wandskulptur, Installation
Dimensions / Maße: 12.5 × 67 cm
3 + 2 AP

A shop sign, most commonly encountered in the UK advertising a sale, has been edited to remove the final 's' in 'reductions' and hung centrally (as if the removed 's' were still intact) on the back wall of a glass-fronted exhibition space.

Ein vor allem in Großbritannien gebräuchliches Schild, mit dem auf Preisreduktionen hingewiesen wird, ist um das »s« von »reductions« gekürzt und in der Mitte (ausgehend von den Maßen des Originalschildes) der Rückwand eines Ausstellungsraumes mit Schaufensterfront installiert.

Genuine Reduction

Mind The Step
2006

Ready-made signs / Vorgefertigte Schilder
Installation, intervention /
Installation, Intervention
Dimensions variable / Maße variabel
Several unique language-specific versions /
Mehrere sprachspezifische Versionen (Unikate)

Each step of a staircase is affixed with a warning sign that reads 'Mind the Step'. Through repetition, a commonplace situation acquires an entirely different meaning.

Installation view: Humboldt Universität, Berlin, 2009

Schilder mit der Aufschrift »Mind The Step« (Vorsicht Stufe) sind an jeder Stufe einer Treppe angebracht. Durch die Wiederholung erhält die alltägliche Situation eine völlig neue Bedeutung.

Installationsansicht: Humboldt Universität, Berlin, 2009

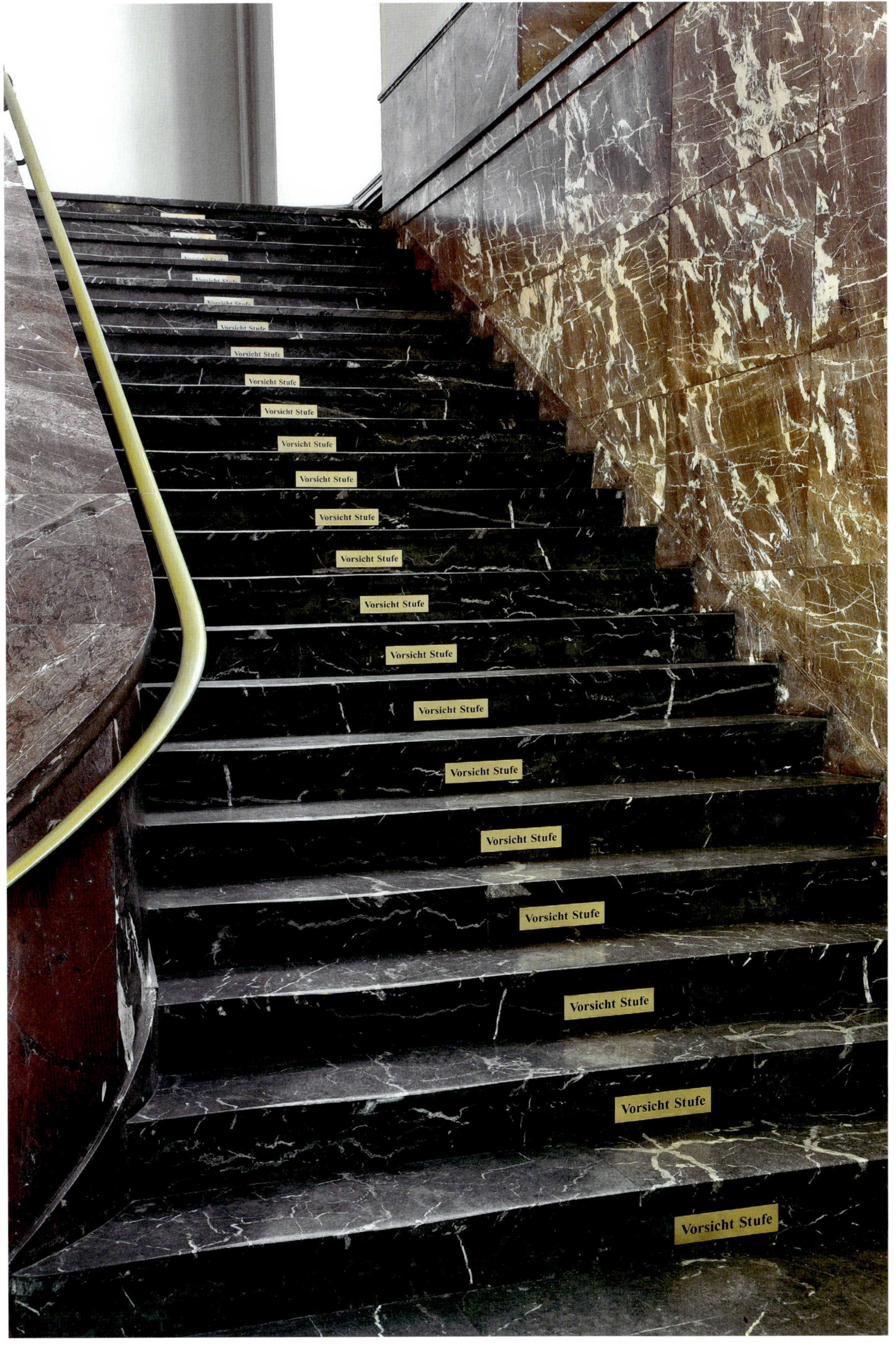

Vorsicht Stufe
Vorsicht Stufe
Vorsicht Stufe
Vorsicht Stufe
Vorsicht Stufe
Vorsicht Stufe
Vorsicht Stufe
Vorsicht Stufe
Vorsicht Stufe
Vorsicht Stufe
Vorsicht Stufe
Vorsicht Stufe
Vorsicht Stufe
Vorsicht Stufe
Vorsicht Stufe
Vorsicht Stufe

Overhead Projection
2006

Incandescent light bulb, overhead projector /
Klare Glühbirne, Overhead-Projektor
Projection / Projektion
Dimensions variable / Maße variabel
3 + 2 AP

Projection of an actual light bulb lying on an overhead projector. The enlarged projection meets the top edge of the wall where it touches the ceiling.

Installation view: DHC / ART Foundation for Contemporary Art, Montreal, 2011

Projektion einer Glühbirne, die auf dem Lichttisch eines Overhead-Projektors liegt. Die vergrößerte Projektion trifft auf die obere Kante der Wand, wo sie die Decke berührt.

Installationsansicht: DHC / ART Foundation for Contemporary Art, Montreal, 2011

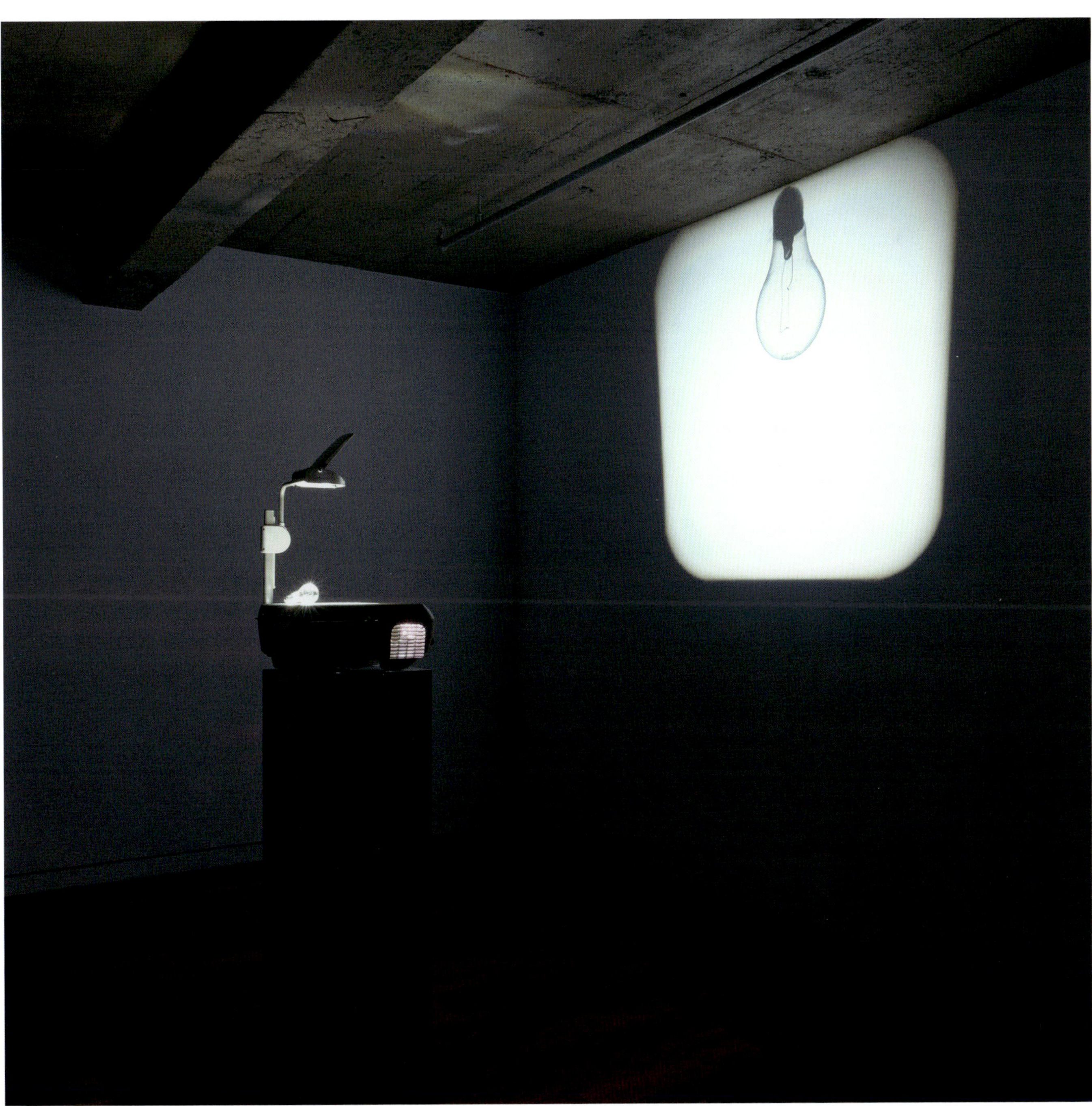

100%
2007

10 vinyl stickers / 10 Vinylaufkleber
Installation
Dimensions variable / Maße variabel
3 + 2 AP

Ten round, red, self-adhesive ‘10%’ sale stickers are stuck on the walls of an empty space.

Installation views: Kabinett für aktuelle Kunst, Bremerhaven, 2007

Zehn runde Aufkleber mit der weißen Aufschrift »10%« auf rotem Grund – wie man sie von Sonderangeboten kennt – sind auf den Wänden eines leeren Raumes verteilt.

Installationsansichten: Kabinett für aktuelle Kunst, Bremerhaven, 2007

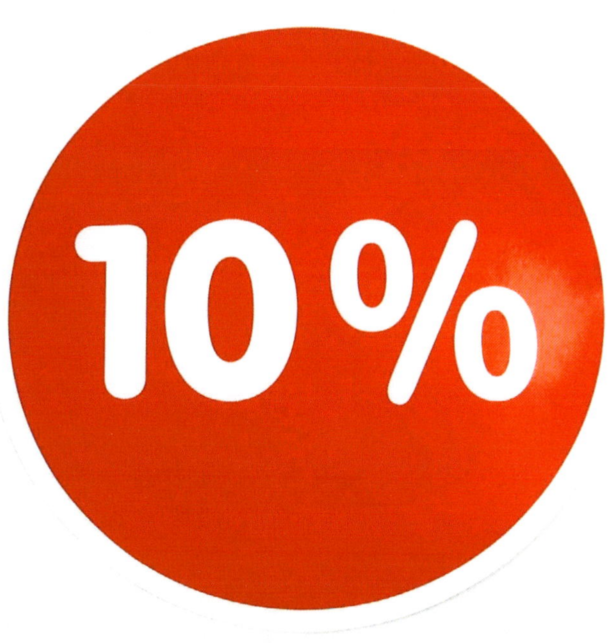
10%

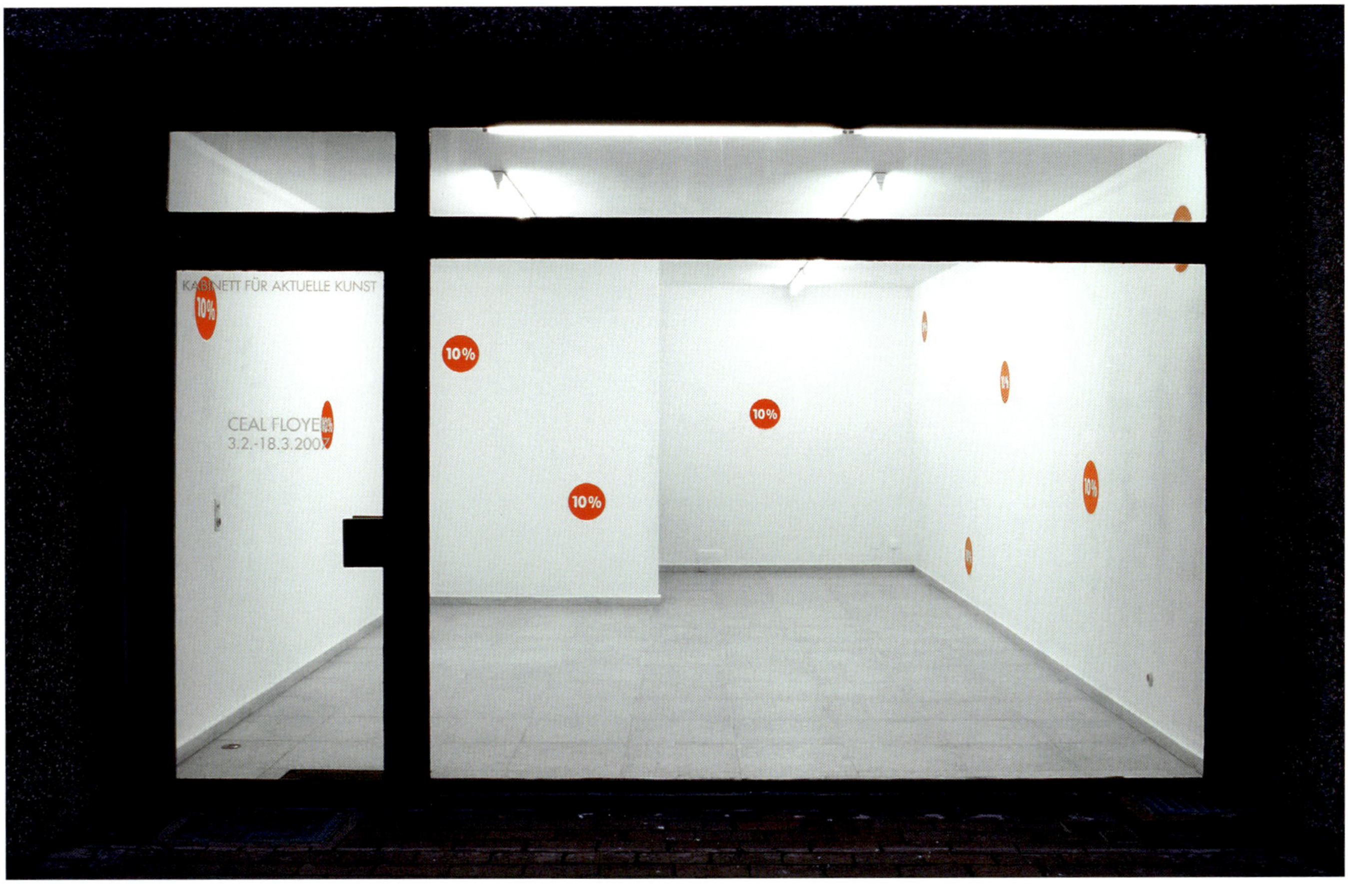

Dancing Flames
2007

DVD, DVD player, projector, MP3 player (with shuffle function), speakers /
DVD, DVD-Spieler, Projektor, MP3-Spieler (mit Zufallswiedergabe-Funktion), Lautsprecher
Audio, video installation /
Audio-, Videoinstallation
Dimensions variable / Maße variabel
3 + 2 AP

A candle flame and its reflection, enlarged to roughly human size by the projection on the wall, appear to dance in synchronicity with themselves and a randomly chosen, attendant soundtrack.

Installation view: Esther Schipper, Berlin, 2008

Eine Kerzenflamme und ihre Spiegelung, die durch die Projektion auf eine Wand auf menschliches Maß vergrößert sind, tanzen scheinbar synchron miteinander und zur zufällig ausgewählten Begleitmusik.

Installationsansicht: Esther Schipper, Berlin, 2008

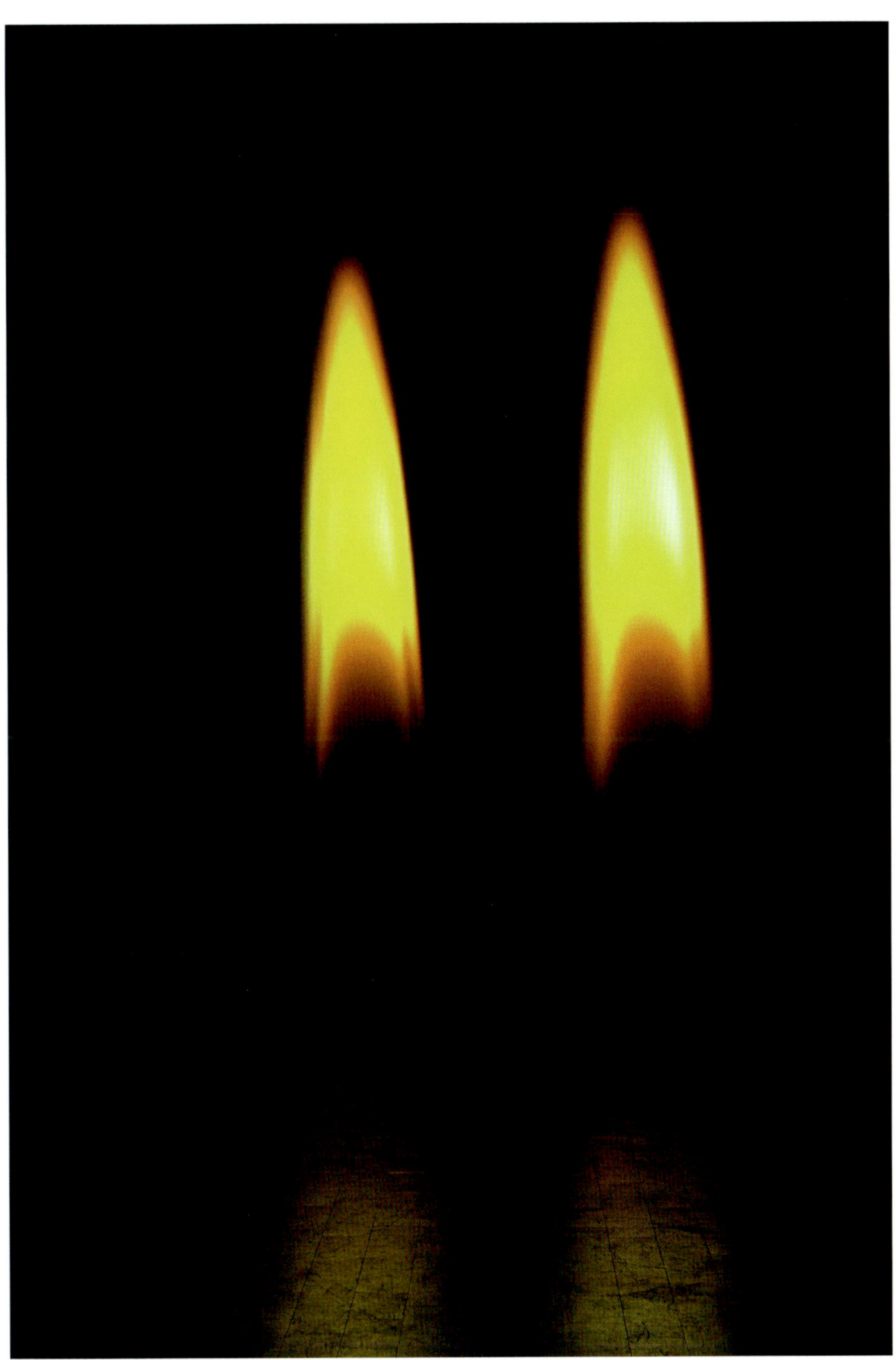

No Positions Available
2007

Plastic signs / Plastikschilder
Sculpture / Skulptur
Dimensions variable (each sign: 35 × 24 cm) /
Maße variabel (jedes Schild: 35 × 24 cm)
3 + 2 AP

Signs usually employed in shop windows to indicate a lack of employment opportunities are crammed to fill an entire wall, thus rendering the sign's meaning literal in relation to space.

Installation view: Esther Schipper, Berlin, 2008

»No Positions Available«-Schilder, die normalerweise in Schaufenstern darauf hinweisen, dass es keine freie Stelle gibt, sind in möglichst geringem Abstand flächendeckend auf einer Wand installiert, sodass ihre Bedeutung wörtlich und konkret wird.

Installationsansicht: Esther Schipper, Berlin, 2008

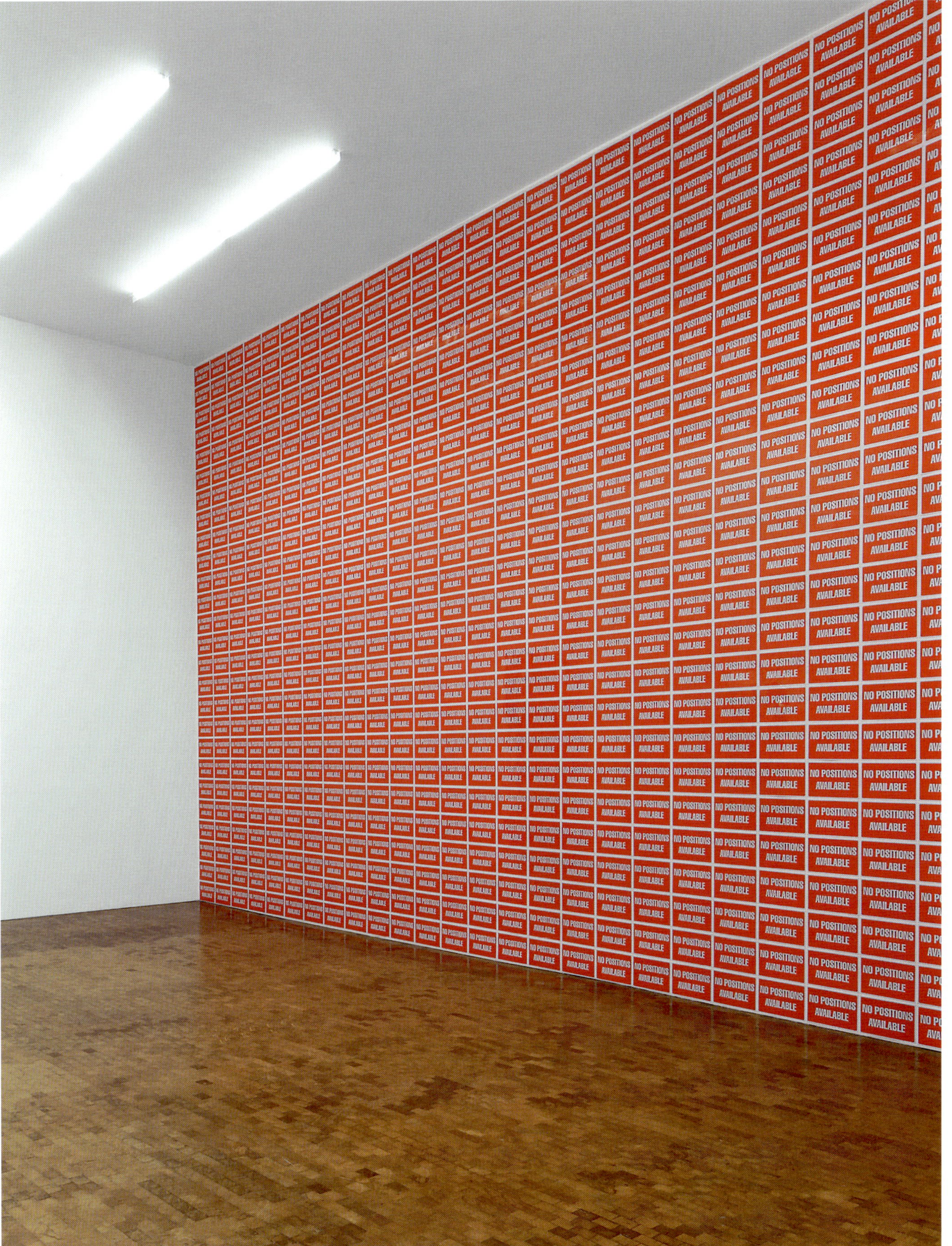
NO POSITIONS AVAILABLE

Order
2007

Index card dividers, rubber support, plinth /
Karteikartenteiler, Gummihalterung, Sockel
Sculpture / Skulptur
Dimensions / Maße: 135 × 40 × 40 cm
3 + 2 AP

Each index card divider is re-positioned so that all the index letters are centred, forming a straight line. The systematic principle of 'order' is made literal, but in an aesthetic sense.

Installation view: Museion, Bolzano, 2014

Jeder Karteikartenteiler ist neu positioniert, sodass alle Buchstabenreiter zentriert sind und eine gerade Linie bilden. Das systematische Ordnungsprinzip ist wörtlich genommen, aber eher in einem ästhetischen Sinn.

Installationsansicht: Museion, Bozen, 2014

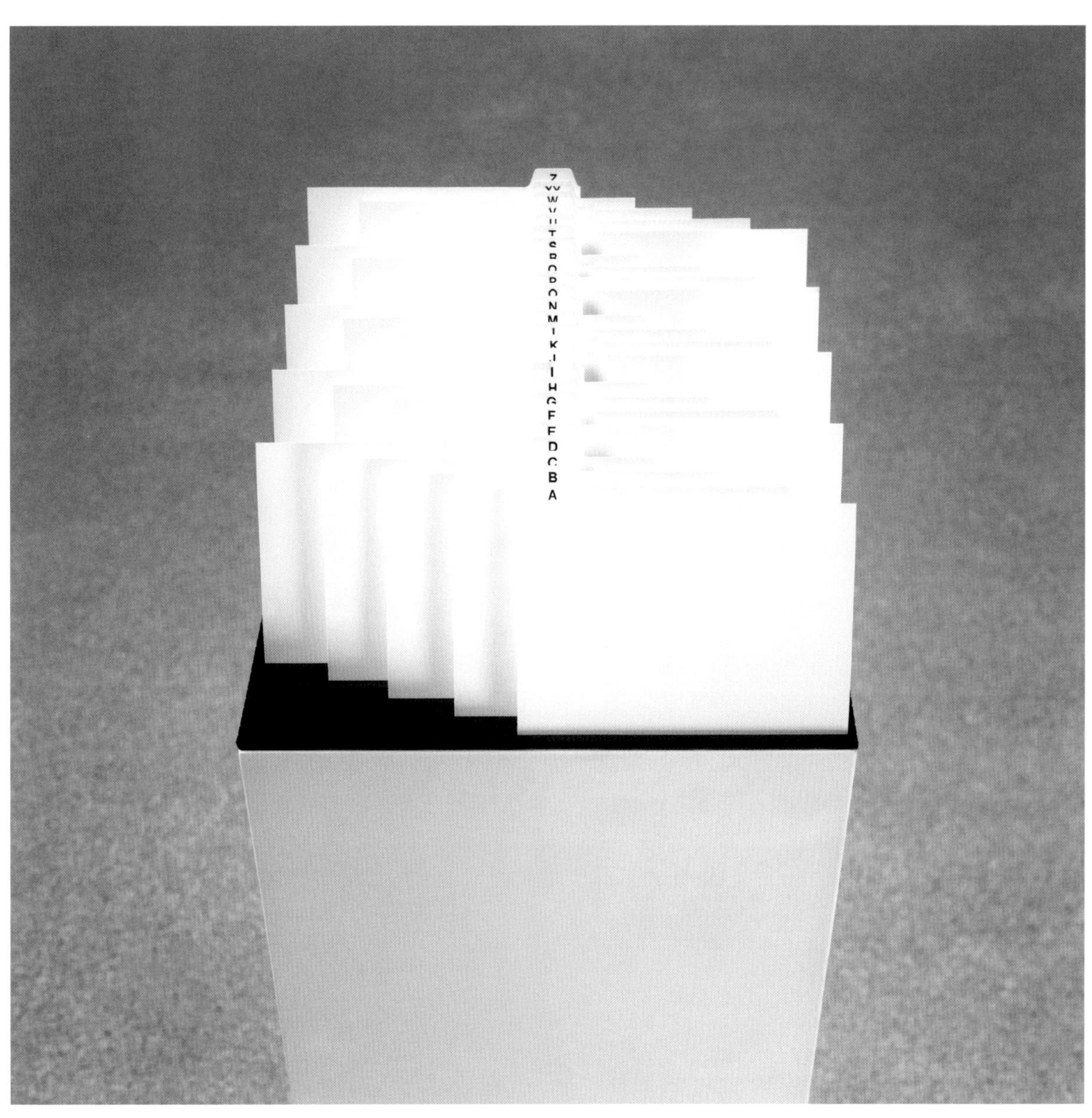

Scale
2007

Even number of mounted speakers, computer, stereo amplifiers, sound file / Gerade Anzahl montierter Lautsprecher, Computer, Stereoverstärker, Sounddatei
Audio sculpture, installation / Audioskulptur, Installation
Dimensions variable, speakers 86 × 20 × 25 cm each / Maße variabel, Lautsprecher je 86 × 20 × 25 cm
3 + 2 AP

An even number of black loudspeakers is attached to a wall. This minimal sculpture—when coupled with its audio component—inevitably creates the illusion of a person repeatedly ascending and descending stairs.

Installation view: Hamburger Bahnhof – Museum für Gegenwart, Berlin, 2007

Eine gerade Anzahl schwarzer Lautsprecher ist an der Wand angebracht. Sobald diese minimalistische Skulptur mit dem dazugehörigen Ton gekoppelt wird, entsteht unweigerlich die Vorstellung einer Person, die wiederholt eine Treppe hinauf- und hinabsteigt.

Installationsansicht: Hamburger Bahnhof – Museum für Gegenwart, Berlin, 2007

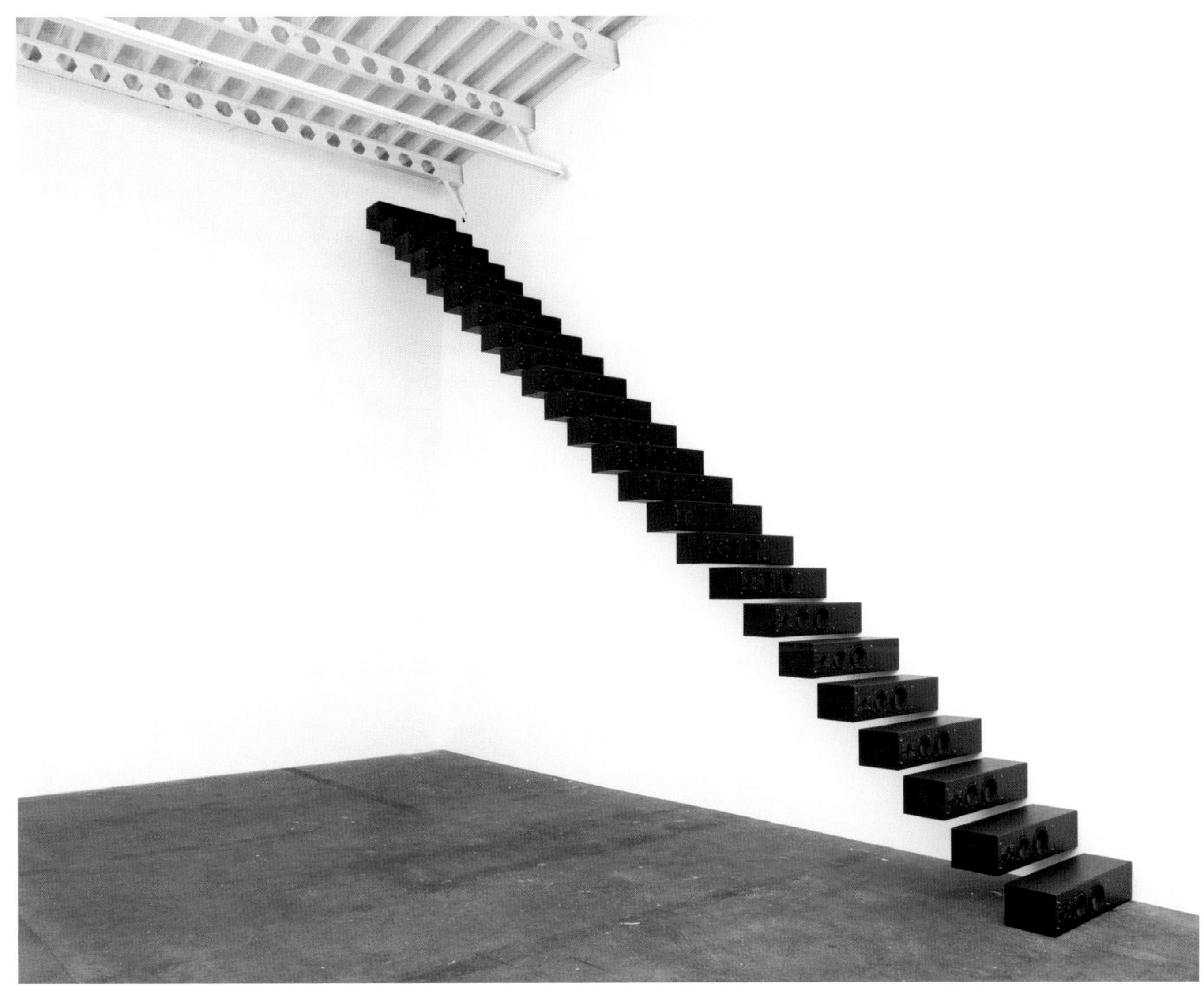

Taking A Line For A Walk
2008

Line-marking paint, line-marking machine /
Markierungsfarbe, Markierungsmaschine
Installation
Dimensions variable / Maße variabel
3 + 2 AP

A marked line with a significant starting point makes a random journey through space, ending logically when the mark-making apparatus runs out of paint. The machine remains in its final position.
This work was initially conceived for the show *5 Minutes Later* at KW Institute for Contemporary Art, Berlin. The original title of the inaugural version, curated by Susanne Pfeffer, was *Taking A Line For A (5 minute) Walk*, and the logistical 'stop' determined the spatial / sculptural outcome. Subsequently, at the Palais de Tokyo in Paris, an alternative premise was chosen, in this case simply the volume of paint in the bucket (i.e., 5 litres).

Installation views: KW Institute for Contemporary Art, Berlin, 2008 (top), Lisson Gallery, Milan, 2013 (lower left and right)

Eine Markierungslinie mit einem auffälligen Anfangspunkt schlängelt sich wie zufällig durch einen Raum und endet, wenn der Markierungsmaschine die Farbe ausgeht. Die Maschine bleibt an der Endposition stehen.
Diese Arbeit wurde ursprünglich für die Ausstellung *5 minutes later* im KW Institute for Contemporary Art, Berlin konzipiert. In der von Susanne Pfeffer kuratierten Ausstellung war die ursprüngliche Fassung dieser Arbeit, *Taking A Line For A (5 minute) Walk*, zu sehen, und das logistische »Ende« bestimmte das räumliche / skulpturale Ergebnis. Später, im Palais de Tokyo in Paris, war die Vorgabe zur Festlegung des Endes beziehungsweise der Ausdehnung der Arbeit einfach die Farbmenge in der Markierungsmaschine (in diesem Fall 5 Liter).

Installationsansichten: KW Institute for Contemporary Art, Berlin, 2008 (oben), Lisson Gallery, Mailand, 2013 (unten links und rechts)

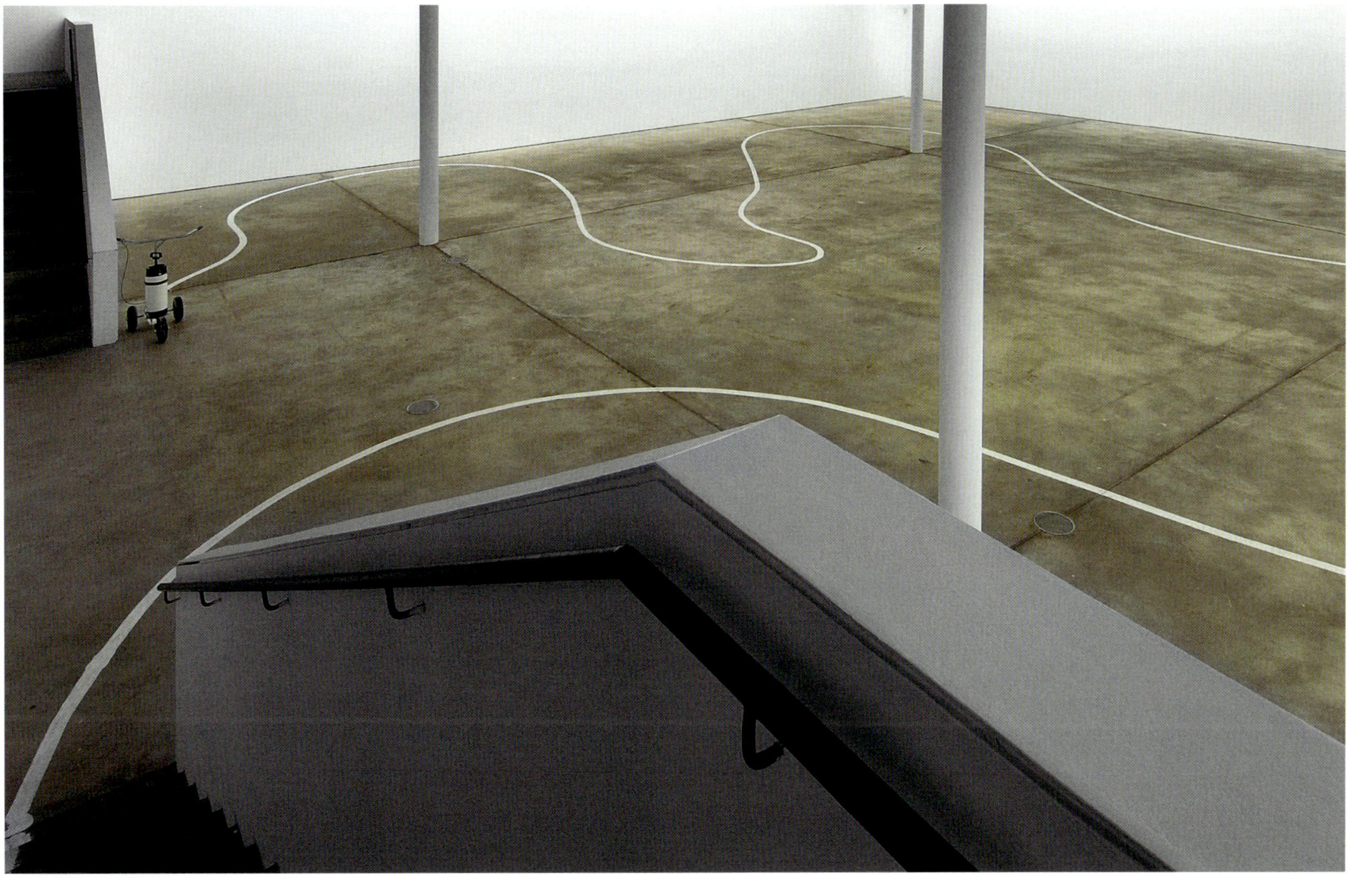

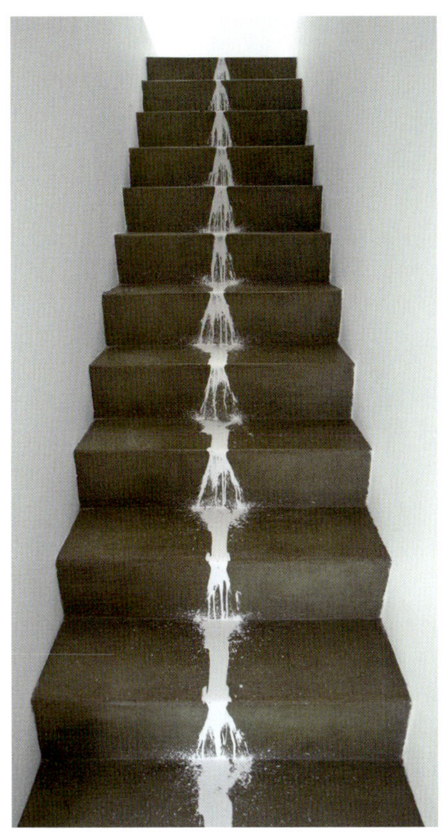

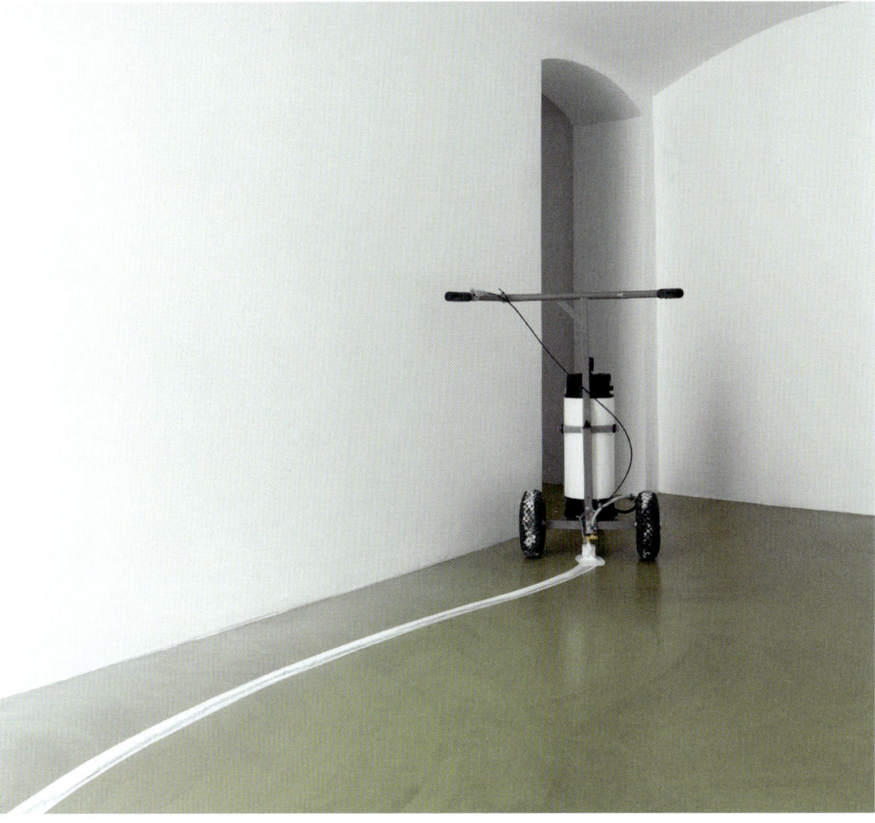

Untitled (Suggestion Box)
2008

Ready-made ‘Suggestion Box’,
ready-made ‘Closed’ sign, chain /
Vorgefertigte »Vorschläge-Box«,
vorgefertigtes »Geschlossen«-Schild, Kette
Sculpture, object / Skulptur, Objekt
Dimensions / Maße: 31 × 30 × 15.5 cm
3 + 2 AP

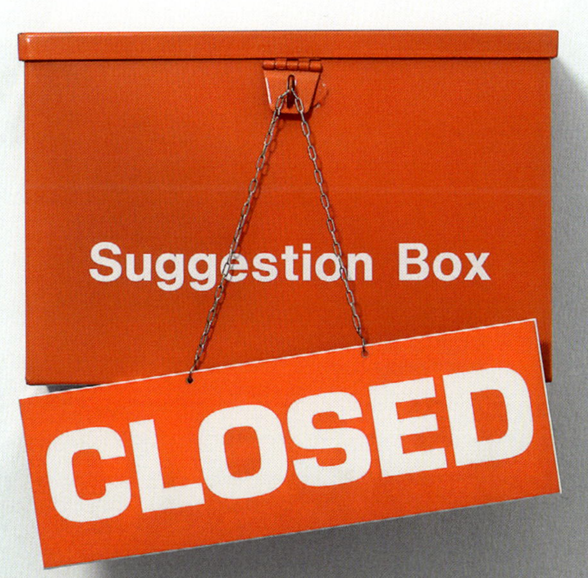
Suggestion Box
CLOSED

Wish you were here
2008

Postcard stand / Postkartenständer
Sculpture, object / Skulptur, Objekt
Dimensions / Maße: 179 × 41.5 × 41.5 cm
3 + 2 AP

‘Wish you were here’ is a clichéd phrase normally seen on postcards. In the case of this sculpture, it refers to the absence of the cards themselves.

Installation view: Esther Schipper, Berlin, 2008

»Wish you were here« (Ich wünschte, Du wärst hier) ist eine Phrase, die man oft auf Postkarten liest. Bei dieser Skulptur bezieht sie sich auf die fehlenden Karten selbst.

Installationsansicht: Esther Schipper, Berlin, 2008

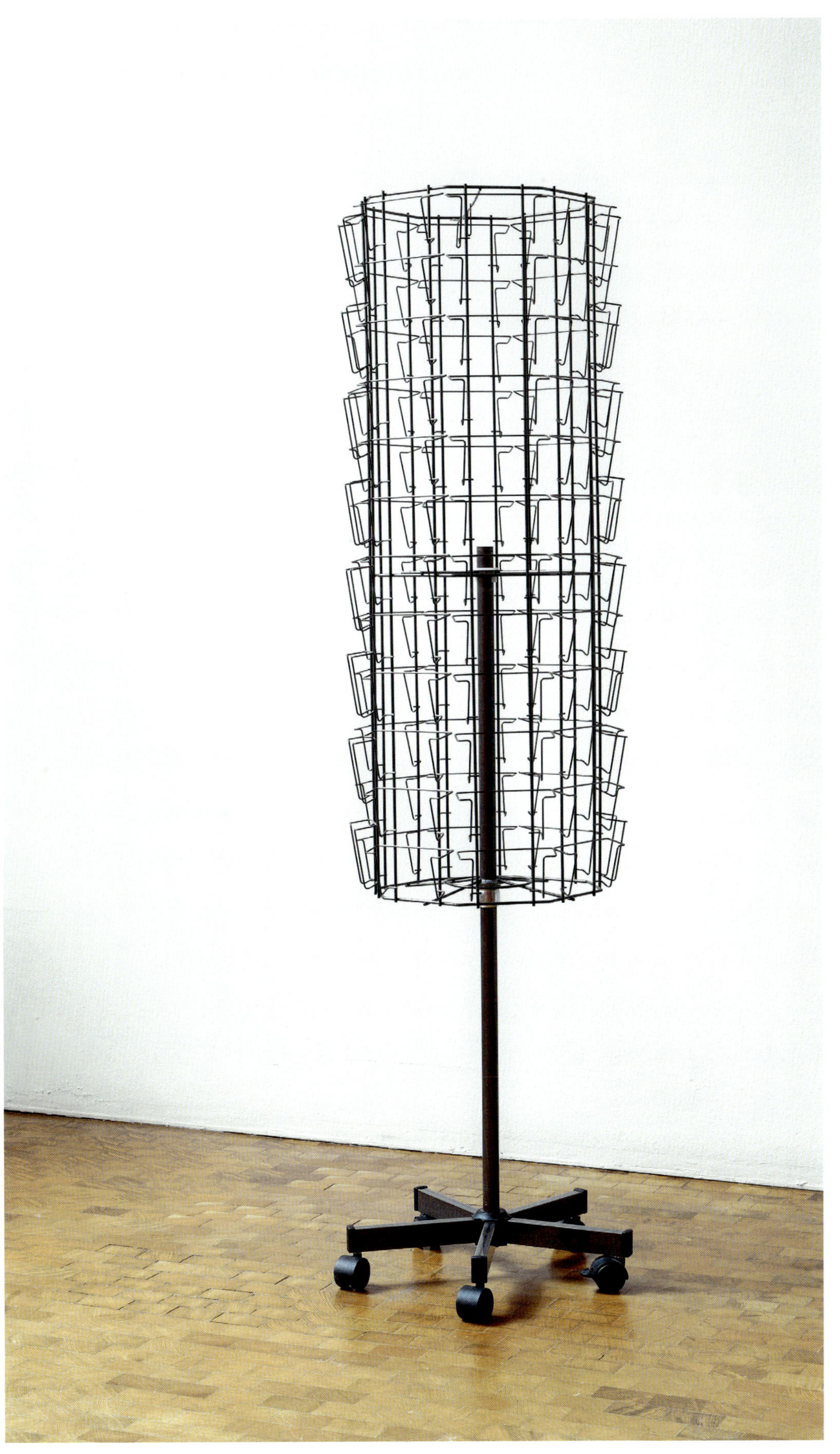

Duck Rabbit
2009

Modified poster, mounted on alu-dibond /
Abgeändertes Plakat auf Alu-Dibond
Print / Druck
Dimensions / Maße: 60 × 60 cm
6 + 2 AP

The iconic *Playboy* image, now square (and cropped to remove the bow tie), is rotated forty-five degrees on its axis to suggest the head of a duck.

Installation view: KW Institute for Contemporary Art, Berlin, 2009

Das bekannte, hier quadratische *Playboy*-Symbol (es ist beschnitten, sodass die Fliege wegfällt) ist um 45 Grad auf seine Spitze gedreht, sodass der Kopf einer Ente darin gesehen werden kann.

Installationsansicht: KW Institute for Contemporary Art, Berlin, 2009

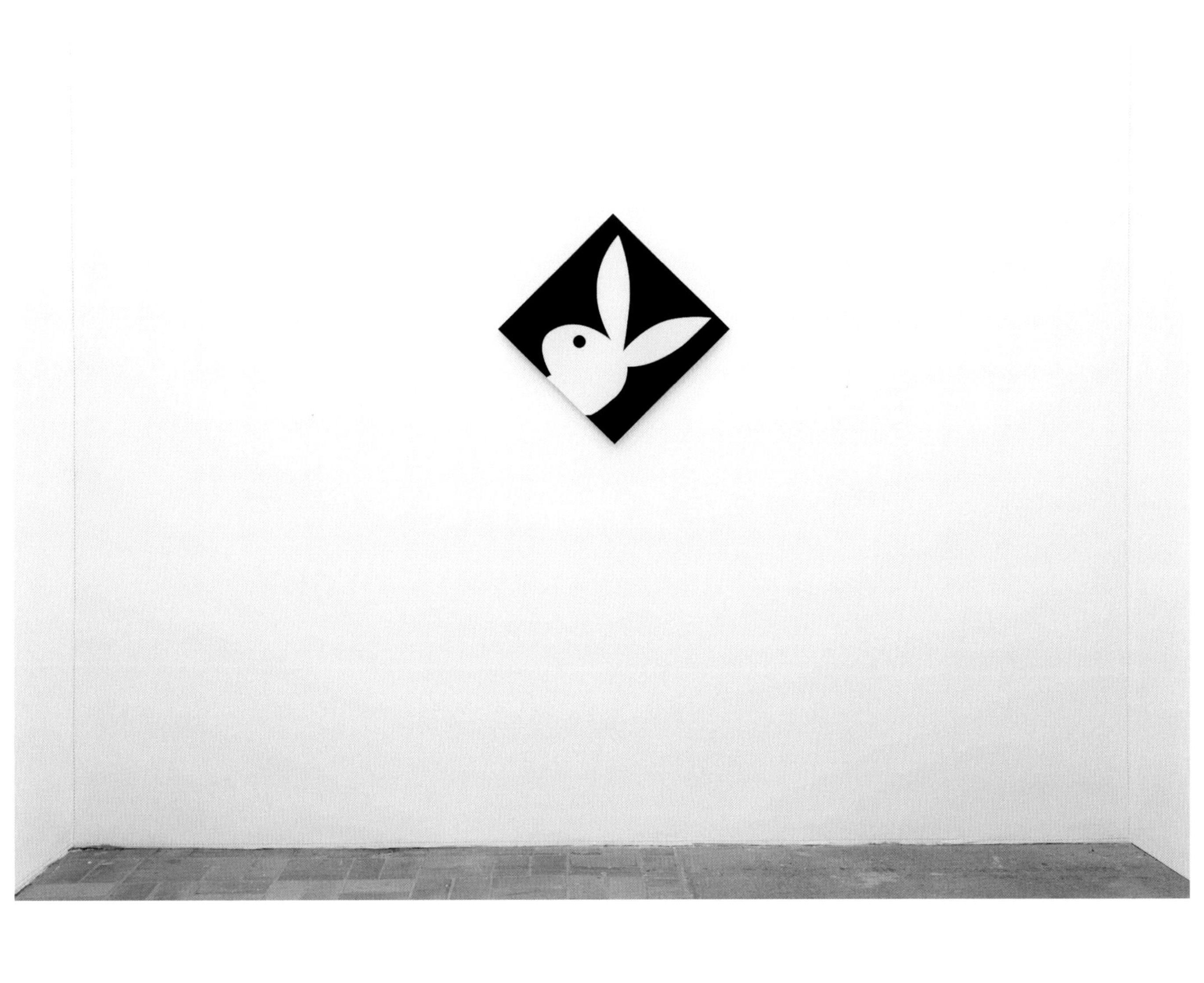

ON AIR
2009

Ready-made 'On Air' sign /
Vorgefertigtes »On Air«-Schild
Sculpture, object / Skulptur, Objekt
Dimensions variable / Maße variabel
3 + 2 AP

The placement of an 'On Air' sign, which is normally found outside the live broadcasting room of a radio / TV station, is shifted to the interior above the main exit doors of the exhibition space.

Installation view: Palais de Tokyo, Paris, 2009

Die Platzierung eines »On Air«-Zeichens – für »Auf Sendung« –, das man normalerweise außen an einem Radio- oder Fernsehaufnahme-Studio findet, ist nach innen über die Hauptausgangstür eines Ausstellungsraums verlegt.

Installationsansicht: Palais de Tokyo, Paris, 2009

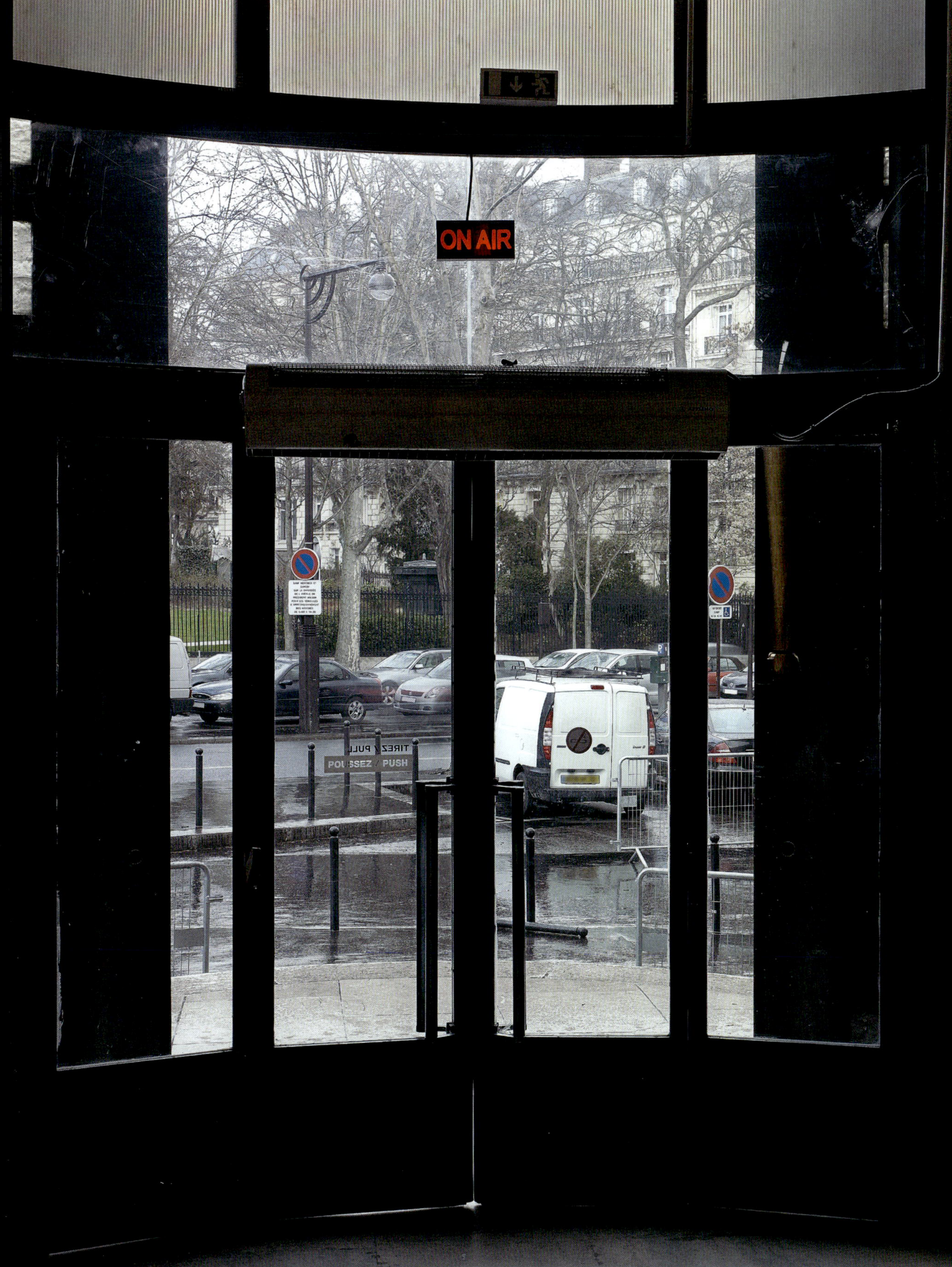
ON AIR
POUSSEZ / PUSH

Things
2009

CDs, CD player, speakers, cables, wood /
CDs, CD-Spieler, Lautsprecher, Kabel, Holz
Audio installation / Audioinstallation
Dimensions variable / Maße variabel
3 + 2 AP

In a room are twenty-five white pedestals with white loudspeakers embedded flush with the top. From each of them, one can hear the word 'thing', as edited out of the following songs:

Kate Nash: 'Nicest Thing' – Lauryn Hill: 'Doo Wop (That Thing)' – Devendra Banhart: 'An Island' – Gwen Stefani: 'The Real Thing' – Dashboard Confessional: 'Ghost of a Good Thing' – Scissor Sisters: 'Everybody Wants the Same Thing' – Aimee Mann: 'Stupid Thing' – Belinda Carlisle: 'We Want the Same Thing' – Bo Diddley: 'Pretty Thing' – Bryan Adams: 'The Only Thing That Looks Good on Me Is You' – Carly Simon: 'The Right Thing to Do' – Diana Krall: 'The Best Thing for You' – Duke Ellington: 'It Don't Mean a Thing' – Ella Fitzgerald: 'Let's Call the Whole Thing Off' – Sheryl Crow: 'Love is a Good Thing' – Suzanne Vega: 'Small Blue Thing' – Simon & Garfunkel: 'We've Got a Groovy Thing Going' – Johnny Cash: 'You're the Nearest Thing to Heaven' – Woody Guthrie: 'The Biggest Thing That Man Has Ever Done' – Isley Brothers: 'It's Your Thing' – James Brown: 'Get up offa That Thing' – Morrissey: 'Such a Little Thing Can Make Such a Difference' – Iron & Wine: 'Passing Afternoon' – Harry Connick Jr.: 'Let's Call the Whole Thing Off' – Jeff Buckley: 'Sweet Thing' – Rod Stewart: 'Until the Real Thing Comes Along' – Travis: 'Funny Thing' – Isaac Hayes: 'Do Your Thing' – Tone Loc: 'Wild Thing' – Incognito: 'Don't You Worry' – Usher: 'Hottest Thing' – The Be Good Tanyas: 'Human Thing' – Bernard Fanning: 'The Strangest Thing' – Rufus and Chaka Khan: 'Sweet Thing' – Pete Yorn: 'Same Thing' – The Black Keys: 'Same Old Thing' – Ocean Colour Scene: 'A Beautiful Thing' – Waterboys: 'Sweet Thing' – Dianne Reeves: 'TV is the Thing' – Frank Sinatra: 'What is This Thing Called Love' – Nancy Sinatra: 'Things' – Fred Astaire: 'Let's Call the Whole Thing Off' – Camouflage: 'Real Thing' – Field Music: 'Luck Is a Fine Thing' – The Plan: 'My Thing' – Pornopop: 'It Doesn't Mean a Thing' – Lisa Ekdahl: 'I've Never Seen Anything Like You' – Candi Staton: 'The Best Thing You Ever Had' – Prince: 'Hot Thing'

Installation view: KW Institute for Contemporary Art, Berlin, 2009

In einem Raum stehen 25 weiße Sockel, in die, bündig mit der oberen Fläche, weiße Lautsprecher eingebaut sind. Sie spielen das Wort »thing«, das aus den folgenden Songs ausgeschnitten wurde:

Kate Nash: »Nicest Thing« – Lauryn Hill: »Doo Wop (That Thing)« – Devendra Banhart: »An Island« – Gwen Stefani: »The Real Thing« – Dashboard Confessional: »Ghost of a Good Thing« – Scissor Sisters: »Everybody Wants the Same Thing« – Aimee Mann: »Stupid Thing« – Belinda Carlisle: »We Want the Same Thing« – Bo Diddley: »Pretty Thing« – Bryan Adams: »The Only Thing That Looks Good on Me Is You« – Carly Simon: »The Right Thing to Do« – Diana Krall: »The Best Thing for You« – Duke Ellington: »It Don't Mean a Thing« – Ella Fitzgerald: »Let's Call the Whole Thing Off« – Sheryl Crow: »Love is a Good Thing« – Suzanne Vega: »Small Blue Thing« – Simon & Garfunkel: »We've Got a Groovy Thing Going« – Johnny Cash: »You're the Nearest Thing to Heaven« – Woody Guthrie: »The Biggest Thing That Man Has Ever Done« – Isley Brothers: »It's Your Thing« – James Brown: »Get up offa That Thing« – Morrissey: »Such a Little Thing Can Make Such a Difference« – Iron & Wine: »Passing Afternoon« – Harry Connick Jr.: »Let's Call the Whole Thing Off« – Jeff Buckley: »Sweet Thing« – Rod Stewart: »Until the Real Thing Comes Along« – Travis: »Funny Thing« – Isaac Hayes: »Do Your Thing« – Tone Loc: »Wild Thing« – Incognito: »Don't You Worry« – Usher: »Hottest Thing« – The Be Good Tanyas: »Human Thing« – Bernard Fanning: »The Strangest Thing« – Rufus and Chaka Khan: »Sweet Thing« – Pete Yorn: »Same Thing« – The Black Keys: »Same Old Thing« – Ocean Colour Scene: »A Beautiful Thing« – Waterboys: »Sweet Thing« – Dianne Reeves: »TV is the Thing« – Frank Sinatra: »What is This Thing Called Love« – Nancy Sinatra: »Things« – Fred Astaire: »Let's Call the Whole Thing Off« – Camouflage: »Real Thing« – Field Music: »Luck Is a Fine Thing« – The Plan: »My Thing« – Pornopop: »It Doesn't Mean a Thing« – Lisa Ekdahl: »I've Never Seen Anything Like You« – Candi Staton: »The Best Thing You Ever Had« – Prince: »Hot Thing«

Installationsansicht: KW Institute for Contemporary Art, Berlin, 2009

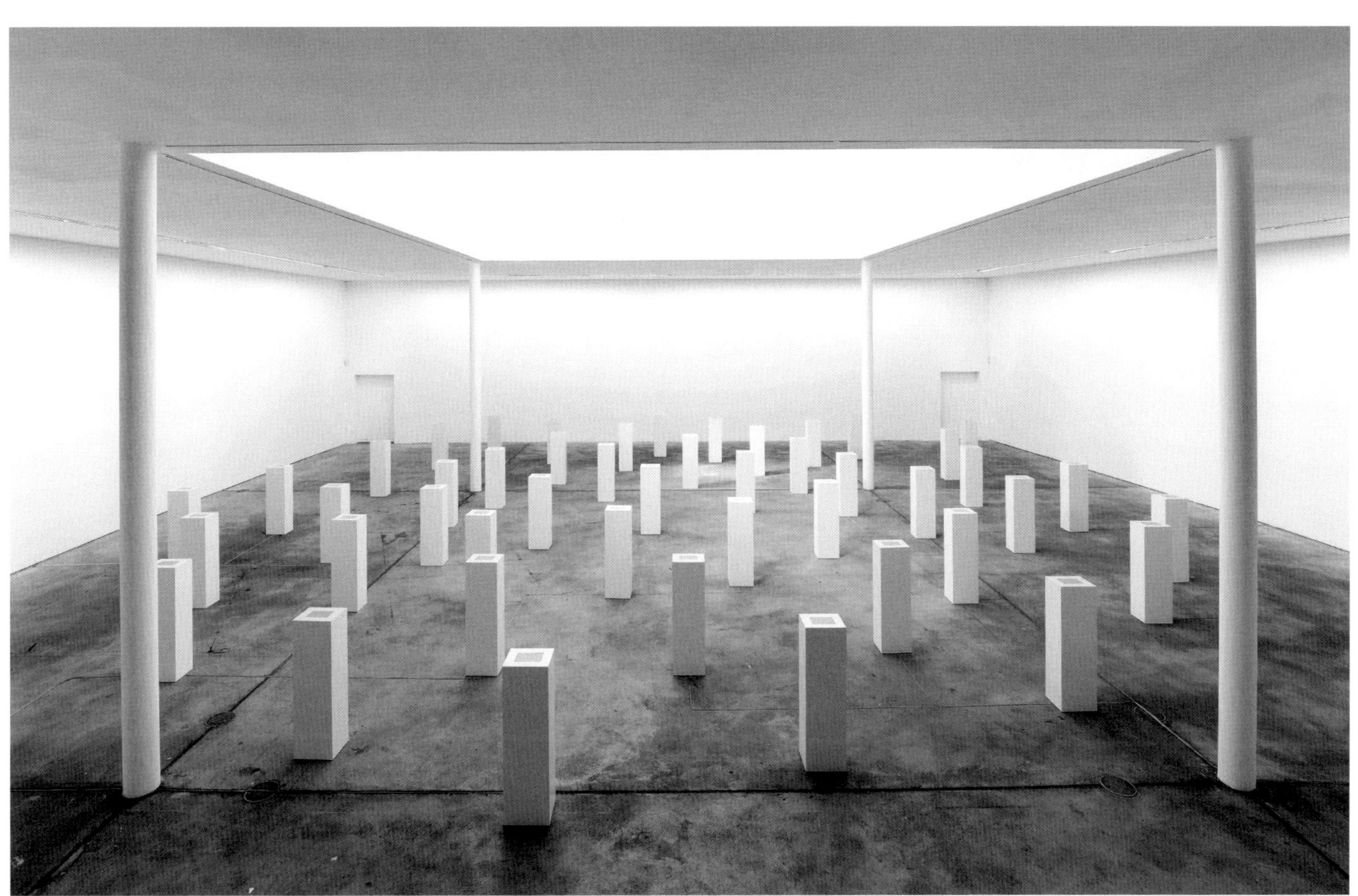

Today's Special
2009

Ready-made two-sided chalkboard, chalk /
Vorgefertigte doppelseitige Tafel, Kreide
Sculpture, object / Skulptur, Objekt
Dimensions / Maße: 52 × 57 × 54 cm
3 + 2 AP

This work plays on a misreading: if the apostrophe were to indicate an abbreviation of the verb 'is', the sign would mean 'Today is special'.

TODAY'S SPECIAL
(on reverse)
TOMORROW'S ANOTHER DAY

Installation views: 303 Gallery, New York, 2009

Das englische »'s« kann auf einen Genitiv hinweisen oder eine Abkürzung für »is« (ist) sein. Das Werk spielt mit dieser Doppeldeutigkeit.

TODAY'S SPECIAL
(auf der Rückseite)
TOMORROW'S ANOTHER DAY

Installationsansichten: 303 Gallery, New York, 2009

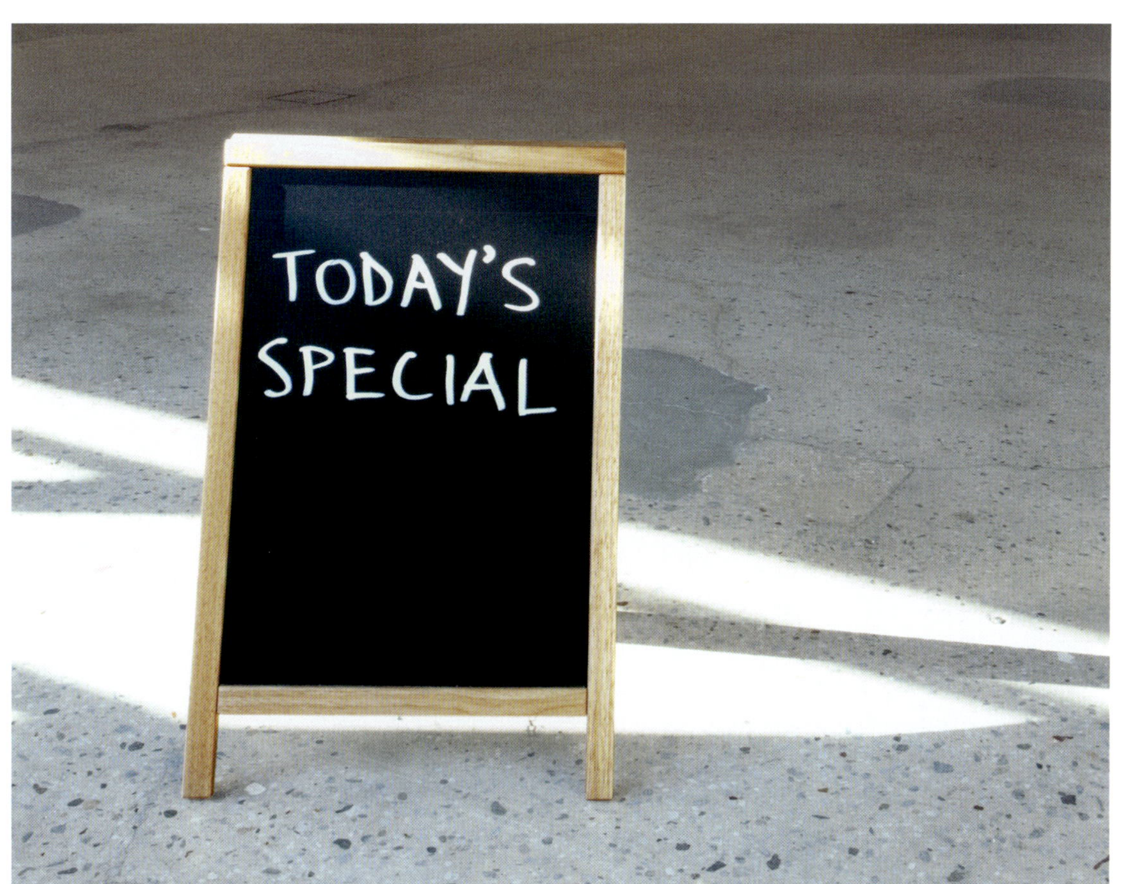
TODAY'S
SPECIAL

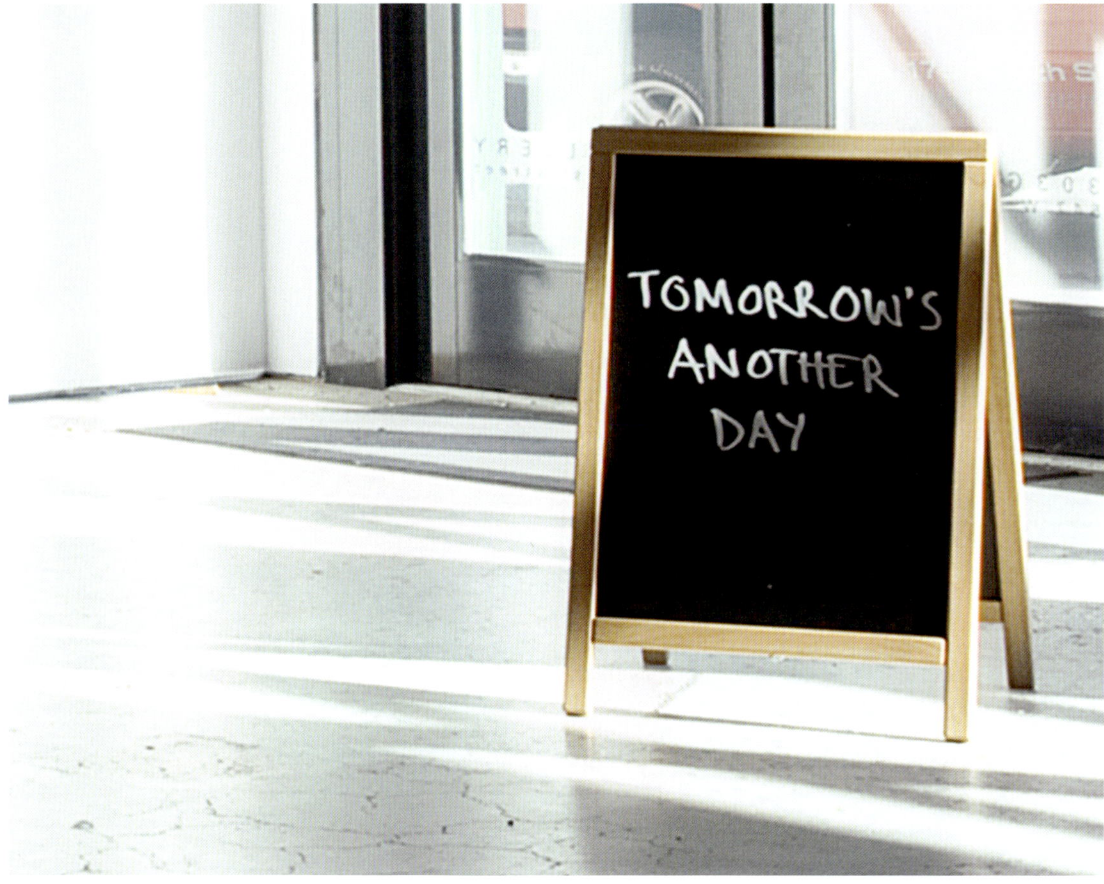
TOMORROW'S
ANOTHER
DAY

Ladder
2010

Modified aluminium ladder /
Abgeänderte Aluminiumleiter
Sculpture, object / Skulptur, Objekt
Dimensions / Maße: 279 × 35 × 5 cm
3 + 2 AP

A standard metal ladder is missing all but the highest and lowest rungs, negating its function as a tool and rendering it a purely minimalist sculpture.

Installation view: Lisson Gallery, London, 2010

Eine Aluminiumleiter lehnt an einer Wand. Mit Ausnahme der untersten und der obersten fehlen alle Sprossen, sodass die Leiter keine Funktion hat und zur minimalistischen Skulptur wird.

Installationsansicht: Lisson Gallery, London, 2010

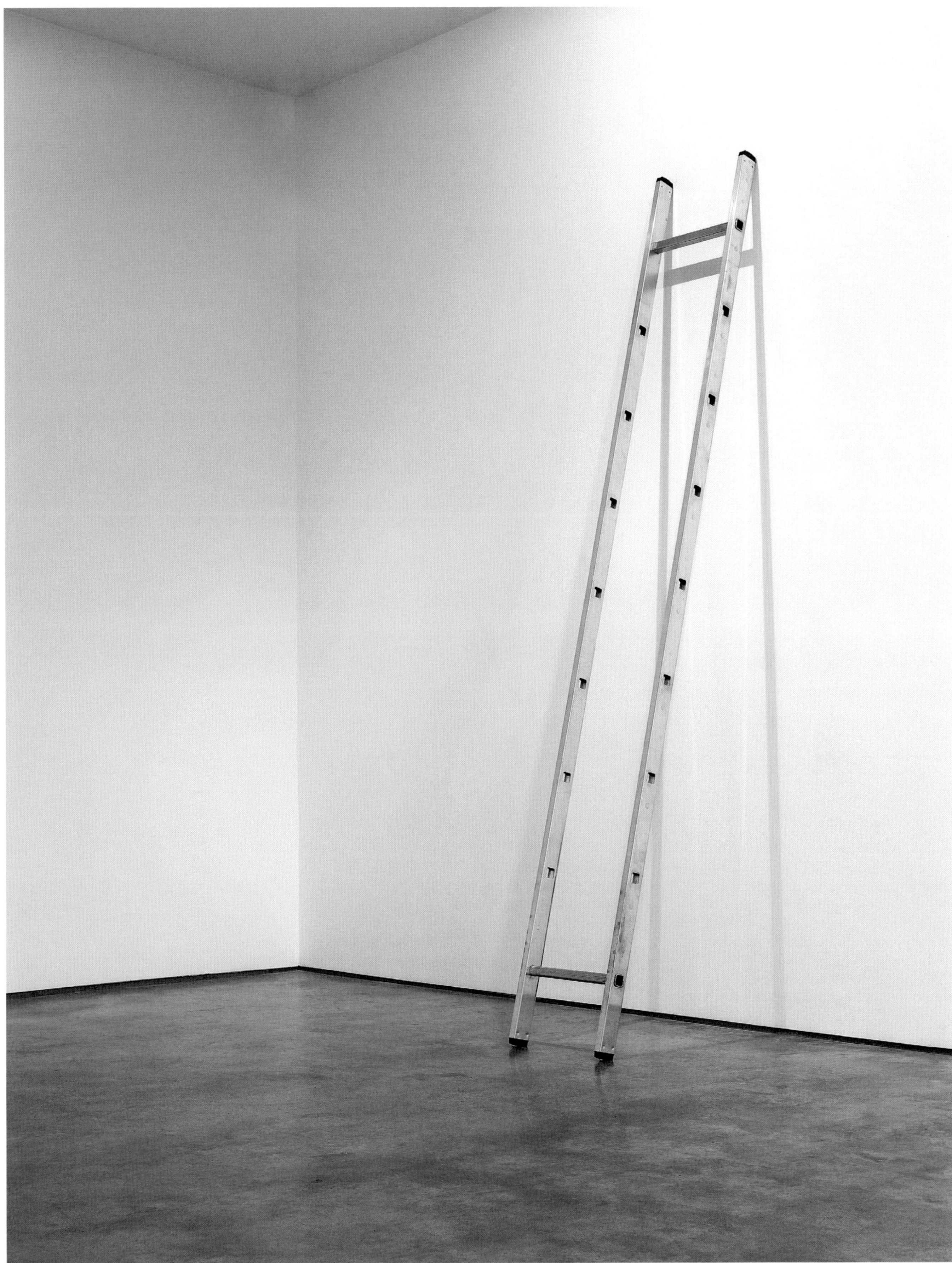

Page 8680 of 8680
2010

Ink on 8,680 sheets of A4-sized paper (90 g/m^2) /
Tinte auf 8680 DIN A4-Blättern (90g/m^2)
Sculpture / Skulptur
Dimensions: 125 × 21 × 29.7 cm (height varies slightly) / Maße: 125 × 21 × 29,7 cm (Höhe leicht unterschiedlich)
3 + 2 AP

The number of sheets, size, and weight of the paper is predetermined: 8680 sheets of paper are printed and numbered continuously from ‘page 1 of 8680’ to ‘page 8680 of 8680’. The sheets of paper are precisely stacked on top of one another with page 8680 uppermost. The form and placement of the stack is reminiscent of a generic plinth.

Installation views: Lisson Gallery, London, 2010

Festgelegt sind die Anzahl der Blätter, ihre Größe und das Gewicht des Papiers. 8680 Blätter sind auf jeweils einer Seite mit einer fortlaufenden Nummerierung von »Page 1 of 8680« bis zu »Page 8680 of 8680« bedruckt. Die Blätter sind präzise aufeinandergestapelt. Blatt 8680 liegt obenauf. Die Form und die Platzierung des Papierstapels im Raum erinnert an einen Sockel in einer Standardgröße.

Installationsansichten: Lisson Gallery, London, 2010

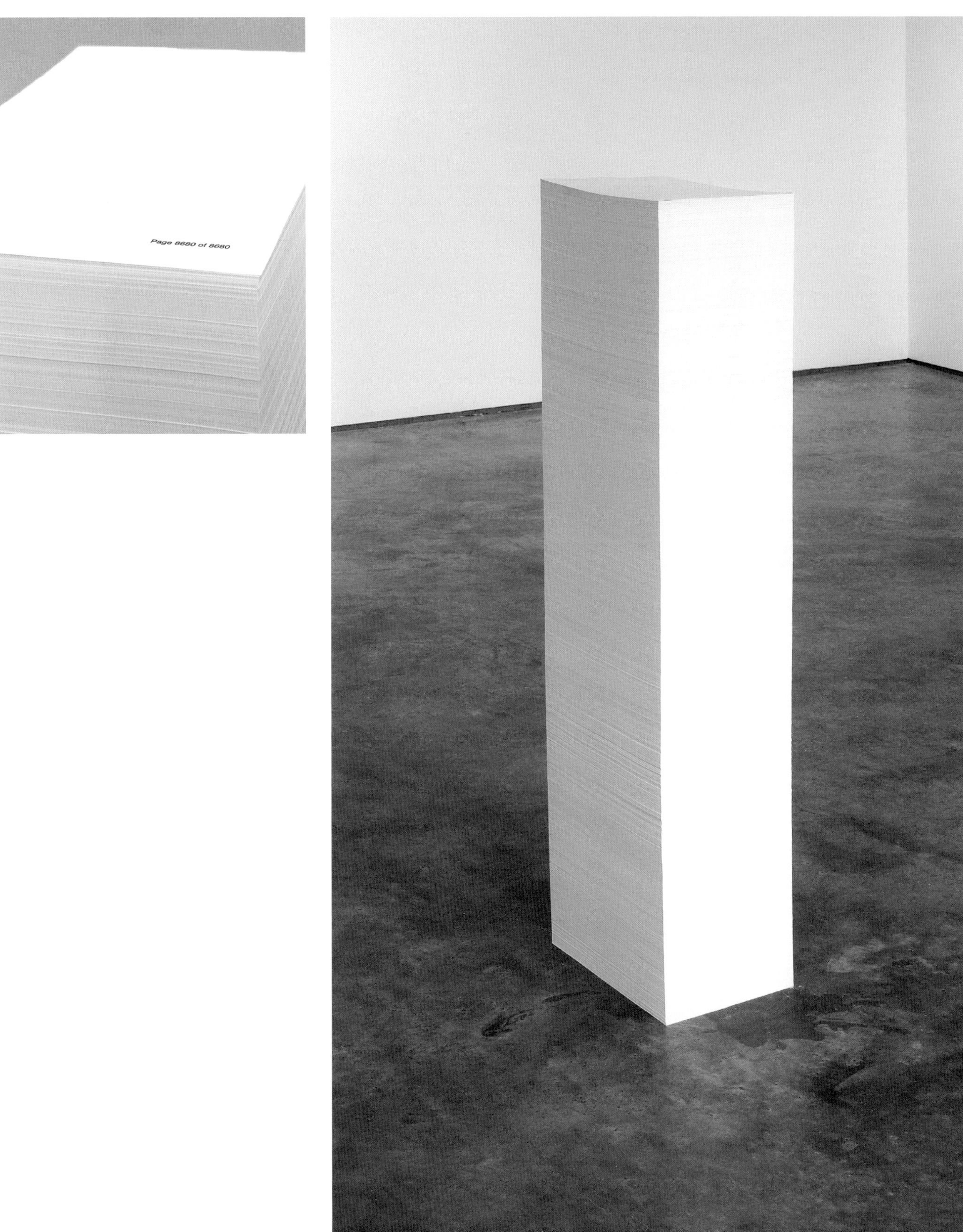
Page 8680 of 8680

Diptych (Pending)
2011

Perforated white paper, 8 metal pins or nails /
Perforiertes weißes Papier, 8 Metallstifte oder Nägel
Wall-based intervention /
Intervention auf einer Wand
Dimensions / Maße: 150 × 220 cm
3 + 2 AP

A vertically perforated sheet of white paper not yet torn.

Ein Blatt Papier mit vertikaler Perforierung, das noch nicht auseinandergerissen ist.

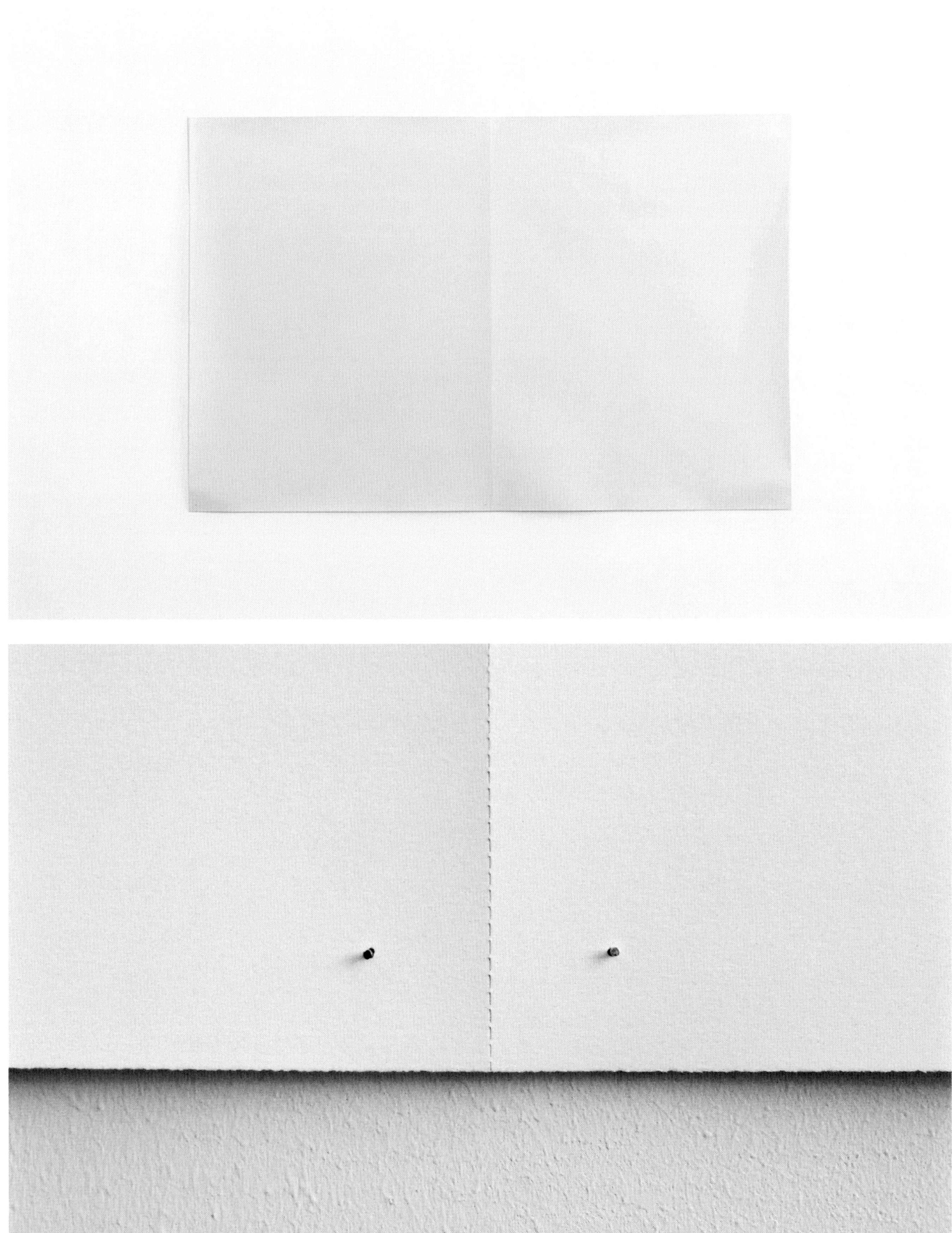

Do Not Remove
2011

Wall with a specified number of holes and dowels (dowel size O5, 32 mm long), 1 plastic sign with the text 'Do not remove' (30 × 20 cm) / Wand mit einer festgelegten Anzahl von Löchern und Dübeln (Dübelgröße O5, 32 mm lang), 1 Plastikschild mit der Aufschrift »Do not remove« (30 × 20 cm)
Wall-based sculpture, installation / Wandskulptur, Installation
Dimensions variable / Maße variabel
3 + 2 AP

A sign reading 'Do not remove' is affixed to a wall marked by a grid of small holes of the type that would be left in the wall after the removal of other such signs.

Installation views: Esther Schipper, Berlin, 2011 (top), 303 Gallery, New York, 2011 (bottom)

An einer Wand hängt ein Schild mit der Aufschrift »Do not remove« (Nicht entfernen), umgeben von einem Netz von kleinen Löchern, als wären weitere dieser Schilder entfernt worden.

Installationsansichten: Esther Schipper, Berlin, 2011 (oben), 303 Gallery, New York, 2011 (unten)

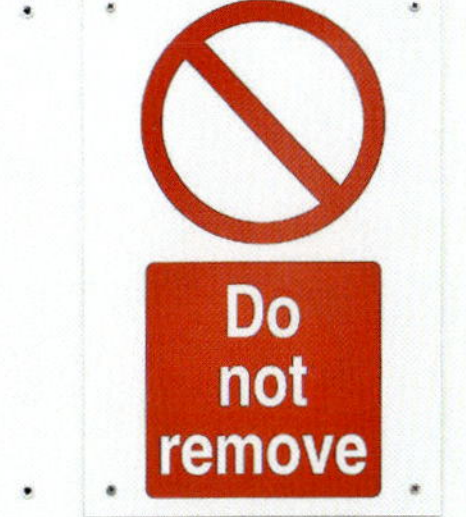
Do
not
remove

Viewer
2011

Door viewer, window / Türspion, Fenster
Sculpture / Skulptur
Dimensions variable / Maße variabel
3 + 2 AP

A door viewer set into a transparent glass windowpane.

Installation view: Esther Schipper, Berlin, 2011

Ein Türspion, der in das Glas einer Fensterscheibe eingesetzt ist.

Installationsansicht: Esther Schipper, Berlin, 2011

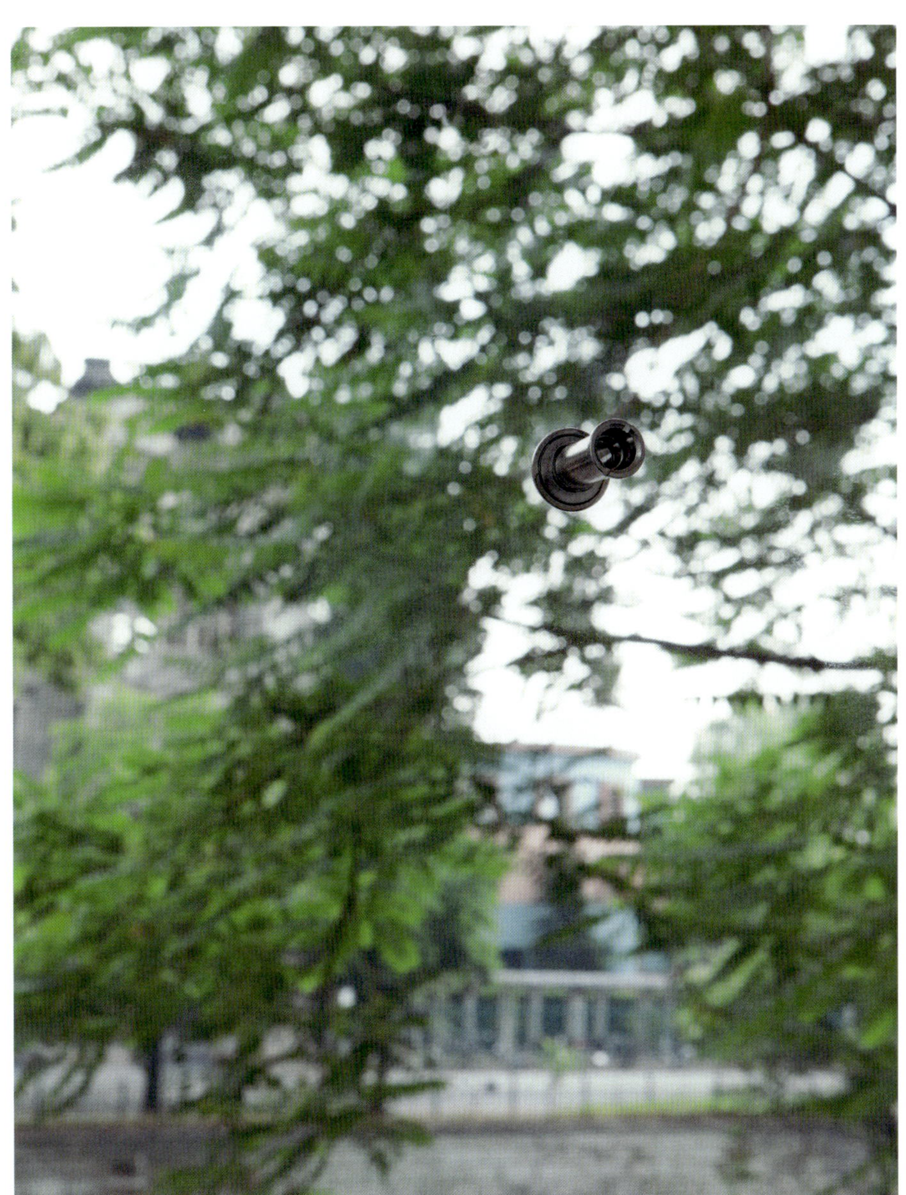

Drop
2013

HD video / HD-Video
Video without sound / Video ohne Ton
Duration / Duration: 11´ 18´´
3 + 2 AP

This video footage depicts a seemingly still image of a line of raindrops suspended from a horizontal railing. Eventually one of the drops drops.

Video still

Ein Videofilm mit einem scheinbar statischen Bild, das eine Reihe von Regentropfen an einem Sims zeigt. Irgendwann tropft ein Tropfen.

Videostill

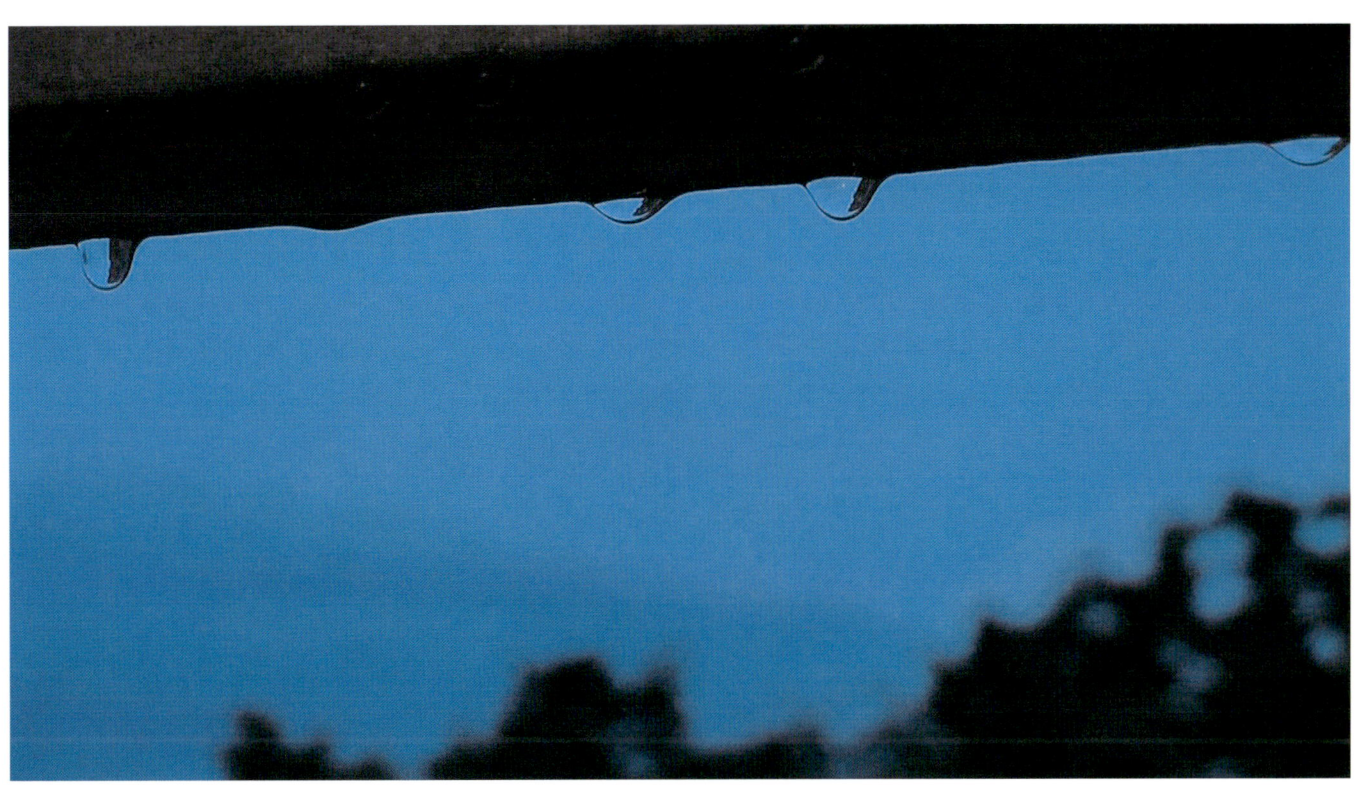

Rock Paper Scissors
2013

Photographic triptych, C-print on alu-dibond /
Foto-Triptychon, C-Print auf Alu-Dibond
Print / Druck
Dimensions (each plate) / Maße (je Tafel):
50 × 50 cm
6 + 2 AP

Rock, paper, scissors

Installation view: Lisson Gallery, London, 2013

Schere, Stein, Papier

Installationsansicht: Lisson Gallery, London, 2013

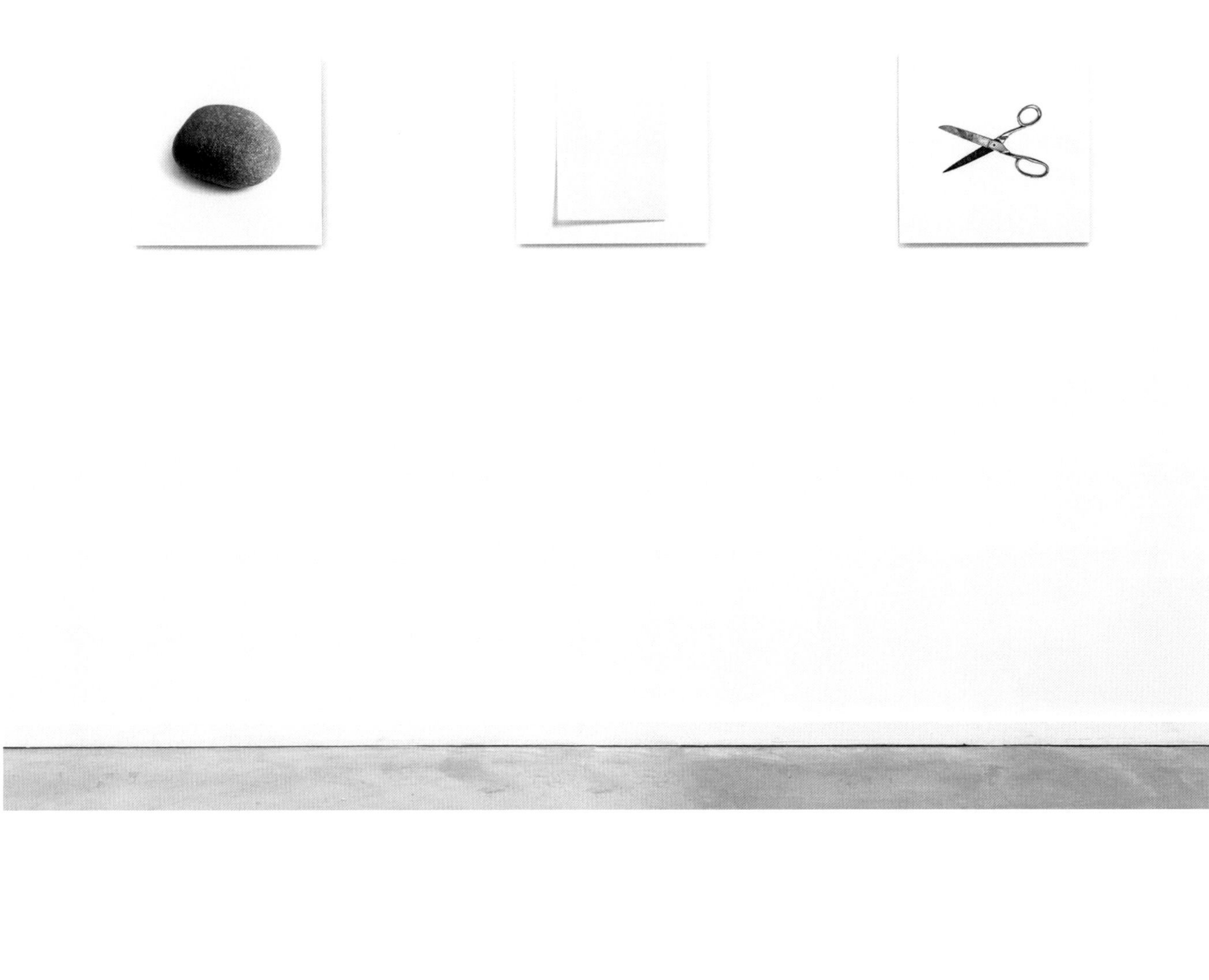

Untitled Credit Roll (. . .)
2013

DVD, DVD player, monitor or projector /
DVD, DVD-Spieler, Bildschirm oder Projektor
Video on monitor or video projection /
Video auf einem Bildschirm oder Video-projektion
Duration variable / Dauer variabel
Several versions + 1 AP, versions to date: /
Mehrere Versionen + 1 AP, bisher:
Untitled Credit Roll (AIW)
Untitled Credit Roll (CA)
Untitled Credit Roll (CMIYC)
Untitled Credit Roll (EPL)

A credit roll, completely out of focus, is re-filmed from a TV monitor.

Installation view: *Untitled Credit Roll (CMIYC),* Museion, Bolzano, 2014, and 6 video stills: *Untitled Credit Roll (CMIYC)*

Der Abspann eines Filmes ist völlig unscharf von einem Fernsehbildschirm abgefilmt.

Installationsansicht: *Untitled Credit Roll (CMIYC),* Museion, Bozen, 2014 und 6 Videostills: *Untitled Credit Roll (CMIYC)*

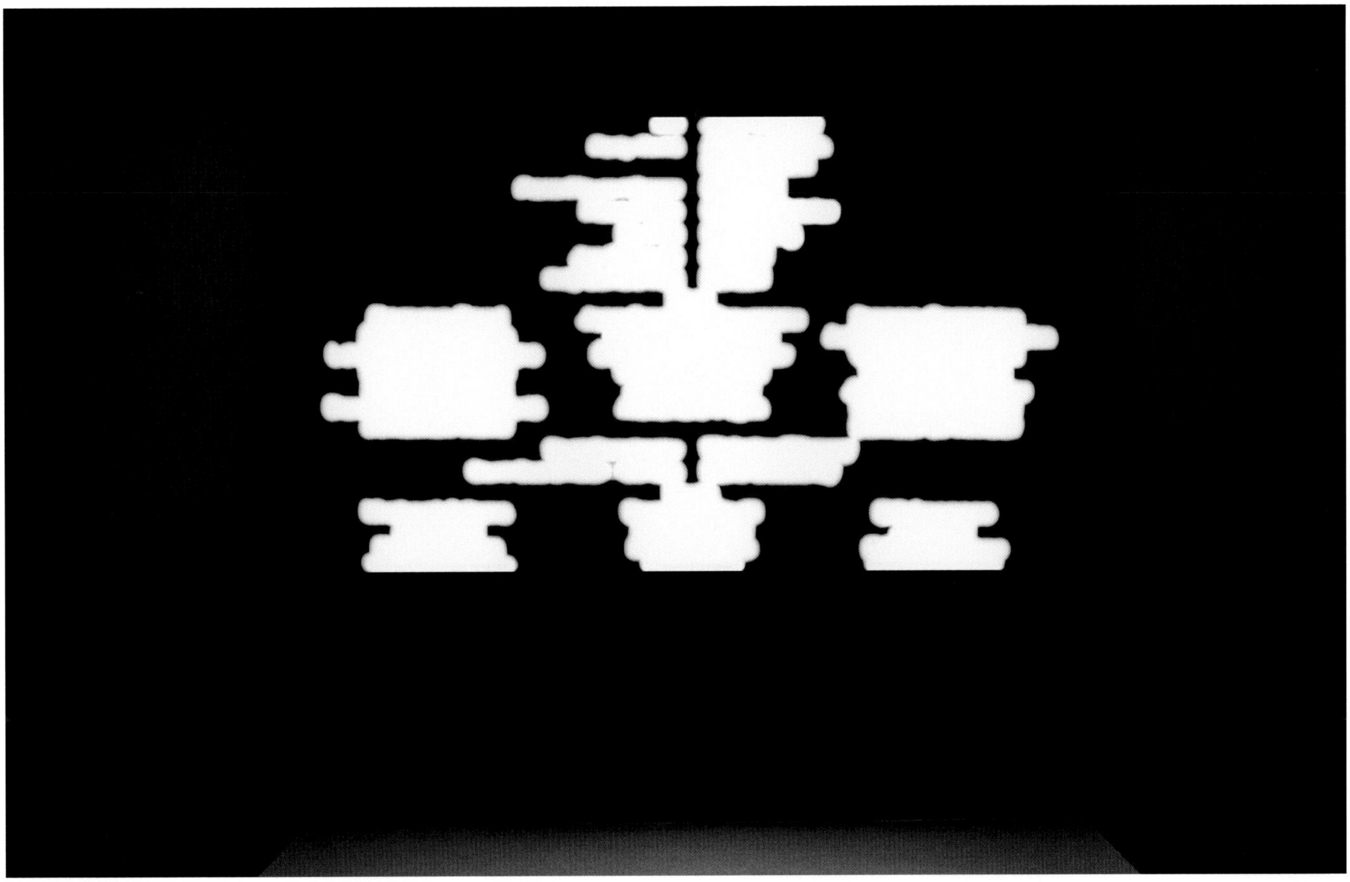

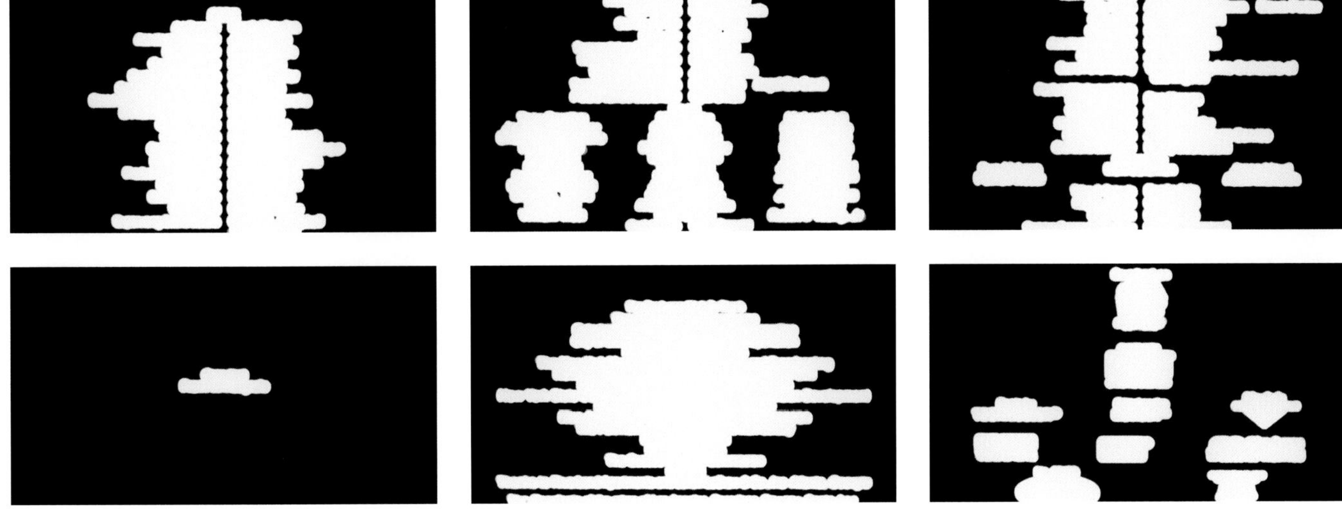

Blick
2014

'Blick' photo-corners, window /
Blick-Fotoecken, Fenster
Site-specific installation /
Ortsspezifische Installation
Dimensions variable / Maße variabel
3 + 2 AP

'Blick' photo-corners placed into corners of a window.

Installation view: Museion, Bolzano, 2014

Fotoecken der Firma Blick, die in den Ecken eines Fensters installiert sind.

Installationsansicht: Museion, Bozen, 2014

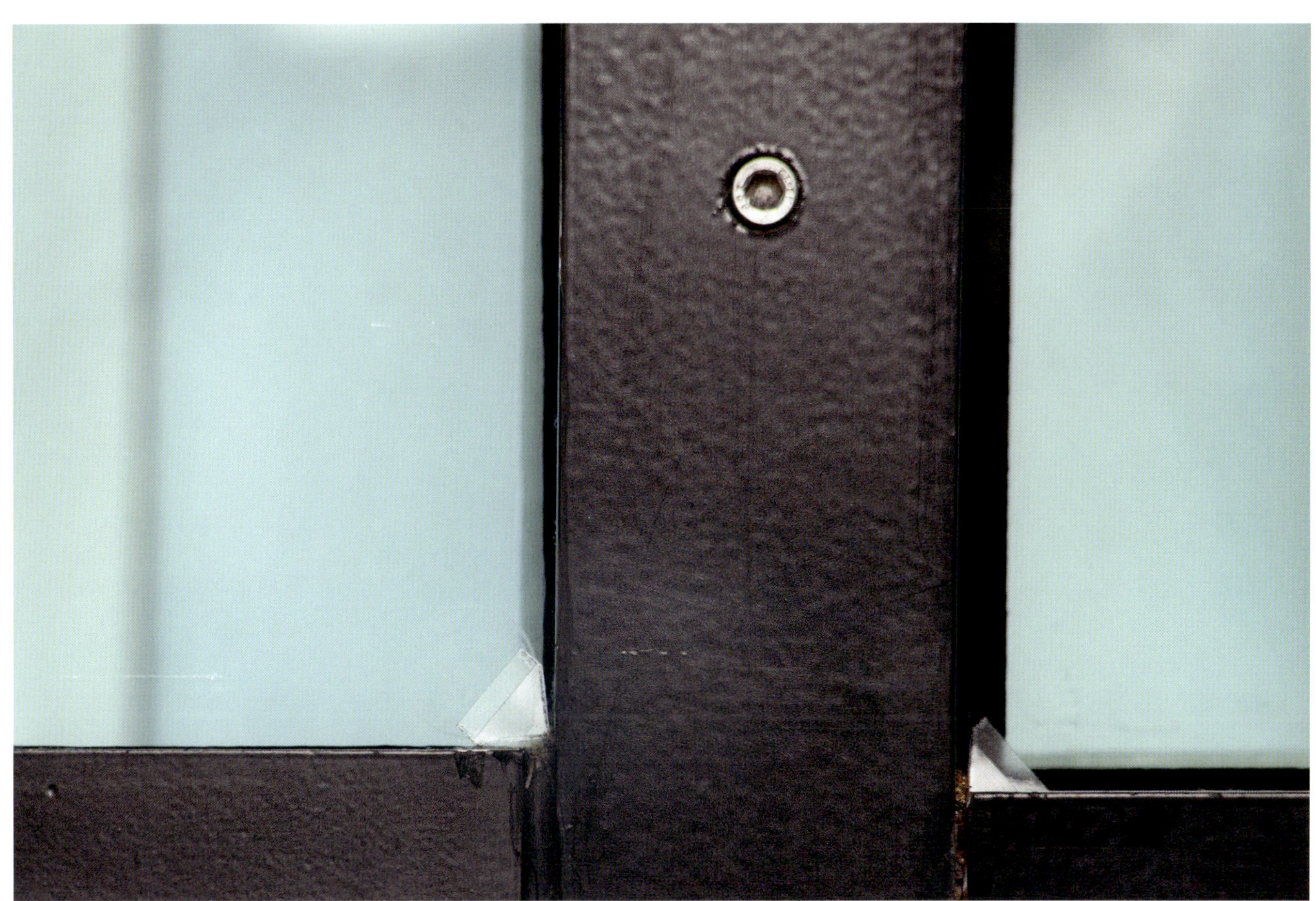

Greener Grass
2014

Turf, green spray-paint, wood /
Gras, grüne Sprühfarbe, Holz
Site-specific installation /
Ortsspezifische Installation
Dimensions variable / Maße variabel
Unique object / Unikat

The proverb 'The grass is always greener on the other side (of the fence)' is rendered quite literally here: in this rectangular plot of grass, one side of each blade (the side not facing the viewer approaching the work) has been spray-painted green.

Installation views: Lisson Gallery, Milan, 2014

Das Sprichwort »Auf der anderen Seite (des Zauns) ist das Gras immer viel grüner« ist hier wörtlich genommen. In einem Hochbeet mit Gras ist eine Seite der Grashalme (diejenige, die der Betrachter nicht sieht, wenn er sich der Arbeit nähert) mit grüner Farbe besprüht.

Installationsansichten: Lisson Gallery, Mailand, 2014

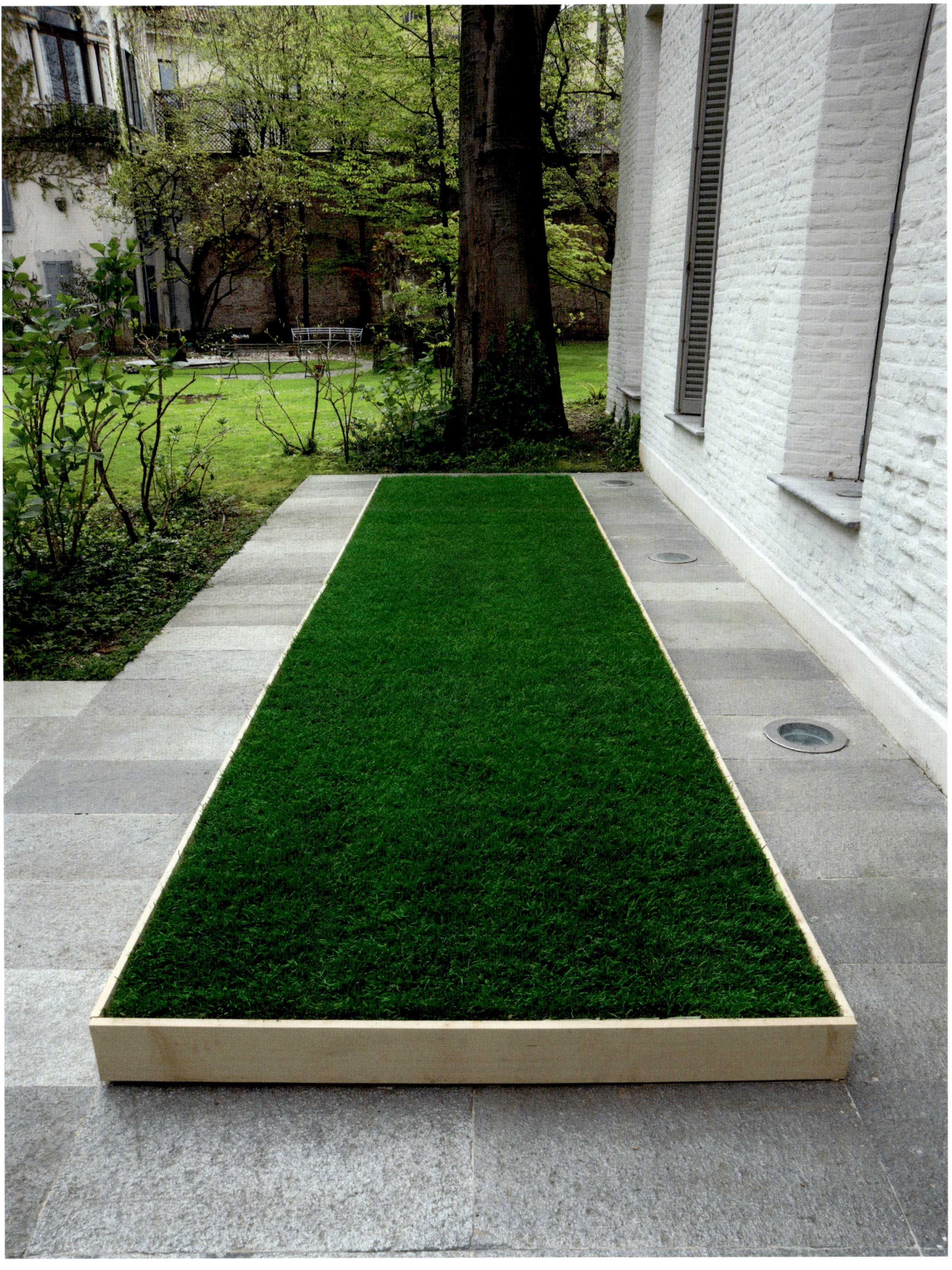

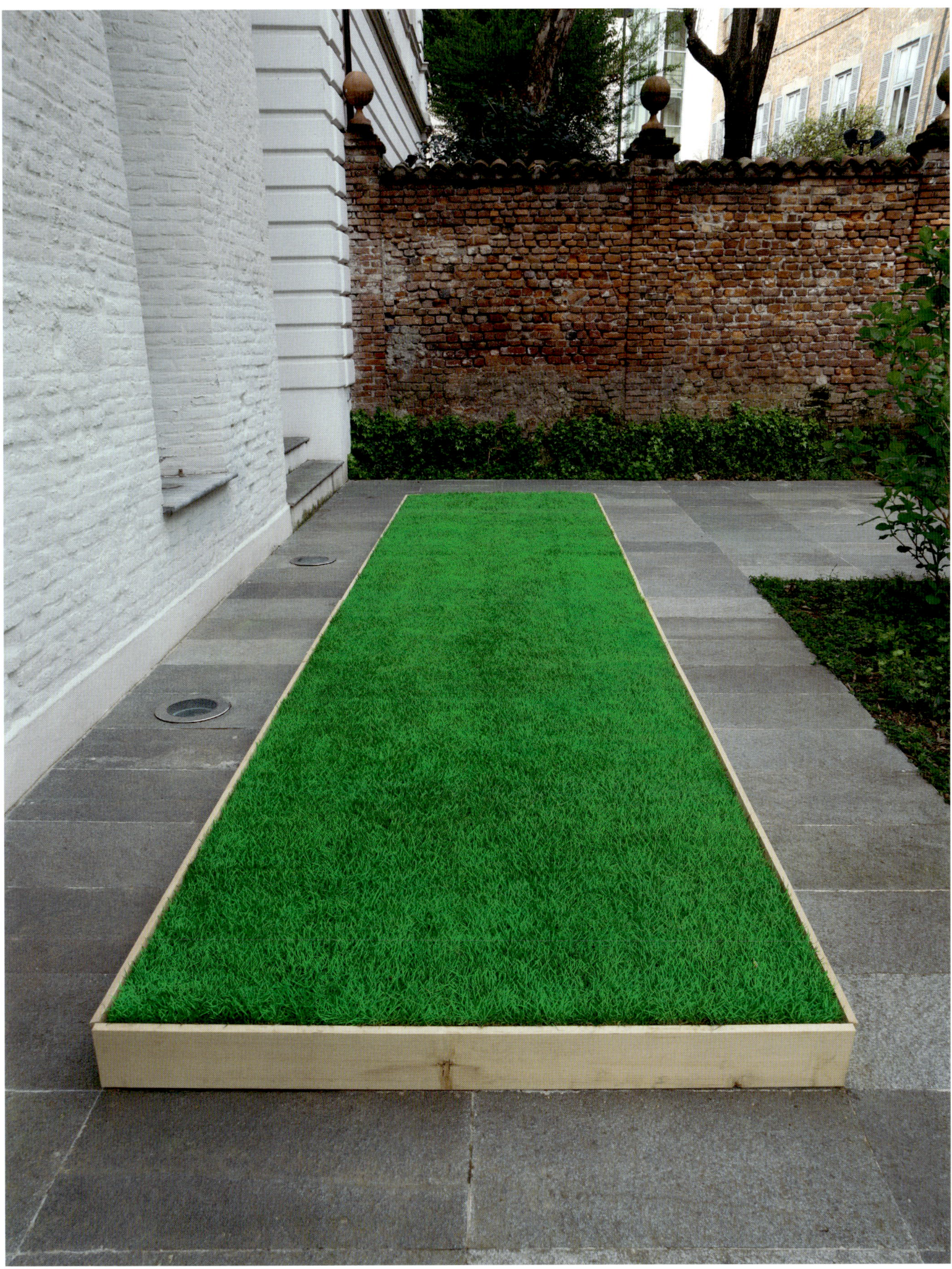

The Answer
2015

Photographic print mounted on aluminum /
Fotoabzug auf Aluminium
Photograph / Fotografie
Dimensions / Maße: 102 × 160 cm
6 + 2 AP

TACITA DEAN: TAUTOLOGICAL CIRCULAR DOT

'It's pronounced Floy-er', Ceal told me after I'd known her for twenty-five years: ER rhyming with HER and not Floyer as in foyer. For some time I tried to find a rhyme for her name as efficient as the one I mistook it for—a task that I knew would have taken Ceal a fraction of a second had she decided to expend any energy on it at all. Inevitably my attempts were clumsy and laboured; I am no competition for Ceal: she is the Dorothy Parker of the rapid response.

So it was just after arriving in Berlin in 2000 that Thomas Demand and I established that we shared the same initials: TCD. Not so surprising in English but rather more unusual in the German language, which does not favour the letter 'c'. What began were the *tcds*: their evolution marked on paper napkins, collected over dinner party after dinner party, and now lost in the back pages of *Parkett* magazine's volume 62:

the common denominator
the cd
the country doctor
the cocked dice
too cool, dammit …

Ceal, the queen of this game, was the inimitable composer of the majority of them, and razor-sharp good at it too:

try com dot
terrible circular dreams
thawing cryogenic Diana
tautological circular dot …

It is not the fault of the wordsmith that writing about the work of Ceal Floyer is nearly pointless. This is no caveat but a statement of fact. Description kills her work because it has already taken too long. What she does is wrought so finely that it operates in fractions of instants, way faster than the time our normal thoughts take. So rapid is the inception and absorption of the work that, at its best, it removes the possibility of reflection.

Ceal works with our cultural and social sensory understanding like a nanotechnologist, crafting idea and response to imperceptible levels of experience-in-time. The best we can do as her commentators is to come plodding along behind her, trying to sum up why it is that light projected on a bulb should become *the* light bulb in memory. Or why her 35-rpm record that plays the click of a slide projector like a scratch is so satisfying in its *Gesamt*-ness, in its completeness. Is it to do with an absence of subjectivity? Is it that her work travels intact through memory, therefore staying as fresh as when it was first encountered?

But with this precision comes a profound relationship to failure, making Ceal's practice precarious, very. Not all pasta is perfectly al dente, even when cooked by the best Italian maestro chefs in the business. If it cooks even a fraction too long, they must throw it away.

There is an ancient and established relationship, neurological or otherwise, that connects the eyes with the hands in the activity of the artist: a circuit that travels via the brain. However, this description is ill fitting for the complex nexuses of Ceal's mind. She is an artisan of consciousness and her brain is no service station in passage elsewhere but the origin and destination of everything. The materials she uses, the *objets trouvés*, the borrowed society of language, the words and sounds and songs, are props for her mind. And it feels like this. Her stark, sparse installations are raw and white and sometimes pleasureless to visit. Do not seek any comfort there. Ceal will not labour with aesthetics or be troubled by metaphor, her concentration is directed upon the purity of the idea and the necessary guise it must assume once it has left her brain. What we experience in her exhibitions is proximity to her mind.

MARK GODFREY: DRAIN

Light Switches

'There is such a thing as a lightness of thoughtfulness', Italo Calvino remarked toward the end of his life, 'just as we all know that there is a lightness of frivolity'.[1] Presenting his comments in a lecture titled 'Lightness', the writer continued 'Lightness for me goes with precision and determination, not with vagueness and the haphazard'.[2] Calvino might well have been describing the work of Ceal Floyer, which takes as its subject objects or phenomena that
we come across in our everyday lives: objects such as a light bulb or a power 18
drill, and phenomena such as a bucket collecting water from an overhead 86, 38
leak or a line of light visible under a door. Floyer eschews the sublime for the 22
pedestrian.

Often Floyer's work is not only light in touch but in material, using illumination
to create simple illusions. One of her earliest pieces, *Light Switch*, first made 12
in 1992, epitomises the simplicity of these gestures: a projector points to a space on a wall where one might expect to find a light switch, perhaps next to an entrance, and projects a slide of a light switch; the slide changes to match the specific kind of switch found in the country where the work is exhibited. The title, then, is not only a deadpan description of the piece but also the
announcement of an artistic strategy. Take *Light*, from 1994, in which four slide 18
projectors are directed at a bulb hanging from the ceiling, its cord disconnected. It has been painted matt white and thanks to the slide projectors is brightly
lit, but the room remains dark. In *Door* (1995), an image projected onto the 22
bottom of a door resembles a crack of light seeping in from the next room.
For *Overhead Projection* (2006), the artist places a light bulb on the glass of 94
an overhead projector; the resulting image makes it appear as if the enlarged bulb were hanging from the ceiling.

Floyer's situations recreate or (to use Jeremy Millar's word) 'impersonate'[3] ordinary objects and phenomena through the use of basic, unpretentious technologies: for instance, a slide machine projecting onto a door. Often the technological apparatus employed is nearly obsolete (slide machines, turntables, overhead projectors), but Floyer attaches little significance to the nostalgic resonance of the apparatus and will also use computer files, CD players, and DVD projectors. More important than the question of digital or analogue is the blunt, unashamed presence of the apparatus. Many works involve the creation of a 'switch', a momentary illusion, but at the very moment the viewer sees this effect, its cause is understood: light apparently shining under a door, and then the slide projector that actually shines this light onto it. We admire the magic of the work no less because the magician reveals her tricks, and this seems contrary to the normal working of 'special effects', which rely on hiding the means of their production. Floyer has spoken of the impact of Fred Sandback's sculpture, his ability to create the illusion of an illusion.[4] Sandback stretched coloured yarn to create the impression that solid planes were leaning against walls; and though we know immediately that the planes are in fact voids, they are no easier to step through. Another work of great importance to her is Charles Ray's *32 x 33 x 35 = 34 x 33 x 35* (1989), a brushed aluminium minimalist cube whose interior is slightly deeper than its exterior, as it is set two inches into the gallery floor. Here the title explains why the work feels so strange but does not explain this strangeness away.

In some cases, the effect of Floyer's 'light switches' relies on formal serendipity and a synesthetic twist. In *Carousel* (1996), a turntable on a plinth plays a

Light Switch, 1992

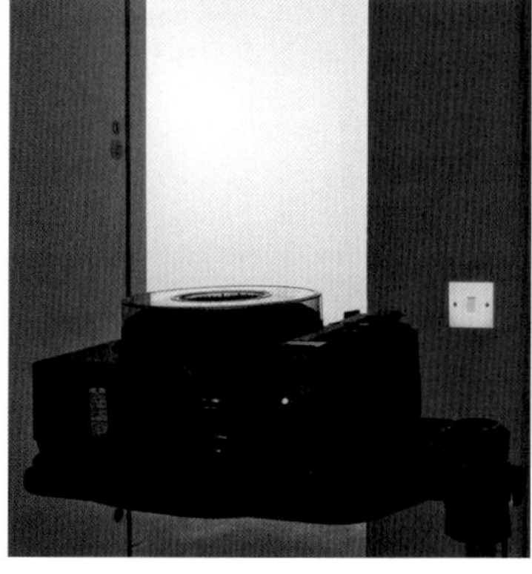

Charles Ray, *32 x 33 x 35 = 34 x 33 x 35*, 1989, aluminium; outside: 32 x 33 x 35 inches; inside: 34 x 33 x 35 inches; © Charles Ray, Courtesy Matthew Marks Gallery

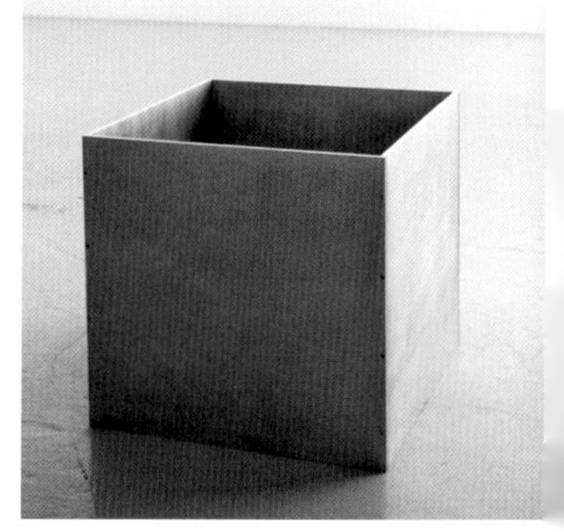

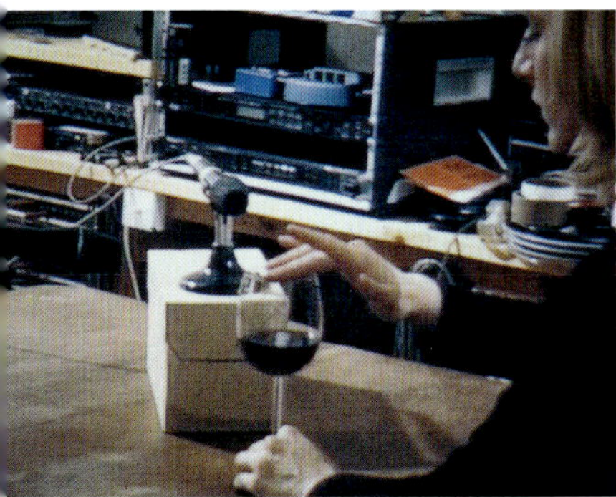

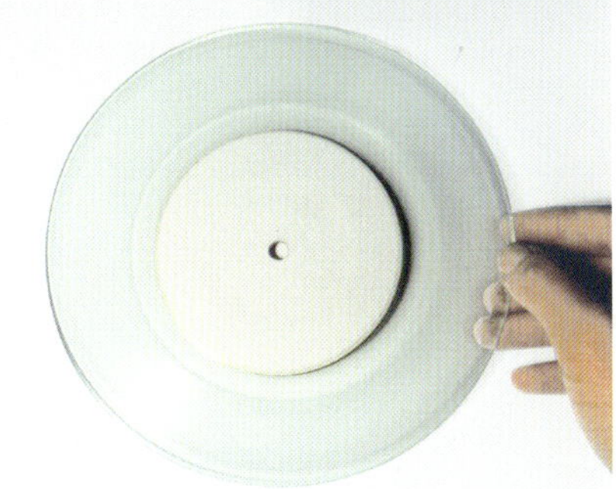

Glass, 1998

Carousel, 1996

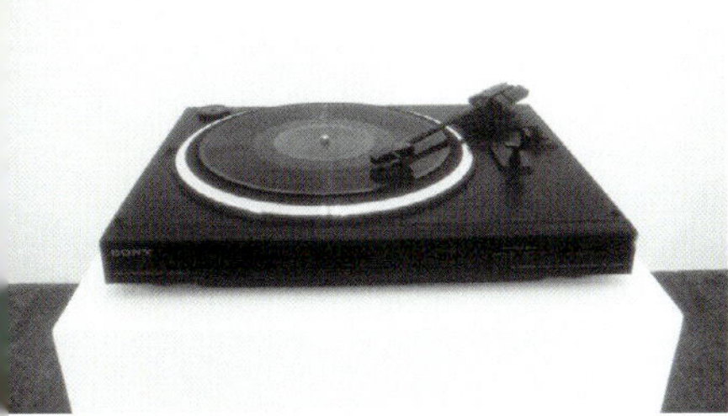

record whose only track is a recording of a slide carousel clicking around; the ten-inch record matches the diameter of a slide carousel. In *Working Title*
26 *(Digging)* (1995), speakers stand on opposite sides of a gallery: one plays the sound of a spade scooping earth; the other, of earth landing on the ground.
104 A series of speakers make up *Scale* (2007), rising from the floor to the ceiling, each one set further back from the last so that the whole resembles a staircase. A soundtrack plays footsteps walking up and down, each speaker emitting a single, identical step in sequence. Equally, a sonic event can become visual, as in *Glass* (1998): as a stylus circles around a clear vinyl record, it plays the sound of a finger tracing the rim of a glass.

Floyer's use of language is incredibly important; often a word or string of words determines a work, which becomes what the artist has called 'stuffing' for its title. Floyer's approach to language is a partly pedantic, partly heroic attempt to do away with ambiguity and metaphor in favour of literalness and precision. A word must mean what it says, she insists, and it must mean everything it can. 'Switch' must mean the thing and the process. If 'throw' is the act of casting something down, and the trade name of a particular kind of lighting, then the work with this title must encapsulate both meanings—as Floyer's *Throw* (1997) does (a theatre lamp with a metal gobo, or circular template, projecting an
86 image of paint onto the floor, as if thrown there). *Drill* (2006) is both a tool and the act of making a hole with this tool—and so both meanings need to be respected (Floyer's drill lies on the floor, its plug inserted not into a socket but into a hole that we guess it drilled—but with what power supply?).

Her puns and switches in signification or syntax recall historical works such as Man Ray's *Featherweight*, a 1960 sculpture in which three feathers stick out of a weight, and Bruce Nauman's 1966 photographs *Waxing Hot* (in which the artist waxes a sign that reads HOT) and *Feet of Clay* (in which his feet
78 are depicted smeared with clay). Similarly, in *Reversed* (2005), Floyer flips a photograph of a restaurant table sign stating RESERVED. The image recalls Giovanni Anselmo's 1970 photograph *Lato Destro* (Right Side), which shows the artist with the title words written on his neck: the words appear on the right side of the photograph, but this means they were written on the left side of his neck.

The affective impact of Floyer's 'light switches' is harder to describe than one would expect. Initially, many of these works prompt a delighted response as the viewer admires their intelligence, their restraint, and the sheer neat brilliance of their conception. Calvino also identified 'quickness' and 'exactitude' as values for future literature, and the light switches espouse these values as much as 'lightness'. But the affective complexity of Floyer's 'light switches' increases as time passes, outlasting the 'aha moment' when we understand when the cause of the work's initial effect is intuited. Lightness then makes way for deflation. *Drain* (2006) is a small speaker shaped like a plug hole, lying on the floor, connected to a CD player and emitting the sound of water pouring down a drain; after we realise that the illusion has relied on the formal proximity of speaker and plug, the sound of water persists, on and on; it seems like everything drains out of the room, as if someone were telling the same one-liner, over and over again. For me this sense of initial delight draining away runs through all Floyer's 'switch' works; indeed the latter affect of disappointment is what I find so compelling about them.

Floyer further underlines this shift from delight to disappointment in works that brilliantly undercut the expectations of spectacular fulfilment and dramatic

1
Italo Calvino, *Six Memos for the Next Millennium* (London, 1996), p. 3.

2
Ibid., p. 16.

3
Jeremy Millar, 'Just Like That', in *Ceal Floyer* (Birmingham, 2001), p. 20.

4
Sandback wrote of his work 'My work is not illusionistic in the normal sense of the word. It doesn't refer away from itself to something that isn't present. Its illusions are simply present aspects of it.' This comment seems particularly pertinent to Floyer's art. See *Fred Sandback* (Munich, 1975), p. 11.

wonder that we have come to expect from so much contemporary art. At first
glance, the 2005 video *Apollinaris* appears to show fireworks exploding against 76
a black sky; in fact, the shot is a close-up of bubbles fizzing off a glass of
the eponymous mineral water. In *Double Act* (2006), a spotlight shines a circle 84
of light onto a red stage curtain along a wall and spills onto the floor below. Standing in the glare, we look up to the spotlight and see it contains a gobo of the curtain. This moment of realisation—that light *and* image come from the same source—is the drama of the work, and we are centre stage. But the curtain stays shut; no further denouement awaits us. Using the language of theatrical spectacle, Floyer resists spectacular theatrics.[5]

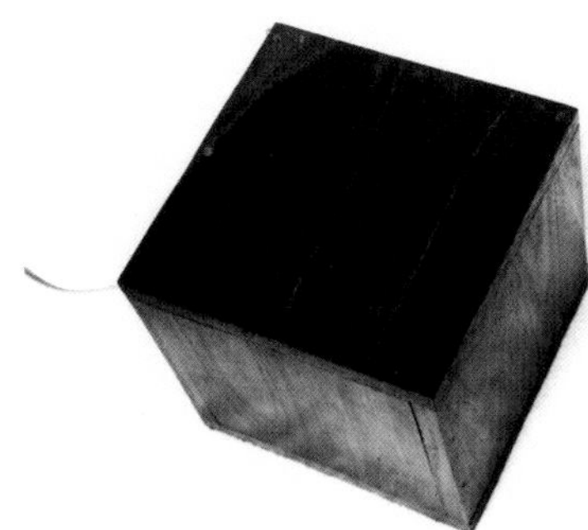

Robert Morris, *Box with the Sound of Its Own Making*, 1961, wood and sound recording; 9 ¾ x 9 ¾ x 9 ¾ inches; Photo Courtesy Castelli Gallery, New York

Another group of Floyer's works addresses the dizzying excesses of the art
economy. Floyer's earliest foray into this terrain was a piece titled *Sold* 1996: 30
she drilled a tiny circular crater in a gallery wall next to a painting, and filled the cavity with cadmium red oil paint to mimic the appearance of brash 'sold' stickers. Only the exhibition's checklist revealed this to be her work, a sculpture (since it was a volume of material) masquerading as a painting—indeed, as a
painting much more humble than the one above it. *Genuine Reduction* 2006 90
is a ready-made sale sign of the kind found in cheap shops, and because its right border has been trimmed, the sign itself is genuinely reduced. When Floyer first showed it at the Lisson Gallery, the work addressed the history of a gallery long associated with minimal art, and her own practice in general. But the work also addressed the particular commercial character of a private gallery. *Genuine Reduction* was installed in the street-facing room of the Lisson Gallery, a location that recalled the position of similar signs in regular shops.

Floyer's most canny intervention of this kind was made for the most moneyed event in the art world calendar—Art Basel. Floyer was allocated a large space in the Art Unlimited section. She took sound boards (flat loudspeakers whose proportions allow them to be embedded in walls), and created a work in which the sound boards played recordings of drilling, sawing, and sanding. These activities would have taken place during the building of this temporary structure; their messy traces were now erased by paint, as the space was now
a generic white cube. Though of course the work nodded to Robert Morris's
Box with the Sound of Its Own Making, its title, *Construction* (2006), suggests 82
other affinities, such as the work of Michael Asher. 'Construction' refers to the labour of building that the soundtrack re-presents, the kind of labour that Asher displayed in many of his installations. Viewers trained by Floyer to look for double meanings might have taken the word to refer beyond the sound of work and to encompass the surrounding scene. For me, the piece suggested that the entire art fair is a construction at whose core might be a void full of sound and fury, just like Floyer's empty cube.

Orders

In an essay titled 'Think/Classify', Georges Perec laments, 'There is something at once uplifting and terrifying about the idea that nothing in the world is so unique that it can't be entered on a list.'[6] Fascinated by systems of organisation and classification, he sought complete, definitive detail, even when describing the contents of one's office—in 'Notes Concerning the Objects That Are on My Work-Table', he lists among other things 'a desk-lamp, a cigarette box, a bud-vase, a matchbox holder, a cardboard box containing little multi-coloured index cards, a large *carton bouilli* inkwell incrusted with tortoiseshell . . .'.[7]

5
Suspense is relevant here as well. For a show at the Domaine de Kerguéhennec (Bignan, France), Floyer created an installation in which a spectator walks down an empty corridor of space towards a loudspeaker, which plays a soundtrack of the kind we hear at key moments of suspense in Hollywood thrillers—screeching, slow strings, crescendos. Here there was no denouement to the suspense; the spectator reached the loudspeaker, found nothing there, and the music stopped.

6
Georges Perec, 'Think / Classify', in *Species of Spaces and Other Pieces* (New York and London, 1999), p. 198.

7
Georges Perec, 'Notes Concerning The Objects That Are On My Work-Table', in *Perec, Species of Spaces*, p. 146.

8
Georges Perec, 'Species of Spaces', in *Perec, Species of Spaces*, p. 50.

9
Perec, 'Think / Classify', p. 190.

10
Perec, 'Think / Classify', p. 196.

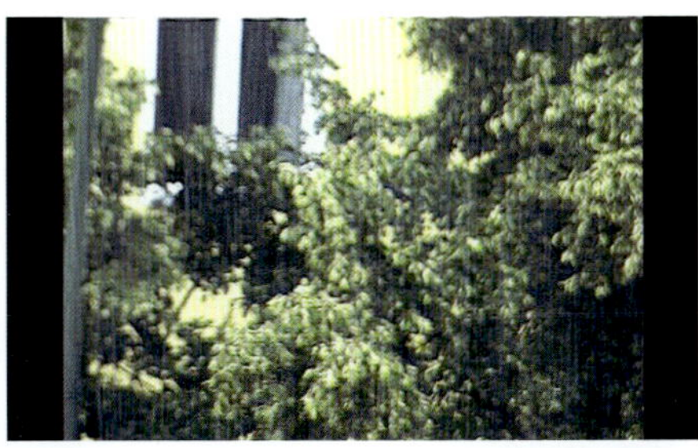

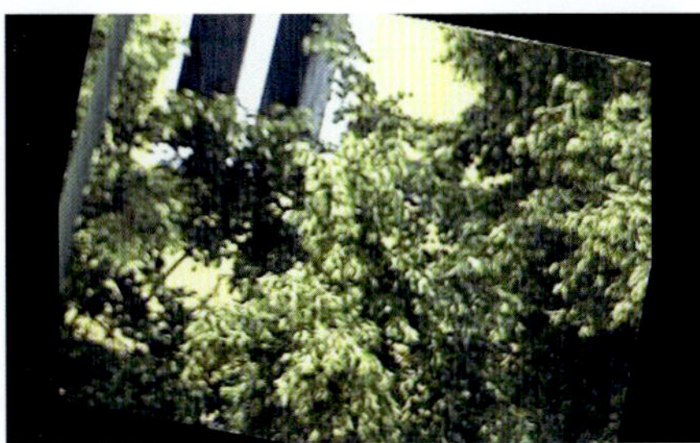

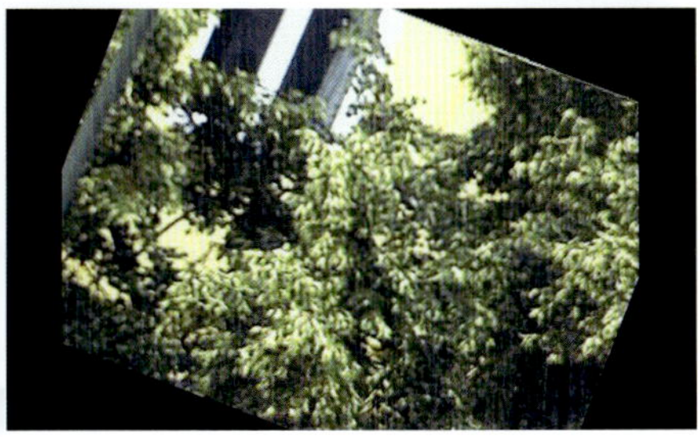

Downpour (Friedrichstrasse), 2004

Throw, 1997

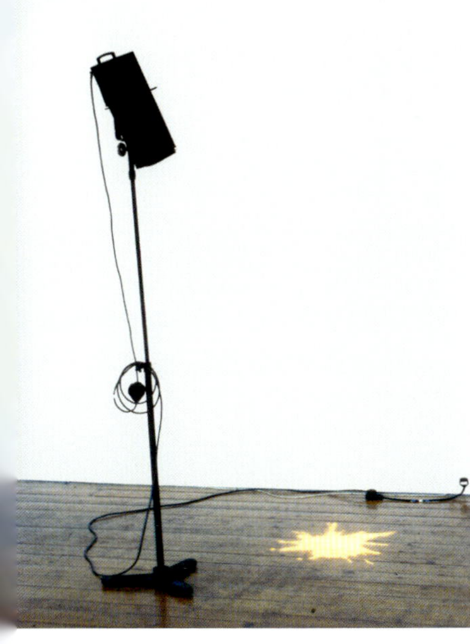

'Don't say, don't write "etc.,"' he commanded: 'Make an effort to exhaust the subject.'[8] Language itself could also be classified: 'How could one classify the following verbs: arrange, catalogue, classify, cutup, divide, enumerate, gather, grade, group, list, number, order, organize, sort?'[9] Yet Perec recognized that the 'problem with classifications is that they don't last; hardly have I finished putting things into an order before that order is obsolete.'[10]

A second family of works by Floyer aims to create order. They are best thought of as processes rather than situations, but like Perec's lists, their ambition is constantly thwarted; the artist herself has termed these pursuits 'Sisyphean'. For *Downpour* (2004), Floyer filmed a windy storm, the rain blown so that it fell at a diagonal, and then tilted the footage to achieve an image of perfectly vertical rainfall; the border of the frame, however, gives away this manipulation. In numerous works, the context for her drive to create order is the chaos of a late-capitalist world characterised by overproduction, noise, speed, techno-
102 logical overload, and excessive material consumption. The simply titled *Order* 2007 is made from one of Perec's working-table objects: a series of tabbed index cards. As manufactured, the tabs are placed in successive positions along the cards' top edges so that the letters run diagonally backward along the box; Floyer, however, has lined up the cards so that the letters stand one behind the next in a column—but now the edges of the cards are unaligned, requiring a specially grooved stand to hold them. The projector in Floyer's *Slide Show* (1995) literally shows slides—images of diagrams of all forty-eight commercially available slide mounts, archived into an order. In this work, medium reflexivity becomes deadpan, literal, and far-fetched, and has little
44 relationship to modernist medium reflexivity. The *Ink on Paper* works, meanwhile, dramatize another dynamic of order and disorder involving an item from the stationer's shop. For each series of drawings, Floyer uses all the pens in a pack of felt-tip markers. She drains each pen on a sheet of blotting paper and pins the latter to the wall in the same order in which the pens come in the packet. Just as *Slide Show* is a show of slides, this is literally 'ink on paper', as in the conventional description of an artistic medium found in a museum caption. But separated out in the process of draining, the inks often appear different in tone from the plastic of the pens, and some pens produce larger circles than others. The work recreates the sequence of the packet, but in the process undoes the order of its appearance.

Removal is another recurrent process that Floyer deploys to organize the world. The best example of this strategy is a series of videos: *Monochrome Edit (White), Monochrome Edit (Red)*, and *Spectrum Edit,* all from 1998. Each video consists of a single shot of an average Berlin street, but the edit is different in each work: watching *Monochrome Edit (White),* we see a series of white cars pass before the camera; all other vehicles have been edited out. Although we cannot see them, we know they were there: Floyer left in the sound of their approach and departure. In *Spectrum Edit*, she recorded her footage so that each successive car is a different colour of the rainbow; she did not spot a purple car, but by chance a pedestrian sporting a purple anorak walked into the frame, so he took the place of the vehicle.

In contrast to these omissions and edits, Floyer also plays with accumulation. In one work from 2004 a dense scrawl of black ink is found at the centre of a blank expanse of paper. The title *again and again* helps us spot repeated forms at the perimeters of this tangle: the upper triangle of an 'A' to the left; a few dots slightly further along. Floyer simply wrote the words 'Again and'

over and over, one on top of the other, as if the phrase were an instruction, until its words became illegible. Repetition is often associated with emphasis and enforcement; alongside reordering, recounting, and removal, it is another means of establishing order. Floyer's works, however, dramatize the ways in which repetition can become a force of cancellation. *again and again* recalls a metaphor Alain Robbe-Grillet used to describe the effect of the descriptive overload in his books: 'The lines of the drawing accumulate, grow heavier, cancel one another out, shift, so that the image is jeopardised as it is created.'[11]
Warning Birds (2002) and *Mind The Step* (2006) are two other examples of this 62
dynamic of repetition and cancellation. The first work uses the kind of stickers 92
that one sees on glass buildings; ideally placed as disparately as possible, their job is to deter birds from flying straight into glass walls. But the vast window of *Warning Birds* is entirely covered in stickers—ensuring that the birds will stay away, but at the cost of the window's transparency. In the latter work, Floyer takes the kind of warning sign that usually appears singly beside solitary steps in places where steps are not expected. She takes a group of 'Mind the Step' signs and fastens them to each rise in a flight of stairs; surprised by this unusual proliferation, it is not unlikely that a viewer, distracted, might actually trip.

Some works, instead of emphasising the repetition of any single motif or object, gather diverse things together and place them in some kind of order.
Helix, first made in 2001, is the most dramatic example of this strategy. The 50
base of the work is a Helix drawing tool, a thin orange sheet of plastic punctured by a grid of circular holes of increasing diameters, which is used for technical drawings and diagrams. In Floyer's custody, however, drawing turns into sculpting as the artist inserts objects with round bases into the appropriate holes of this template. Dissimilar things sit next to one another in utterly unexpected juxtapositions, predicated on the unquestionable sequence of their diameters: coins, candies, torches, medicine bottles, light bulbs, pen tops, washers, and batteries.

In addition to bringing together a host of unrelated objects, Floyer unites previously disconnected sculptural practices. Most obviously, *Helix* is a collection of Readymades, but it is also indebted to Duchamp's random measurements, such as *Three Standard Stoppages* (1913–14). With its sequence of ordered holes, *Helix* also refers to the serial progressions of Minimalism, but its everyday objects suggest the work of Arman and early Christian Boltanski as well as Alighiero Boetti's *Cubo* 1968, in which disparately shaped materials all fit together in a neat box.

Monochrome Till Receipt (White), originally created in 1998, is one of Floyer's 34
most conceptually elegant pieces and justly among her most renowned. The work is a humble receipt, neither white nor monochrome but printed out in purple ink on fading beige paper. Listing disparate shopping goods in a column—lard, cream cheese, detergent, salt, and so on—the receipt is as ordinary as the items; Floyer continually remakes the work from a supermarket local to the country of exhibition, so that the receipt hardly seems to deserve attention. But soon the reason for the title becomes clear: everything purchased is white. *Monochrome Till Receipt* evokes a plethora of artistic genres and traditions—still life, sculptural accumulations, the documents of conceptual artworks, and even concrete poetry. But more than anything else, the receipt invites us to imagine a world of purity and order associated with modernist monochrome paintings and architecture, the early twentieth-century Utopianism

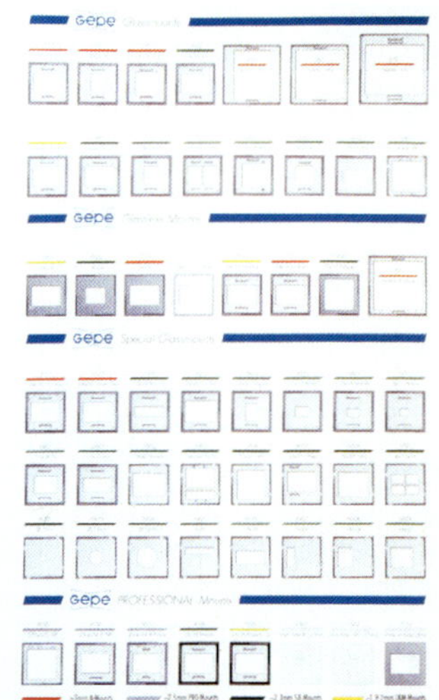

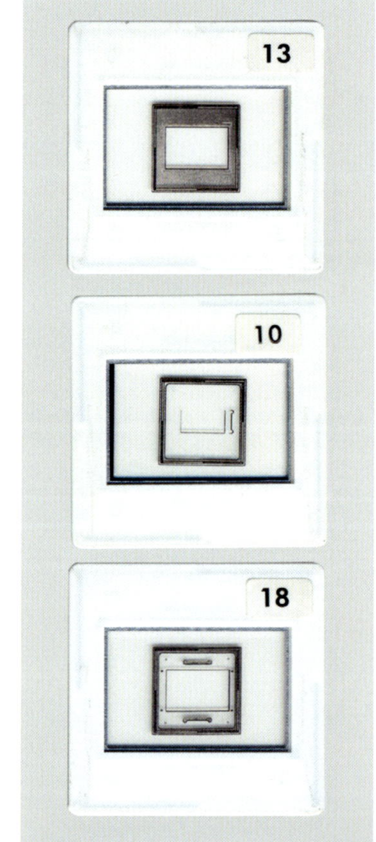

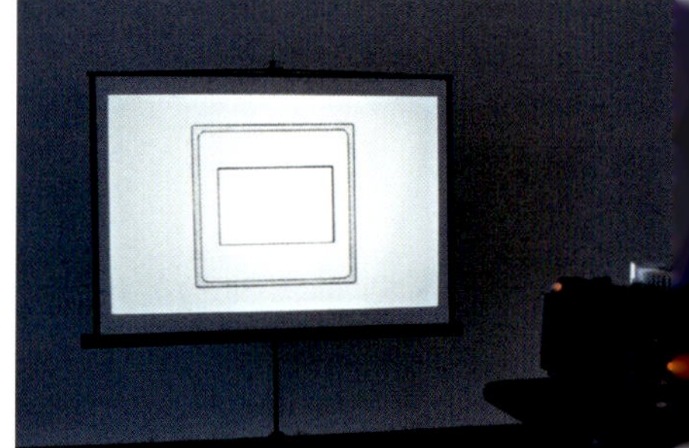

Slide Show, 1995

of Malevich (who first painted white on white) and Le Corbusier. But does *Monochrome Till Receipt* really suggest the possibility of bleaching a world of cheap commerce? More than modernist purity, the work evokes the clutter of the supermarket—the graveyard of modernist dreams, a place of corruption and colour, where bright, catchy logos attack the eye. We end up feeling that the work, by so transiently evoking the monochrome and its associations, only underscores our distance from a world in which such an artistic innovation could hold Utopian promise.

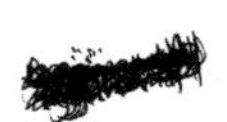

gain and again, 2004

Time Pieces

In her essay 'Some Translucent Substance, or the Trouble with Time', Briony Fer looks back to the late nineteen-sixties to consider the different ways that time was at stake in art and critical discourse. She contests Michael Fried's reductive distinction between the 'instant' in which modernist works could be perceived and the 'duration' that Minimalist works demanded, and insisted that there was a much greater range of approaches to time, manifest in the work of artists such as Eva Hesse and Robert Smithson. In a work by Hesse, one might sense moments of 'arrest, of time being suddenly cut' as well as a sense of 'time just going on and time draining out.'[12] Smithson imagined infinities, but 'the kind of infinity that was interesting [to him] did not have a capital "I" and was not Sublime.' For Smithson, Donald Judd's work evoked 'sheer inertia and endlessness'; as is well known, many of Smithson's own works suggest the slow waste of entropy.[13]

The question of time is equally crucial to Floyer's practice, defining a third body of work. Some of these pieces explicitly address time: In *15 Minutes Ago* (2002), a speaker installed on a wall where a clock might be placed plays a fifteen-minute recording of the sound of a clock—but plays it backward, producing a strange yet unmistakable tock-ticking, as if forward time were being sucked into reverse. The two records playing at thirty-three and forty-five rotations per minute, respectively, in *Twin Decks* (1999) have only one groove each, silent but for a single bump, which means the sound of the speed of revolutions is discernible even though the two clicks are always out of synch.
66 The work *1–25* (2003) is a projection of the written words of each number in a sequence, each of which appears on the wall for the equivalent number of seconds; we realize the logic of the piece only after the first few numbers have disappeared. *Time Piece* (2003) relays all the chimes (quarters and hours) of a clock-tower bell, with the intervals between them taken out: a whole day reduced to a sequence of meaningless markers. In such works, to use Hamlet's words, 'time is out of joint', and they make us feel disjointed too.

In some works, however, Floyer creates situations that we can only comprehend after a delay; the moment of understanding reverses the assumptions we have made already and requires us to rethink our encounter with the entire piece to this point. An early example of this temporal structure is a work first
16 made in 1993, *Untitled Installation (Dotted Line)*. Upon walking down a corridor into a room, we see a slide viewer on a plinth; the screen shows a pair of scissors, which seems innocuous enough until we leave the space and notice a broken line at the perimeter of the walls, windows, and doors—the kind of line that stands for 'cut here'. This line has surrounded us from the moment of entry but we failed to notice; once it is perceived, however, we feel our relation to the space around us change. The walls suddenly appear paper thin, and we feel 'cut out' of space and time.

11
Alain Robbe-Grillet, 'Time and Description in Fiction Today', in *For a New Novel* (Evanston, Illinois, 1989), p. 148.
12
Briony Fer, 'Some Translucent Substance, or the Trouble with Time', in *Time and the Image*, ed. Carolyn Gill (Manchester, 2000), p. 69.
13
Fer, 'Some Translucent Substance', p. 73.

This experience of slowly dawning realisation often marks Floyer's time-based
works. The image in the video *Blind* (1997) is at first opaque, suggesting ob- 32
scured or blinded vision. A white surface pulses in and out, and at times a dark shape appears behind it. Suddenly, we realize that we are looking not at an abstract image but at a real object: a blind pulled down over a window frame,
pushed in and out by air currents. *Waterline* (2002) starts with a single line 64
ascending the frame of the image; soon another line appears, rising just below it, and then the two lines switch positions. Prompted by the title, toward the end of the video, we understand that Floyer recorded the image from halfway up a glass that was being filled with water. Initially, from above the waterline, we saw a line appear on the far side of the glass, followed by the line on the near side; when the level of water rose above the camera, the far waterline switched under the near one as we were looking at the surface of the water from below.

In discussing these works, Floyer has said that viewers must 'back-map' their experience; she describes a kind of 'retrospective choreography' that takes place as we realise the falsity of our initial understanding. This kind of plot twist or 'surprise ending' is familiar from literature and film, usually providing an exciting climax. In Floyer's hands, however, the moment of recognition is accompanied by a sense of bathos.

In other works, there is no denouement. Time is perfectly linear and has no moment of rise and fall but instead seems both to thicken and stretch out. Some works use the iconography of waiting; others just make us feel what it
is like to wait. *Unfinished* (1995) is a video of twiddling thumbs, usually pro- 24
jected onto a wall in a lobby space. *H_2O Diptych* (2002) presents two screens: in one, water boils away in a pot; in the other, a glass of fizzy mineral water gradually goes flat. Each video is sixty minutes, and we know exactly what
will unfold. In *Ink on Paper (Video)* (1999) Floyer holds a pen's felt tip to a sheet 46
of paper, and the circle of ink grows as the minutes pass.

Floyer employs a similar strategy in *Nail Biting Performance* (2001), the only 54
live work in her oeuvre to date. Prior to the opening of her exhibition at Ikon Gallery, in Birmingham, UK, the artist stood alone on the stage at the Birmingham Symphony Hall in front of a microphone and proceeded to bite her nails. Audience members might well have gasped as they realized that Floyer was taking a clichéd phrase at face value and making it literally describe an activity; as she bit into the second nail, some people may have groaned. With eight fingers still to trim, the groans would have turned to silence as the auditorium filled, instead, with biting sounds and the nervous shuffling of the audience's feet.

These works put me in mind of Harold Schweizer's account of *Waiting for Godot* in *On Waiting*: 'This is not waiting for something that would validate, cancel or fulfil waiting. This is the kind of waiting we fear that waiting—or living—might amount to: just waiting.'[14] Schweizer recalls that for Henri Bergson, 'we experience time only when it is not exactly calibrated to the will, when it is other than, or in conflict with, how we *thought* time should run.'[15] In waiting, time becomes uncomfortable because there is nothing we can do to control it. Part of the unnerving effect of Floyer's waiting works is that they proceed at their own undifferentiated pace, however hurried or patient we might be. To cite Fer again, 'This is the kind of time that goes on, and on, which cannot be salvaged or redeemed.'

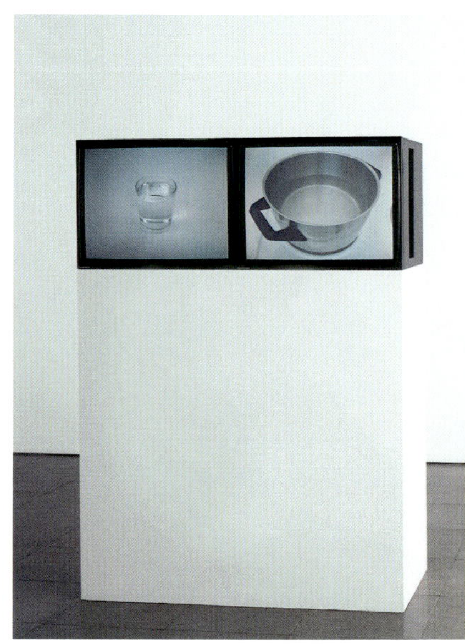
H_2O Diptych, 2002

14
Harold Schweizer, *On Waiting* (London, 2008), p. 12.
15
Schweizer, *On Waiting*, p. 16.
16
Rosalind Krauss, 'The Im/pulse to See', in *Vision and Visuality*, ed. Hal Foster (New York, 1988), p. 51.
17
Rosalind Krauss, 'Pulse', in Yve-Alain Bois and Rosalind Krauss, *Formless* (New York, 1997), pp. 161–65.
18
Tammy Wynette, vocal performance of 'Till I Get it Right', by Red Lane and Larry Henley, released December 1972 on *My Man*, Epic Records.

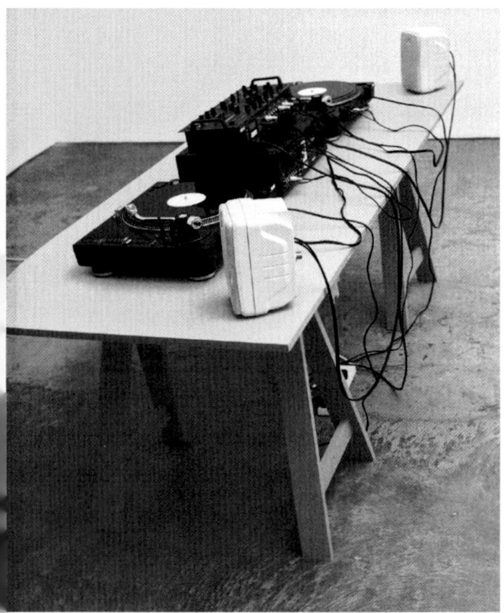

15 Minutes Ago, 2002
Twin Decks, 1999

A slightly different model of time is suggested in works that stage the repetition of identical visual or sonic events in rapid succession; here time is mechanical,
58 endless, and maddening. The most powerful of these works is *Auto Focus* (2002). Facing a wall, a slide projector has neither a carousel nor a slide in its gate. It is set to its autofocus function, but with no image to focus, it beams an empty octagon of light that expands and contracts on the wall, losing definition, sharpening, and blurring again, in and out, ad infinitum. It can be tempting to anthropomorphise the work and to imagine that the projector is breathing, but the movement is far more consistent and unceasing than that of lungs. Rather than empathising with the movement of the lens, we are chilled by its sheer, inhuman repetition. If the first monochrome paintings were an assault on every painting in art history, this slide piece might similarly reference all projections of Conceptual Art, from Marcel Broodthaers's to Dan Graham's, but we can also think about its targets in wider terms. Rosalind Krauss had looked at 'the issue of rhythm, or beat, or pulse' in Duchamp's *Rotoreliefs* (1935) and Max Ernst's *La Femme 100 Têtes* (1929), opposing the temporality of such works to the instantaneity of modernist painting, and showing how the former erodes the latter. Krauss writes, 'A kind of throb of on/off on/off on/off . . . acts against the stability of visual space in a way that is destructive and devolutionary. . . . This beat has the power to decompose and dissolve the very coherence of form on which visuality may be thought to depend.'[16] Elsewhere, addressing James Coleman's *Box (ahhareturnabout)* 1977, a film made up of pulsing sections of boxing footage and black leader, Krauss associates the pulse with the Bataillian idea of the 'formless' and its assault on all kinds of order.[17] Although the work might seem to exemplify stability through the complete regularity of its action, *Auto Focus* has an erosive impact similar to these works. Literally, the perpetual un-focusing that the work performs erodes the possibility of a coherent form; meanwhile, its repetitive mechanical temporality completely erodes ideas about time that persist in culture—both the time of nostalgia and the time of progress. Instead, we have the temporality of repetition, and of the death drive.

Having started this account of Ceal Floyer's work with lightness, *Auto Focus* seems a dark place to end, but an appropriate one, I believe. For it is in pieces like this that we can best sense a fine balance in her work between a conceptual, material, and formal concision and economy that is often a source of surprise and even delight, and a critical negativity. Just as her light switches deflate the conventions of spectacular art, and her order works play out the inevitable frustrations of attempts to make coherence in a world of capitalist excess, Floyer's time pieces undo notions of romantic nostalgia and confident progress by insisting on the banal reality of stasis and the monotony of repetition. In 2005, Floyer looped a lyric of a country song: 'I'll just keep on falling
74 in love 'til I get it right', cutting out the words 'falling in love'.[18] The edit does not grate because the percussion matches at both ends, but the constant repetition of the phrase grows increasingly disturbing as we realise that the peaceful resolution for which the singer hopes is perpetually withheld. Floyer herself realistically represents the on-going repetitions of daily life, but because she does so without descending into gloom, and while making works that are so precise, she manages to keep on getting it right.

MARK GODFREY: DRAIN

Light Switches

»Es [gibt] eine Leichtigkeit der Nachdenklichkeit«, bemerkte Italo Calvino gegen Ende seines Lebens, »so wie es bekanntlich eine Leichtigkeit der Frivolität gibt.«[1] In seinem Vortrag mit dem Titel »Leichtigkeit« fuhr Calvino fort: »Für mich verbindet sich Leichtigkeit mit Präzision und Bestimmtheit, nicht mit Vagheit und Vertrauen auf den Zufall.«[2] Calvino könnte hier auch das Werk von Ceal Floyer beschreiben, das sich Objekten und Phänomenen widmet, denen wir in unserem täglichen Leben begegnen: Gegenständen wie einer
18, *86* Glühbirne oder einer Bohrmaschine oder Phänomenen wie einem Eimer, in
38, *22* dem sich Wasser aus einem Loch in der Decke sammelt, oder einem Licht-
streifen unter einer Tür. Floyer vermeidet das Erhabene und bevorzugt das Prosaische.

Häufig ist Floyers Werk nicht nur leicht und hell in der Anmutung, sondern auch hinsichtlich des Materials – durch Beleuchtung erzeugt sie einfache Illusionen.
12 Eines ihrer frühesten Werke, *Light Switch* von 1992, veranschaulicht die Ein-
fachheit dieser Gesten: Ein Projektor ist auf den Ort an einer Wand gerichtet, wo man einen Lichtschalter erwarten würde, vielleicht neben einem Eingang, und projiziert ein Dia eines Lichtschalters. Das Dia wird je nach Ausstellungsort ausgewechselt, sodass es immer der Art von Lichtschalter entspricht, die in dem Land üblich ist, in dem die Arbeit gezeigt wird. Der Titel ist nicht nur eine trockene Beschreibung des Werks, sondern gleichzeitig die Offenlegung
18 einer künstlerischen Strategie. Nehmen wir *Light* von 1994: Hier sind vier Dia-
projektoren auf eine von der Decke hängende, mit mattweißer Farbe überzogene Glühbirne gerichtet, deren Kabel nicht angeschlossen ist; folglich ist die
22 Glühbirne hell erleuchtet, aber der Raum bleibt dunkel. In *Door* (1995) ähnelt
ein unten an eine Tür projiziertes Bild einem Lichtstrahl, der vom nächsten
94 Zimmer hereinscheint. Für *Overhead Projection* (2006) legte die Künstlerin eine
Glühbirne auf das Glas eines Overhead-Projektors; das resultierende Bild wirkt so, als würde die vergrößerte Glühbirne von der Decke hängen.

Floyers Situationen erschaffen oder (um Jeremy Millars Ausdruck zu verwenden) »verkörpern«[3] gewöhnliche Gegenstände und Phänomene durch den Einsatz von einfachen, schlichten Technologien neu: beispielsweise durch einen auf eine Tür gerichteten Diaprojektor. Oft ist das verwendete Gerät fast veraltet (Diaprojektoren, Plattenspieler, Overhead-Projektoren), doch ist für Floyer der nostalgische Nachklang des verwendeten Apparats nicht sehr bedeutend, sie verwendet ebenso Computerdateien, CD-und DVD-Spieler. Wichtiger als die Frage von digital und analog ist ihr die unübersehbare, ganz offene Präsenz des Apparats. Bei vielen Arbeiten geht es um das Schaffen einer Verschiebung oder eines Wechsels (»switch«), um eine kurzzeitige Illusion, aber genau in dem Moment, in dem der Betrachter diesen Effekt sieht, versteht er auch seine Ursache: Licht, das scheinbar unter einer Tür hindurchscheint, und dann den Diaprojektor, der dieses Licht tatsächlich auf die Tür projiziert. Wir bewundern den Zauber der Arbeit keineswegs weniger, weil die Zauberin ihre Tricks offenlegt, und dies ist konträr zur üblichen Funktionsweise von Spezialeffekten, welche ihr Zustandekommen verstecken. Floyer hat vom Einfluss von Fred Sandbacks Skulpturen gesprochen, von dessen Fähigkeit, die Illusion einer Illusion zu schaffen.[4] Sandback hat farbigen Faden so gespannt, dass der Eindruck entsteht, eine feste Ebene würde an einer Wand lehnen; und obwohl wir sofort wissen, dass diese Ebenen tatsächlich Leerräume sind, fällt es keineswegs leichter, durch sie hindurchzugehen. Eine weitere für Floyer sehr wichtige Arbeit ist Charles Rays *32 x 33 x 35 = 34 x 33 x 35* (1989), ein minimalistischer Würfel aus gebürstetem Aluminium, dessen Inneres etwas tiefer ist als sein Äußeres, da er zwei Zoll tief in den Boden des Ausstellungsraums eingelassen wird. Der Titel erklärt, warum die Arbeit sich so merkwürdig anfühlt, aber er erklärt diese Merkwürdigkeit nicht weg.

In manchen Fällen basiert der Effekt von Floyers Verschiebungen auf formalen Zufällen und einem synästhetischen Dreh. In *Carousel* (1996) spielt ein Plattenspieler auf einem Sockel eine Platte, deren einziger Track eine Aufnahme des Klickens eines Diakarussells ist; der Durchmesser der Platte (10 Zoll) entspricht
dem Durchmesser des Diakarussells. Bei *Working Title (Digging)* (1995) stehen 26
zwei Lautsprecher auf gegenüberliegenden Seiten des Ausstellungsraums, aus dem einen ist das Geräusch eines Erde schaufelnden Spatens zu hören,
aus dem anderen das Geräusch von auf den Boden fallender Erde. *Scale* (2007) 104
besteht aus einer Reihe von Lautsprechern, die vom Boden bis zur Decke emporsteigen; jeder ist gegenüber dem vorherigen ein wenig zurückversetzt, sodass der Eindruck einer Treppe entsteht. Man hört Schritte, die auf und ab gehen, alle Lautsprecher spielen in Folge einen einzigen, immer identischen Schritt. Aber das akustische Ereignis kann auch visuell werden. Dies ist bei *Glass* (1998) der Fall: Eine Nadel dreht sich auf einer durchsichtigen Vinylschallplatte, zu hören ist das Geräusch eines Fingers, der sich oben auf einem Glasrand im Kreis bewegt.

Floyers Verwendung von Sprache ist unglaublich wichtig; oft bestimmen ein Wort oder eine Wortreihe eine Arbeit, wobei die Künstlerin die Wörter so lange »verknetet«, bis sich der Titel daraus ergibt. Floyers Herangehensweise an Sprache ist ein teils pedantischer, teils heroischer Versuch, Mehrdeutigkeit und Metapher durch Buchstäblichkeit und Präzision zu ersetzen. Sie besteht darauf, dass ein Wort bedeuten muss, was es aussagt, und es muss alles bedeuten, was es bedeuten kann. »Switch«, Schalter, muss den Gegenstand bezeichnen, aber auch die Tätigkeit, da es im Englischen auch ein Verb sein kann: schalten, umtauschen, umschalten, verschieben. Wenn »throw« die Tätigkeit des Herunterwerfens bezeichnet, aber auch der Handelsname einer bestimmten Art von Beleuchtung ist, dann muss eine Arbeit mit diesem Titel beide Bedeutungen umfassen – wie dies bei Floyers *Throw* (1997) der Fall ist (es handelt sich um eine Theaterlampe mit einem Gobo aus Metall, einer runden Maske oder Schablone, die ein Bild von Farbe auf den Boden projiziert,
als ob sie da hingeschüttet worden wäre). *Drill* (2006) ist sowohl das Werkzeug 86
Bohrmaschine als auch der Akt des Bohrens mit diesem Werkzeug – und somit müssen beide Bedeutungen respektiert werden. (Floyers Bohrer liegt auf dem Boden, aber der Stecker steckt nicht in einer Steckdose, sondern in einem Loch, von dem wir vermuten, es wurde mit ebendiesem Bohrer gebohrt – aber woher kam der Strom dafür?)

Ihre Wortspiele und Bedeutungs- oder Syntaxverschiebungen erinnern an ältere Arbeiten wie Man Rays *Featherweight* (1960), eine Skulptur, bei der drei Federn in einem Gewicht stecken, und zwei Fotografien Bruce Naumans von 1966, *Waxing Hot* (der Künstler, der ein Schild mit der Aufschrift »HOT« wachst) und *Feet of Clay* (Naumans mit Lehm beschmierte Füße). Ganz ähnlich bei
Reversed (2005), für das Floyer die Fotografie eines Schildes auf einem 78
Restauranttisch mit der Aufschrift »RESERVED« spiegelbildlich abgezogen hat. Das Bild erinnert an Giovanni Anselmos Fotografie *Lato Destro* (Rechte Seite) von 1970, das den Künstler mit dem Titel auf seinem Hals zeigt: Die Wörter erscheinen auf der rechten Seite des Fotos, aber dies bedeutet, dass sie auf die linke Seite seines Halses geschrieben wurden.

1
Italo Calvino, *Sechs Vorschläge für das nächste Jahrtausend*, Frankfurt am Main: Fischer Taschenbuch, 2012, S. 25.

2
Ebd., S. 31.

3
Jeremy Millar, »Just Like That«, in: *Ceal Floyer*, Ausst.-Kat. Ikon Gallery, Birmingham 2001, S. 20.

4
Sandback schrieb über sein Werk: »Meine Arbeit ist nicht im üblichen Sinne des Wortes illusionistisch. Sie verweist nicht weg von sich selbst auf etwas, das nicht da ist. Ihre Illusionen sind einfach anwesende Aspekte von ihr.« Dieser Kommentar scheint mir für Floyers Werk besonders relevant zu sein. Siehe *Fred Sandback*, Ausst.-Kat. Kunstraum München 1975, S. 11.

Die affektive Wirkung von Floyers »leichten Verschiebungen« oder »Umkehrungen« – »light switches« – ist schwieriger zu beschreiben als erwartet. Zunächst rufen viele dieser Arbeiten eine erfreute Reaktion hervor: Als Betrachter bewundert man ihre Intelligenz, ihre Zurückhaltung und einfach die präzise Brillanz ihrer Konzeption. Calvino hat zudem »Flinkheit« und »Genauigkeit« als Werte zukünftiger Literatur identifiziert, was auf Floyers Arbeiten ebenso zutrifft wie Leichtigkeit. Aber die affektive Komplexität von Floyers »leichten Umkehrungen« wird im Laufe der Zeit stärker, sie überdauert den Aha-Effekt, wenn wir verstehen, dass die Ursache der ursprünglichen Wirkung der Arbeit intuitiv erfasst wird. Aus Leichtigkeit wird dann ein Luftablassen. *Drain* (2006) ist ein kleiner Lautsprecher, der wie ein Abfluss aussieht, auf dem Boden liegt, an einen CD-Spieler angeschlossen ist und das Geräusch von durch einen Abfluss spülendem Wasser spielt; auch nachdem uns klar wird, dass die Illusion auf der formalen Ähnlichkeit von Lautsprecher und Abfluss basiert, läuft das Wassergeräusch immer weiter – es scheint, als würde alles aus dem Raum ablaufen, als würde jemand immer wieder den gleichen Witz erzählen. Für mich wiederholt sich der erste Moment des Vergnügens, der dann verrinnt, bei allen Arbeiten von Floyer, in denen es um »leichte Umkehrungen« geht; und tatsächlich ist es dieser später auftretende Affekt der Enttäuschung, der mich an ihnen besonders fasziniert.

Floyer unterstreicht diese Umkehrung von Vergnügen zu Enttäuschung in Arbeiten, die auf brillante Art und Weise die Erwartungen nach spektakulärer Befriedigung und dramatischem Staunen unterlaufen, mit der wir heute einem Großteil der zeitgenössischen Kunst zu begegnen gelernt haben. Auf den
76 ersten Blick scheint das Video *Apollinaris* (2005) ein Feuerwerk vor schwarzem Himmel zu zeigen; tatsächlich handelt es sich um eine Nahaufnahme der Blasen, die aus einem Glas mit dem gleichnamigen Mineralwasser sprudeln.
84 In *Double Act* (2006) wirft ein Spotlight einen Lichtkreis auf einen roten Bühnenvorhang an einer Wand, der sich weiter auf dem Boden darunter erstreckt. Stehen wir in dem blendenden Licht und schauen in das Spotlight, sehen wir, dass es ein Gobo des Vorhangs enthält. Dieser Moment des Erkennens – dass Licht *und* Bild aus derselben Quelle kommen – ist das Dramatische dieser Arbeit, und wir sind mitten auf der Bühne. Aber der Vorhang bleibt geschlossen; es gibt keine weitere Auflösung. Mit der Sprache des theatralischen Spektakels widersteht Floyer spektakulärer Theatralik.[5]

Eine weitere Gruppe von Floyers Werken widmet sich den schwindelerregenden Exzessen der Kunstwirtschaft. Floyers frühester Vorstoß auf dieses Terrain
30 war die Arbeit *Sold* (1996): Die Künstlerin bohrte einen winzigen runden Krater in eine Galeriewand neben einem Gemälde und füllte das Loch mit cadmiumroter Ölfarbe, ähnlich den roten »Verkauft«-Aufklebern, die man manchmal in Galerien sieht. Nur auf der Checkliste der Galerie konnte man sehen, dass dies ihre Arbeit war, eine Skulptur (da dreidimensional), die sich als Gemälde verkleidet hatte – als ein in der Tat sehr viel bescheideneres Gemälde als das,
90 was darüber hing. *Genuine Reduction* (2006) ist ein vorgefertigtes Ausverkaufsschild, wie man es in Billigläden findet, und da die rechte Seite des Schildes ein Stück beschnitten ist, ist das Schild selbst stark reduziert. Als Floyer diese Arbeit zum ersten Mal in der Lisson Gallery zeigte, sprach sie damit auch die Geschichte einer Galerie an, die lange mit der Minimal Art in Verbindung gebracht wurde, aber auch ganz allgemein ihre eigene künstlerische Praxis. Zudem setzte sich die Arbeit mit dem Wesen einer privaten Galerie als kommerzieller Einrichtung auseinander: *Genuine Reduction* wurde in einem zur

5
Auch *Suspense* ist hier von Belang. Für eine Ausstellung in der Domaine de Kerguéhennec im französischen Bignan schuf Floyer eine Installation, bei der ein Besucher einen leeren Korridor entlang auf einen Lautsprecher zugeht, der einen Soundtrack spielt, wie man ihn aus spannenden Momenten in Hollywood-Thrillern kennt – ein kreischendes Geräusch, langsame Streichercrescendos. Was hier anders ist: Es gibt keine Auflösung der Spannung; der Besucher kommt zum Lautsprecher, findet dort nichts, und die Musik hört auf.

6
Die Zitate in diesem Absatz nach: George Perec, *Penser / Classer*, Paris: Hachette, 1985.

Straße gelegenen Raum der Lisson Gallery installiert, dort wo in normalen Geschäften ähnliche Schilder auch hängen würden.
Floyers raffinierteste Intervention dieser Art wurde 2006 für das kommerziell wichtigste Ereignis im Kunstweltkalender geschaffen – die Kunstmesse Art Basel. Der Künstlerin stand ein großer Raum in der Sektion Art Unlimited zur Verfügung. Sie realisierte ein Werk, bei dem Soundboards (flache Lautsprecher, deren Maße es ermöglichen, sie in Wände einzubauen) Aufnahmen von Bohren, Sägen und Schleifen abspielen. Diese Maßnahmen fanden beim Bau dieser temporären Konstruktion für die Kunstmesse statt; ihre schmutzigen Spuren waren längst mit Hilfe von Farbe beseitigt, da der Raum inzwischen ein typischer White Cube war. Obwohl die Arbeit natürlich auf Robert Morris'
Box with the Sound of Its Own Making anspielt, weist ihr Titel, *Construction*, 82
auf andere Wesensverwandtschaften hin und lässt beispielsweise an die Werke von Michael Asher denken. »Construction« bezieht sich auf Bauarbeiten, die der Soundtrack wiedergibt, eine Art von Arbeit, die Asher in vielen seiner Installationen darbot. Betrachter, die von Floyer gelernt haben, nach Doppelbedeutungen zu suchen, könnten das Wort so verstehen, dass es sich über den Klang der Arbeit hinaus auf die gesamte Umgebung bezieht. Für mich deutete die Arbeit darauf hin, dass die ganze Kunstmesse eine Konstruktion ist, in deren Kern eine Leerstelle voller Klang und Wut sein könnte, genau wie Floyers leerer White Cube.

Ordnungen

In seinem Essay *Denken / Ordnen*[6] klagt Georges Perec: »Der Gedanke, dass auf der Welt nichts so einzigartig ist, dass es nicht in eine Liste eingetragen werden kann, ist faszinierend und beängstigend zugleich.« Fasziniert von Organisations- und Klassifizierungssystemen, strebte er danach, bestimmte Details vollkommen zu erfassen, selbst wenn er sein Büro beschrieb. In »Notizen, die die Dinge auf meinem Schreibtisch betreffen« listet er unter anderem »eine Lampe, ein Zigarettenetui, eine Vase für eine Blume, ein Feuerzeug, ein Karton mit kleinen vielfarbigen Karteikarten, ein großes Tintenfass aus Carton bouilli mit Schildpattverzierungen […]« auf. »Sagen Sie und schreiben Sie nicht ›etc.‹«, ordnete er an. »Strengen Sie sich an, den Gegenstand erschöpfend zu behandeln.« Auch die Sprache selbst lässt sich klassifizieren. »Wie könnte man die folgenden Verben sortieren: anordnen, katalogisieren, einordnen, kleinschneiden, teilen, aufzählen, sammeln, einstufen, gruppieren, auflisten, nummerieren, ordnen, organisieren, sortieren?« Dabei erkannte Perec auch, dass das »Problem bei Einordnungen darin liegt, dass sie nicht lange gültig bleiben; kaum bin ich fertig, Dinge in eine Ordnung zu bringen, dann ist diese Ordnung auch schon wieder überholt.«
Eine zweite Familie von Floyers Werken will Ordnung schaffen. Man denkt sie sich am besten eher als Prozesse denn als Situationen, aber wie bei Perecs Listen wird ihr Ehrgeiz ständig vereitelt; die Künstlerin selbst hat diese Projekte als »sisyphosmäßig« bezeichnet. Für *Downpour* (2004) filmte Floyer einen Sturm, der Regen so verwehte, dass er in einer Diagonalen fiel, und neigte die Aufnahme dann so, dass sie ein Bild von exakt vertikalem Regen erhielt; der Rand des Filmbildes allerdings offenbart die Manipulation. In zahlreichen Arbeiten hängt ihr Bestreben, Ordnung zu schaffen, mit dem Chaos unserer spätkapitalistischen Welt zusammen, mit Überproduktion, Lärm, Hochgeschwindigkeit, technologischer Überfrachtung und exzessivem materiellen
Konsum. Die einfach *Order* betitelte Arbeit (2007) besteht aus einem der 102

Objekte auf Perecs Schreibtisch: einem Satz von Registerpappen für Karteikarten. Vom Hersteller werden die Reiter oben an den Registerpappen nebeneinander sortiert, sodass die Buchstaben im Kasten in einer Diagonale verlaufen; Floyer allerdings hat die Registerpappen so hintereinander aufgereiht, dass die Buchstaben eine Spalte bilden – jetzt aber sind die Ränder nicht mehr auf einer Linie, und es bedarf eines besonderen, gerillten Ständers, um sie zu halten. Der Projektor in Floyers *Slide Show* (1995) zeigt Dias, »slides«, im eigentlichen Sinne des Wortes – Bilder und Diagramme aller 48 kommerziell verfügbaren Diarahmen, nach einer bestimmten Ordnung archiviert. In dieser Arbeit wird Medienreflexivität auf trockene Art witzig, sie ist wörtlich genommen und weit hergeholt, und sie hat kaum Beziehung zur modernen Medien-
44 reflexivität. Die Arbeiten mit dem Titel *Ink on Paper* (1999) dramatisieren eine weitere Dynamik von Ordnung und Unordnung, diesmal mit Hilfe eines Gegenstands aus dem Schreibwarengeschäft: Für jede Serie von Zeichnungen benutzt Floyer alle Stifte aus einer Packung Filzstifte. Sie entleert jeden Stift auf ein Stück Löschpapier, und diese Papiere heftet sie genau in der Reihenfolge an die Wand, die der Reihenfolge der Stifte in der Packung entspricht. So wie *Slide Show* eine Show von Diarahmen ist, handelt es sich hier buchstäblich um »Tinte auf Papier«, wie auch die übliche Angabe zum künstlerischen Medium in Museen lautet. Beim Auslaufen wird die Unterschiedlichkeit der Filzstifttinten deutlich, die Tinte unterscheidet sich im Ton oft von der Farbe der Plastikhülle der Stifte, und einige Stifte laufen in einem größeren Kreis aus als andere. Die Arbeit bildet die Folge des Filzstiftpakets nach, aber in diesem Prozess löst es das Erscheinungsbild des Farbsortiments auf.

Das Entfernen ist ein weiteres Verfahren, das Floyer immer wieder anwendet, um die Welt zu ordnen. Das beste Beispiel für diese Strategie ist eine Gruppe von 1998 entstandenen Videos: *Monochrome Edit (White)*, *Monochrome Edit (Red)* und *Spectrum Edit*. Jedes Video besteht aus einer einzigen Einstellung einer gewöhnlichen Berliner Straße, aber der Schnitt ist in jeder Arbeit unterschiedlich. In *Monochrome Edit (White)* sieht man eine Folge weißer Autos, die vor der Kamera vorbeifahren, alle anderen Fahrzeuge wurden herausgeschnitten. Obwohl wir sie nicht sehen können, wissen wir, dass sie da waren: Das Geräusch der sich nähernden und wegfahrenden Autos hat Floyer beibehalten. In *Spectrum Edit* sind die Aufnahmen so angeordnet, dass jedes der aufeinanderfolgenden Autos eine andere Farbe des Regenbogens hat; Floyer sah kein lila Auto, aber zufällig lief ein Fußgänger mit einem lila Anorak ins Bild, der den Platz dieses Autos erhielt.

Im Gegensatz zu diesen Auslassungen oder Schnitten spielt Floyer auch mit der Akkumulation. In einer Arbeit aus dem Jahr 2004 befindet sich ein dichtes Gekritzel schwarzer Tinte im Zentrum einer leeren Papierfläche. Der Titel *again and again* hilft uns, Formen an den Rändern dieses Gewirrs zu erkennen, die sich wiederholen: Das obere Dreieck eines »A« links; ein bisschen weiter ein paar Punkte. Floyer schrieb einfach die Wörter »Again and« immer wieder, eins auf dem anderen, als wäre dies eine Anweisung, bis die Wörter unlesbar wurden. Wiederholung wird oft mit Betonung oder Nachdruck in Verbindung gebracht; zusammen mit dem Neuordnen, Neuzählen und Entfernen ist sie ein weiteres Mittel, um Ordnung zu schaffen. Floyers Arbeiten verleihen den Arten, in denen Wiederholung eine Kraft des Auslöschens sein kann, allerdings auch Dramatik. *again and again* erinnert an eine Metapher, die Alain Robbe-Grillet verwendete, um den Effekt der deskriptiven Überfrachtung in seinen Büchern zu beschreiben: »Die Linien der Zeichnung häufen sich, überdecken einander,

heben einander auf oder verschieben sich, so daß das Bild in dem Maße, in
dem es entsteht, in Zweifel gezogen wird.«[7] *Warning Birds* (2002) und *Mind* 62
The Step (2006) sind zwei weitere Beispiele dieser Dynamik von Wiederholung 92
und Auslöschung. Die erste Arbeit verwendet Aufkleber, wie sie an Gebäuden
mit Glasflächen verwendet werden; idealerweise werden sie ganz unregel-
mäßig aufgeklebt und sollen Vögel davon abhalten, in die Glasscheiben zu
fliegen. Das riesige Fenster von *Warning Birds* aber ist vollkommen mit Aufklebern bedeckt – so bleiben zwar die Vögel weg, aber um den Preis, dass
man nicht mehr aus dem Fenster schauen kann.

In einigen Arbeiten geht es nicht darum, ein einziges Motiv oder Objekt betont
zu wiederholen, sondern darum, unterschiedliche Dinge zu kombinieren und
ihnen irgendeine Ordnung zu geben. *Helix*, dessen erste Fassung 2001 ent- 50
stand, ist das auffälligste Beispiel für diese Strategie. Die Basis der Arbeit bildet
ein Zeicheninstrument der Firma Helix, eine dünne orange Plastikschablone,
deren runde Löcher einen immer größer werdenden Durchmesser haben und
die für technische Zeichnungen und Diagramme verwendet wird. In Floyers
Händen wird jedoch das Zeichnen zu einer skulpturalen Aktivität, da die Künstlerin Gegenstände mit runden Böden in die passenden Löcher der Schablone
steckt. Ganz unterschiedliche Dinge befinden sich vollkommen unerwartet
nebeneinander, bedingt durch die nicht in Frage zu stellende Aufeinanderfolge
ihrer Durchmesser: Münzen, Bonbons, Taschenlampen, Medizinflaschen,
Glühbirnen, Kappen von Stiften, Dichtungsringe und Batterien.

Floyer bringt hier nicht nur eine Menge Gegenstände zusammen, die nichts
miteinander zu tun haben, sondern sie kombiniert auch bisher nicht zusammen-
hängende bildhauerische Praktiken. Am offensichtlichsten ist *Helix* eine
Sammlung von Readymades, aber es verweist ebenso auf Duchamps willkür-
lich festgelegte Eichmaße wie in *3 Stoppages étalon* (1913/14). Mit seiner Folge
von geordneten Löchern bezieht sich *Helix* ebenso auf die seriellen Abläufe
des Minimalismus, aber seine Alltagsgegenstände erinnern eher an die
Arbeiten von Arman, an den frühen Christian Boltanski und auch an Alighiero
Boettis *Cubo* (1968), in dem Objekte unterschiedlicher Form in einer Kiste
säuberlich ineinandergeschoben sind.

Monochrome Till Receipt (White), erstmals 1998 ausgeführt, ist eine von Floyers 34
konzeptionell elegantesten Arbeiten, und zu Recht eine ihrer bekanntesten. Die
Arbeit ist ein bescheidener Kassenzettel, weder weiß noch monochrom,
sondern lila Tinte auf verblassendem beigem Papier. Die verschiedenartigsten
Einkäufe werden aufgelistet – Schmalz, Frischkäse, Waschmittel, Salz usw. –,
die Quittung ist so gewöhnlich wie die aufgelisteten Einkäufe. Floyer schafft das
Werk immer wieder neu, nach Einkäufen aus einem Supermarkt in dem Land,
in dem sie ausstellt, sodass die Quittung kaum Aufmerksamkeit zu verdienen
scheint. Aber bald wird der Grund für den Titel klar: Alle erworbenen Produkte
sind weiß. *Monochrome Till Receipt* lässt an eine Vielzahl von künstlerischen
Traditionen und Gattungen denken – an Stillleben, skulpturale Akkumulationen,
die Dokumente zu Konzeptkunstwerken und sogar an die konkrete Poesie.
Aber mehr als alles andere lädt uns der Kassenzettel ein, uns eine Welt der
Reinheit und Ordnung vorzustellen, die mit der monochromen Malerei und
Architektur der Moderne assoziiert ist, mit dem Utopismus des frühen 20. Jahr-
hunderts, von Malewitsch (der als Erster weiß auf weiß malte) und Le Corbusier.
Aber verweist *Monochrome Till Receipt* wirklich auf die Möglichkeit, eine
Welt des billigen Kommerzes zu bleichen? Mehr als modernistische Reinheit
evoziert die Arbeit den Wirrwarr eines Supermarkts – der Friedhof der Träume

7
Alain Robbe-Grillet, *Argumente für einen neuen Roman*, übers. von Marie-Simone Morel und Helmut Scheffler, München: Hanser, 1965, S. 98.

der Moderne, ein Ort der Verfälschung und der Farbe, an dem grelle und griffige Logos das Auge angreifen. Zum Schluss haben wir das Gefühl, dass die Arbeit, indem sie so flüchtig das Monochrome und seine Assoziationen evoziert, nur unsere Distanz zu einer Welt unterstreicht, in der eine solche künstlerische Innovation noch ein utopisches Versprechen sein konnte.

Zeitarbeiten

In ihrem Essay »Some Translucent Substance, or the Trouble with Time« blickt Briony Fer auf die späten 1960er-Jahre zurück, um die unterschiedlichen Arten zu erörtern, in denen die Zeit in der Kunst und im kritischen Diskurs zur Diskussion stand. Sie hinterfragt Michael Frieds reduktive Unterscheidung zwischen dem »Moment«, in dem moderne Arbeiten wahrgenommen werden konnten, und der »Dauer«, die Werke des Minimalismus erforderten, und besteht darauf, dass es ein viel breiteres Spektrum an Herangehensweisen an die Zeit gab, die sich beispielsweise in Werken von Künstlern wie Eva Hesse und Robert Smithson manifestierten. In einer Arbeit von Hesse könne man Momente des »Stillstands, in denen die Zeit plötzlich abgeschnitten wird« spüren, wie auch das Gefühl haben, »die Zeit gehe einfach weiter, und Zeit läuft ab«.[8] Smithson stellte sich Unendlichkeiten vor, aber »die Art von Unendlichkeit, die ihn interessierte, war nicht groß geschrieben und war nicht erhaben«. Für Smithson evozierte Donald Judds Werk »schiere Trägheit und Endlosigkeit«; und, wie wohlbekannt ist, verweisen viele von Smithsons eigenen Arbeiten auf Entropie, den allmählichen Energieverlust.[9]

Die Frage der Zeit ist auch für Floyers Vorgehensweise entscheidend und definiert einen dritten Werkkorpus. Einige der dazugehörigen Arbeiten widmen sich ganz explizit der Zeit: In *15 Minutes Ago* (2002) spielt ein Lautsprecher an einer Wand (dort, wo man auch eine Uhr aufhängen würde) eine 15-minütige Aufnahme des Tickens einer Uhr – rückwärts abgespielt, was ein merkwürdiges, aber dennoch unverwechselbares Tack-Tick bewirkt, als ob die voranschreitende Zeit in den Rückwärtsgang geschaltet worden wäre. Die beiden Platten, die in *Twin Decks* (1999) mit 33 respektive 45 Umdrehungen pro Minute abgespielt werden, haben jede nur eine Rille, sie spielen keinen Ton außer einem einzigen Stoß, was bedeutet, dass anhand dieses Geräusches das Tempo der Umdrehungen erkennbar ist, obwohl die beiden Klicks nie
66 synchron sind. *1–25* (2003) ist die Projektion einer Folge ausgeschriebener Zahlen, von denen jede die der Zahl entsprechende Anzahl von Sekunden lang gezeigt wird; man versteht die Logik des Werks erst, wenn die ersten paar Zahlen schon wieder verschwunden sind. *Time Piece* (2003) überträgt alle Schläge (volle Stunden und Viertelstunden) einer Kirchturmuhr, aber die dazwischenliegenden Intervalle sind herausgenommen: Ein ganzer Tag wird auf eine Folge bedeutungsloser Markierungen reduziert. In solchen Werken ist, in den Worten von Shakespeares Hamlet, »die Zeit aus den Fugen«, und sie rufen in uns dasselbe Gefühl hervor.

In einigen Arbeiten allerdings schafft Floyer Situationen, die wir erst mit einiger Verzögerung verstehen können; der Moment des Verstehens kehrt das von uns bereits Angenommene um und verlangt, dass wir unsere Begegnung mit der Arbeit noch einmal ganz neu überdenken. Ein frühes Beispiel für diese zeitliche Struktur ist die erstmals 1993 realisierte Arbeit *Untitled Installation*
16 *(Dotted Line)*. Wir gehen einen Flur entlang und gelangen in ein Zimmer; dort sehen wir einen Diabetrachter auf einem Sockel, dessen Bildschirm eine Schere zeigt. Dies erscheint erst einmal harmlos, bis wir den Raum verlassen

8
Briony Fer, »Some Translucent Substance, or the Trouble with Time«, in: Carolyn Gill (Hrsg.), *Time and the Image*, Manchester: Manchester University Press, 2000, S. 69.
9
Ebd., S. 73.

und eine Strichellinie am Rand der Wände, Fenster und Türen bemerken – die Art von Linie, die bedeutet: »hier schneiden«. Diese Linie hat uns vom Moment des Betretens dieses Zimmers an umgeben, blieb aber unbemerkt; sobald wir sie allerdings wahrnehmen, spüren wir, wie sich unsere Beziehung zum Raum um uns herum verändert. Die Wände erscheinen plötzlich dünn wie Papier, und wir fühlen uns, als wären wir aus Raum und Zeit »ausgeschnitten«.

Diese Erfahrung, dass uns etwas erst langsam, nach und nach klar wird, zeichnet Floyers zeitbasierte Arbeiten häufig aus. Das Bild im Video *Blind* (1997) 32
ist anfänglich opak und suggeriert ein verschleiertes oder halbblindes Sehen. Eine weiße Oberfläche pulsiert, und manchmal erscheint dahinter eine dunkle Form. Plötzlich wird uns klar, dass wir kein abstraktes Bild betrachten, sondern einen realen Gegenstand: eine heruntergezogene Jalousie vor einem Fensterrahmen, die vom Luftstrom nach vorne und hinten bewegt wird. *Waterline* 64
(2002) beginnt mit einer einzigen Linie, die in der ganzen Breite des Bildes emporsteigt; bald erscheint eine zweite Linie, die direkt darunter aufsteigt, und im weiteren Verlauf tauschen die beiden Linien ihre Positionen. Der Titel lenkt unsere Wahrnehmung, und gegen Ende des Videos wird uns klar, dass Floyer einen Glasbehälter aufgenommen hat, der mit Wasser gefüllt wird. Anfangs, solange wir von der Kameraposition in der Mitte des Glases aus auf die Wasseroberfläche schauen, erscheint eine Linie am hinteren Ende des Glases, gefolgt von einer Linie an der Vorderseite; wenn der Wasserspiegel über die Kamerahöhe steigt, verschiebt sich die weiter entfernte Wasserlinie unter die nähere, da wir die Wasseroberfläche von unten betrachten.

Floyer selbst hat in Bezug auf diese Arbeiten angemerkt, dass Betrachter ihre Erfahrung »rückwärts kartieren« müssen; sie beschreibt das als eine Art »retrospektive Choreografie«, die stattfindet, wenn wir erkennen, dass unsere anfängliche Interpretation falsch war. Diese Art von einer überraschenden Wendung in der Handlung, oder von einem überraschenden Ende, ist aus Literatur und Film bekannt, wo sie normalerweise für einen spannenden Höhepunkt sorgt. In Floyers Händen allerdings wird der Moment der Erkenntnis von einem Gefühl des Bathos begleitet. In anderen Werken gibt es gar keine Auflösung. Die Zeit ist vollkommen linear, es gibt keinen Moment des Ansteigens und Fallens, stattdessen scheint sie sich sowohl zu verdichten als auch auszudehnen. Einige Arbeiten verwenden die Ikonografie des Wartens, andere geben uns ein Gefühl dafür, was es heißt zu warten. *Unfinished* (1995) ist ein 24
Video, das Däumchendrehen zeigt und üblicherweise auf eine Wand in einem Foyer projiziert wird. *H_2O Diptych* (2002) arbeitet mit zwei Bildschirmen, auf dem einen verkocht Wasser in einem Topf, auf dem anderen verschwinden nach und nach die Sprudelblasen aus einem Glas Wasser. Jedes Video dauert 60 Minuten, und wir wissen genau, was passieren wird. In *Ink on Paper (Video)* 46
(1999) hält Floyer die Spitze eines Filzstifts auf ein Stück Papier, und der Kreis der Farbe wächst im Verstreichen der Minuten.

Eine ähnliche Strategie verfolgt Floyer in *Nail Biting Performance* (2001), 54
ihrer bisher einzigen Live-Performance. Vor der Eröffnung ihrer Ausstellung in der Ikon Gallery im britischen Birmingham stand die Künstlerin alleine auf der Bühne der Birmingham Symphony Hall an einem Mikrofon und begann, an ihren Fingernägeln zu kauen. Das Publikum hat wahrscheinlich nach Luft geschnappt, als klar wurde, dass Floyer eine klischeehafte Redewendung für bare Münze und als Vorlage für eine konkrete Aktivität genommen hatte; als sie in den zweiten Nagel biss, haben wohl einige Leute aufgestöhnt. Da aber

noch acht Fingernägel darauf warteten, gekaut zu werden, dürfte das Stöhnen verstummt sein, während sich das Auditorium mit den Geräuschen des Nägelknabberns und nervösen Fußescharrens des Publikums füllte.

Bei diesen Arbeiten kam mir Harold Schweizer in den Sinn, der in seinem Buch *On Waiting* Folgendes über *Warten auf Godot* schreibt: »Dies ist kein Warten auf etwas, was das Warten validieren, widerrufen oder erfüllen könnte. Dies ist die Art von Warten, bei der wir fürchten, dass Warten – oder Leben – genau das sein könnte: einfach warten.«[10]

Schweizer erinnert daran, dass wir Henri Bergson zufolge »Zeit nur erleben, wenn sie nicht genau nach dem Willen kalibriert wird, wenn sie anders ist oder im Konflikt dazu steht, wie wir dachten, dass die Zeit verlaufen sollte«.[11] Beim Warten wird die Zeit unangenehm, weil wir nichts tun können, um sie zu steuern. Zum Beunruhigenden von Floyers Arbeiten über das Warten gehört, dass sie in ihrem eigenen undifferenzierten Tempo verlaufen, gleichgültig, wie eilig wir es gerade haben oder wie geduldig wir sind. Um noch einmal Briony Fer zu zitieren: »Dies ist die Art von Zeit, die immer weiterläuft, die nicht zurückgewonnen oder wettgemacht werden kann.«

Ein etwas anderes Zeitmodell kommt in Arbeiten zum Tragen, die die Wiederholung von identischen visuellen oder akustischen Ereignissen in schneller Folge präsentieren; hier ist die Zeit mechanisch, endlos und macht einen verrückt.
58 Die eindruckvollste davon ist *Auto Focus* (2002). Ein Diaprojektor ist auf eine Wand gerichtet, enthält aber weder ein Karussell noch ein Dia in seinem Schieber. Er ist so eingestellt, dass er sich automatisch scharf stellt, aber ohne Dia wirft er ein leeres Lichtoktagon an die Wand, das sich weitet und wieder zusammenzieht, an Schärfe verliert, scharf wird, dann wieder verschwimmt, hin und her, ad infinitum. Es wäre verlockend, die Arbeit zu vermenschlichen und sich vorzustellen, der Projektor würde atmen, aber die Bewegung ist viel gleichbleibender und kontinuierlicher als die der Lunge. Statt sich also in die Bewegung des Objektivs einzufühlen, erschrecken wir angesichts der schieren, unmenschlichen Wiederholung. Wenn die ersten monochromen Gemälde ein Angriff auf jedes vorherige Gemälde der Kunstgeschichte waren, dann verweist diese Projektion auf alle Projektionen der Konzeptkunst, von den Werken Marcel Broodthaers' bis hin zu denen von Dan Graham, aber man kann ihr Ziel weiter gefasst denken. Rosalind Krauss untersuchte »die Frage von Rhythmus oder Beat oder Puls« in Duchamps *Rotoreliefs* (1935) and Max Ernsts *La femme 100 têtes* (1929), stellte die Temporalität solcher Arbeiten der Gegenwärtigkeit der modernen Malerei gegenüber und zeigte, wie Ersteres Letzteres erodiert. Krauss schrieb: »Eine Art von an/aus, an/aus, an/aus-Pochen oder Pulsieren arbeitet destruktiv und degenerativ gegen die Stabilität des Bildraums. […] Dieser Beat hat die Kraft, gerade die Kohärenz der Form zu zersetzen und aufzulösen, von der man dachte, dass sie die Voraussetzung für eine bildliche Darstellung wäre.«[12] Andernorts schrieb Krauss über James Colemans *Box (ahhareturnabout)* (1977), einen Film, der aus pulsierenden Boxkampf-Sequenzen und schwarzem Startband besteht; hier assoziierte sie den Puls mit dem Bataille'schen Begriff des »Formlosen« und dessen Angriff auf alle Arten von Ordnung.[13] Obwohl die Arbeit durch die vollkommene Regelmäßigkeit ihrer Handlung exemplarisch für Stabilität sein könnte, hat *Auto Focus*, ähnlich wie diese Arbeiten, eine erodierende Wirkung. Buchstäblich erodiert das ständige Entfokussieren dieses Werks die Möglichkeit einer kohärenten Form, während seine repetitive mechanische Temporalität die in der Kultur fortbestehenden Ideen über Zeit erodiert – sowohl die Zeit der

10
Harold Schweizer, *On Waiting*, London: Routledge, 2008, S. 12.
11
Ebd., S. 16.
12
Rosalind Krauss, »The Im/pulse to See«, in: Hal Foster (Hrsg.), *Vision and Visuality*, New York: Dia Art Foundation, 1988, S. 51.
13
Rosalind Krauss, »Pulse«, in: Yve-Alain Bois und Rosalind Krauss, *Formless*, New York: Zone Books, 1997, S.161–165.

Nostalgie als auch die Zeit des Fortschritts. Stattdessen erhalten wir die Temporalität der Wiederholung und des Todestriebs.

Nachdem ich diese Erörterung von Ceal Floyers Werk mit Helle und Leichtigkeit begonnen habe, scheint *Auto Focus* ein düsterer Ort für ihr Ende zu sein, aber es ist, wie ich meine, ein passender Ort. Denn in Arbeiten wie dieser verspüren wir am besten das genau austarierte Gleichgewicht zwischen konzeptueller, materieller und formaler Präzision und Ökonomie, die oft Quelle von Überraschung und Freude sind, und einer kritischen Negativität. So wie ihre Interventionen mit Licht (Lichtschalter usw.) die Konventionen spektakulärer Kunst in sich zusammenfallen lassen und ihre Ordnungs-Arbeiten die unvermeidlichen Frustrationen vorführen, die mit den Versuchen einhergehen, in einer Welt der Exzesse des Kapitals Kohärenz zu schaffen, machen Floyers Zeitarbeiten Begriffe von romantischer Nostalgie und Fortschrittsglauben zunichte, indem sie auf der banalen Realität des Stillstands und der Monotonie der Wiederholung bestehen. 2005 hat Floyer eine Textzeile aus einem Country-Song in einer Endlosschleife wiederholt: »I'll just keep on falling in love 'til I get it right«, die Worte »falling in love« aber herausgeschnitten. Diese Bearbeitung *74*
hat nichts Störendes, weil das Schlagzeug an beiden Enden rhythmisch passt, aber die ständige Wiederholung der Phrase wird immer beunruhigender, sobald wir merken, dass die von der Sängerin erhoffte friedliche Auflösung ihr ewig vorenthalten bleiben wird. Floyer selbst stellt die ständigen Wiederholungen des täglichen Lebens realistisch dar, aber weil sie dies tut, ohne in Schwermut zu versinken, und dabei solch präzise Arbeiten schafft, gelingt es ihr in der Tat, es immer wieder richtig zu machen.

SERGIO EDELSZTEIN: SPACE, WHATSOEVER

Unless you are an experienced Ceal Floyer viewer, on entering one of her shows for the first time you will probably feel disconcerted. Side by side with identifiable works of art (i.e., works on paper and videos on monitors) you will find a rather empty space presenting a number of objects of eclectic character. There could be signs and stickers, common daily objects and all kinds of projectors. At this stage, a feeling of 'what's-going-on-here?' might arise inside you. This might be prompted by the discrepancy between the space the viewer knows he or she has entered—which is supposedly consecrated to high art—and the eclecticism and inconspicuousness of the display in place.

This feeling would be heightened by the 'provenance' of these unremarkable objects, most of them clearly belonging to another realm than a gallery space: to the street, to the vernacular. Among these commonplace items, we are
likely to find a garbage bag, a bucket, a drill lying on the floor, a hanging plumb *28, 38, 86, 70*
line, an empty postcard rack, a pub-like, double-sided blackboard announcing *110*
'today's special', an EXIT sign, and more. *118, 88*

Among these objects, the conspicuous placement of projectors around the room immediately grabs your attention. In contemporary art spaces these machines are usually isolated, out of sight, hanging from the ceiling, or concealed inside perfectly camouflaged boxes (a 'white box' is the obvious device). In Floyer's installation, though, projectors do not simply co-exist in with their effects; their sculptural presence is actually in dialogue with the other objects in the space. A projected work is both the projector and the projection.
A good example is *Overgrowth*, a work that shows a large-scale screening of *68*
a midget tree (usually called 'bonsai'). In this work, the most important element is the distance of the projector to the screen, the tree serving solely as a Deleuzian 'opsign'. Most of these projectors cast a single image that is seldom
a 'moving' one. A light switch (*Light Switch*), a crack of light under an existing *12*
door (*Door*), a computer trash bin (*Trash*), four slide projectors rendering a dull *22, 80*
light bulb incandescent (*Light*), or one of these 'Sysiphically' trying to focus *18*
(*Auto Focus*). Another machine, especially cumbersome, casts the gigantic *58*
image of a light bulb high on the wall (*Overhead Projection*). These projectors *94*
project light, and many of them deal with light and its mechanisms, effectively reversing the cause and effect of the operating apparatus and the object depicted. The light switch and the light bulb are 'illuminated' rather than illuminating. In these projections the artist compromised the visual quality of the image by screening them in the fully lit space, endowing them with a rather phantasmagorical quality. Video and slide projections screened in this way lose sharpness, but in Floyer's work, they gain meaning by exposing the screening apparatus, turning it into a sculptural presence in space—and also by redefining the perceptive conventions of the art space, straining its definition and limits. Your expectations demand that a contemporary art space either be well lit, illuminating evenly artworks hanging on the walls or standing on the floor, or pitch dark, declaring that you are entering a video or film projection room, a 'moving image' work.

In fact, you are also likely to find this 'black box' feature in Floyer's installation and will enter it just as predisposed for a certain type of narrative as you did the 'white box'. Your eagerness for a 'movement-image' work becomes Floyer's playground. Her works in this representational context comment on and unfold the language of cinema—beginning with the mechanism of the camera and
our perception of cinematic magic. *Apollinaris*, for instance, is a static frame *76*

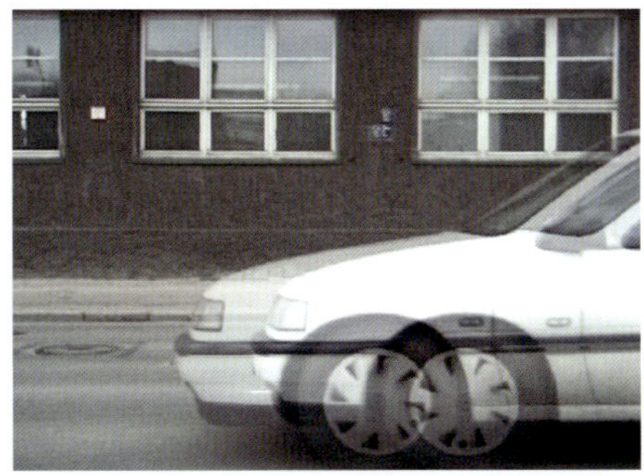
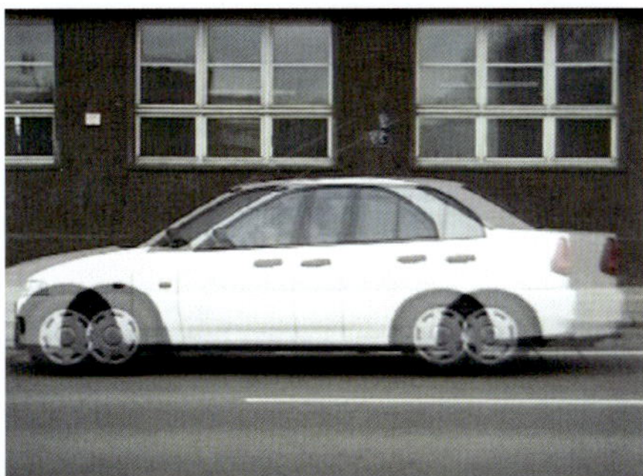
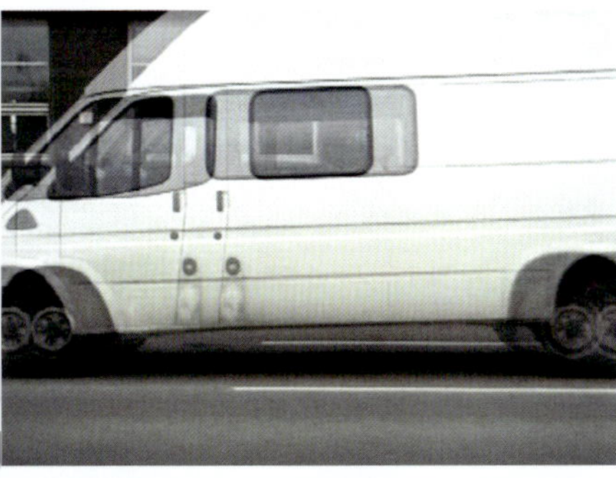
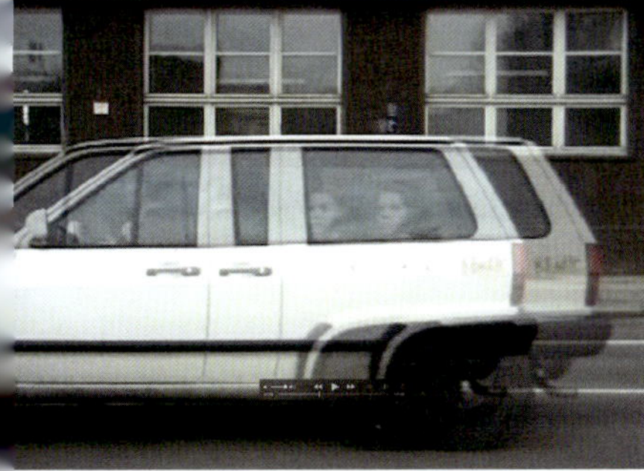
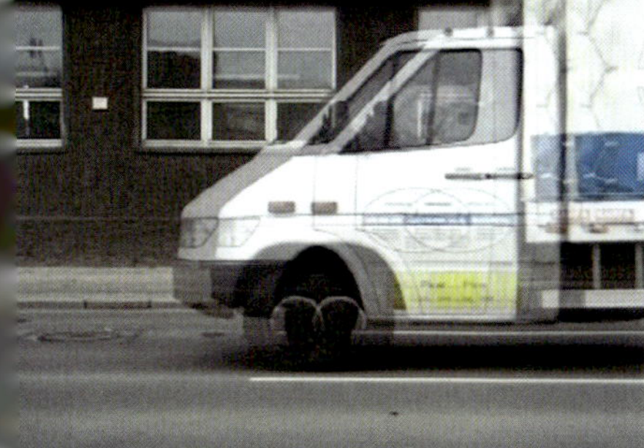
Monochrome Edit (White), 1998

showing bubbles exploding over a glass of sparkling water. The frame is monumentally enlarged, floor-to-ceiling and wall-to-wall, such that the bubbles acquire an astral quality. The title alludes to sparkling mineral water, but also to the Apollo spaceships. It might take a minute or two for the viewer to understand what he or she is looking at—but the sudden knowledge (aided by the title) that this sublime landscape is, in fact, a glass of sparkling water is undoubtedly one of those 'Floyerian' moments we could call the 'epiphany of the mundane'.

134 *Untitled Credit Roll* also takes an index of cinema: the credit roll at the end of the movie. The morphology of this feature is archetypical, aligned in the middle and asymmetrical in the sides. Floyer's, though, is shot out of focus, making it illegible yet still retaining the character of an accomplished sign that encompasses the whole narrative medium of cinema, giving away the narrative but placing in the centre our associative powers and knowledge of the medium. The association will also take us to the realm of abstract painting: on second viewing, *Untitled Credit Roll* looks more like a never-ending Rothko painting than a filmic device.

130 Questioning the mere perception of the 'moving image' is the subject of *Drop*. In the frame we see a vague landscape within a windowsill from which raindrops delicately depend; nothing seems to be moving. The culmination of the work occurs in a fraction of a second, as one of the drops finally, well—drops. The possibility of missing 'the whole story' while selfishly wondering why nothing is moving in this 'moving image' work is very real. In fact, playing with the viewer's stamina is one of Floyer's strategies of engagement. Another example of filmic endurance—of taking the term 'time based' to the level of 'ad absurdum'—occurs in the work *Minute*, a sixty-second, thirty-five millimetre segment that is meant to be spliced between the film trailers and the main feature. The work shows a monumental frame filled with sixty seconds-worth of relentless finger drumming as the hand's owner waits for the film to start. It is indeed a test of endurance.

Another conceptual 'time piece' that comments on the technicalities of video
66 as a medium is *1–25*. This work addresses the frame rates of different video systems (twenty-five frames per second for PAL, twenty-four frames per second for NTSC). The image shows the *spelled* numbers one to twenty-four or -five (according to the region in which the work is screened); each number is seen for the number of seconds we read in the frame. The viewer—who cares very little about frame rates—is forced to remain in front of the screen for several minutes in order to understand the conceptual subtext of the work.

In other videos, Floyer prefers to play with the image itself, editing in or out elements according to pre-established conceptual parameters. Some works play with the editing out of sounds and images. *Monochrome Edit (White)* and *Monochrome Edit (Red)* show a street where all the cars but those in the specified colours were edited out. In another video, *Spectrum Edit*, she waited in real time for the passing of cars in the colours and sequence of the rainbow in order to film them. *Silent Movie* shows a metal detector as it moves from left to right in search of metal in the floor. Floyer edited out all the 'beeps' signalling the presence of metal, thereby undermining the machine's utility.

These cinematic works reflect what Gilles Deleuze has called the principle of the 'time-image', which—as Ina Blom has pointed out in relation to Floyer—involves some type of image disrupting the causal temporality of action and reaction, which ultimately shatters the unity of cinema's representational space. In doing so, it generates a new construction that shifts the operations of perception and human thought processes to the centre of cinematic activity.

Years ago, I used to take my young daughter to the movies. This was no easy feat. Throughout the film, any time a figure exited the frame—through a door, for instance—my daughter, who was about eight at the time, would lean towards me and whisper: 'Where did she (or he) go?' It was useless to urge her to continue looking at developments on the screen. 'Never mind,' I would whisper, 'what matters is what we see now, this character will come back later . . .' But still she insisted: 'Yes, I know, you are right—but where did she (or he) go?'

It took me years to appreciate this kind of thinking, and to understand that in cinema—as in life—what is out of the frame is as important as what we actually see. Modernism discovered and developed 'negative space' as an additional realm of significance, a perceptual space that echoed quantum theories and other scientific discoveries of the early twentieth century. Cinema, however, relying heavily on editing, could present all possible narratives at once, showing what happens in several places at once, or according to the director's desire to build drama. Edited commercial film never fully took advantage of 'what is not seen' but has to be 'known' in order to appreciate a narrative.

My young daughter's perception of the cinematic frame comes to mind whenever I think of the way Ceal Floyer's work functions as a narrative in both time and space, in which the object represents the 'frame', but where most of the meaning resides in other fields—cultural, linguistic, geographic, or art-world parochial. Or in which the objects 'depicted' simply exist outside the frame or use these 'framing capacities'—as does the hand in *Minute*, which occupies the corner of the filmic frame—to hint at the larger space behind it.

The cinematic aspect of Floyer's work is also the basis of her sound pieces, which rely chiefly on syncretic sound—i.e., 'a convergence of meaning organized according to gestalt laws and contextual determinations' that unifies sound and object, a concept developed by Michel Chion in his book *Audio Vision*. 'For some situations that set up precise expectations of sound,' Chion writes, 'a character walking, for example—synchresis is unstoppable, and we can therefore use just about any sound effects for these footsteps that we might desire. In *Mon Oncle* [Jaques] Tati drew on all kinds of noises for human steps, including Ping-Pong balls and glass objects.' Floyer's sound pieces
almost inevitably play with these 'Pavlovian' effects. The indistinct ascending
and descending knocks that are heard from the speakers that compose *Scale* *104*
make us believe that someone was actually recorded climbing it. The speakers
inevitably sound like what they look like—scale steps. An equally arbitrary
sound coming out of a bucket (*Bucket*) creates the impression of water dripping *38*
inside, although the noise has no relation to water. The sound of digging and
earth falling in *Working Title* (*Digging*), heard alternately from two speakers *26*
placed a certain distance from each other, makes us believe someone was
recorded while actually digging. In the videos *Monochrome Edit (White)* and *Monochrome Edit (Red)* mentioned earlier, cars in non-conforming colours were edited out, while the sound of their approaching and passing was left in the film, thereby maintaining the sonic imprint of the passing cars—even though their images had been extracted.

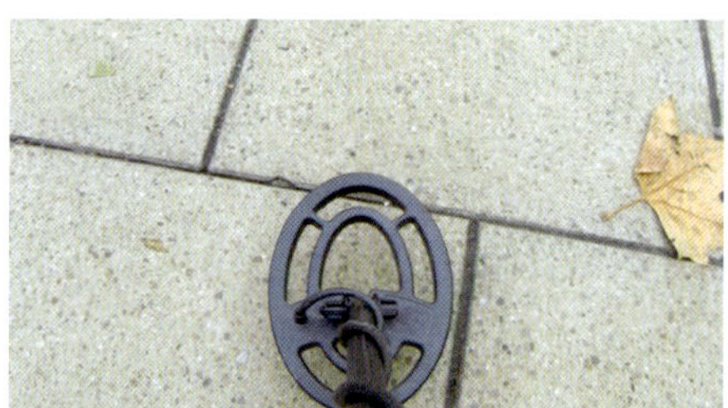
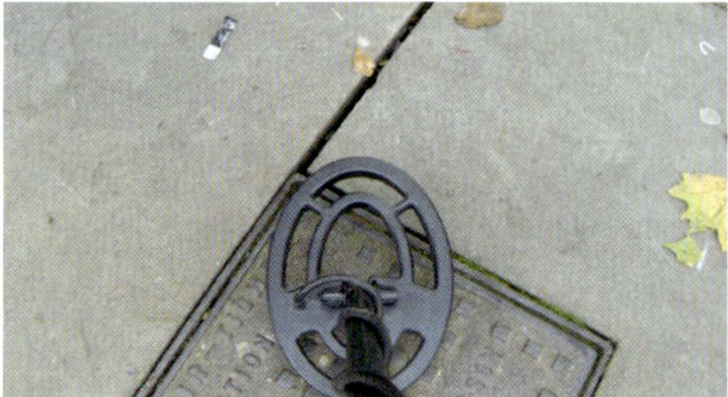
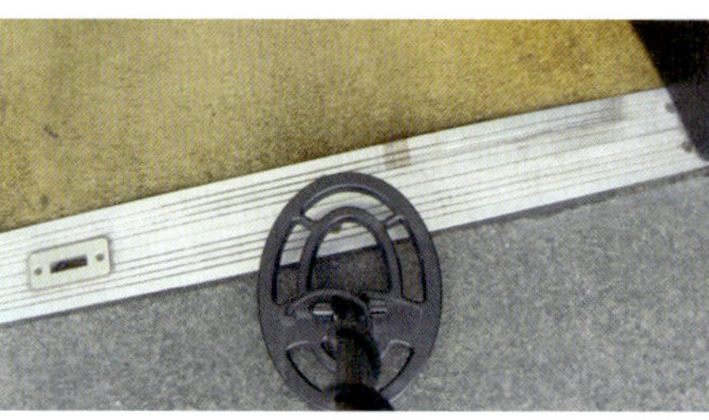
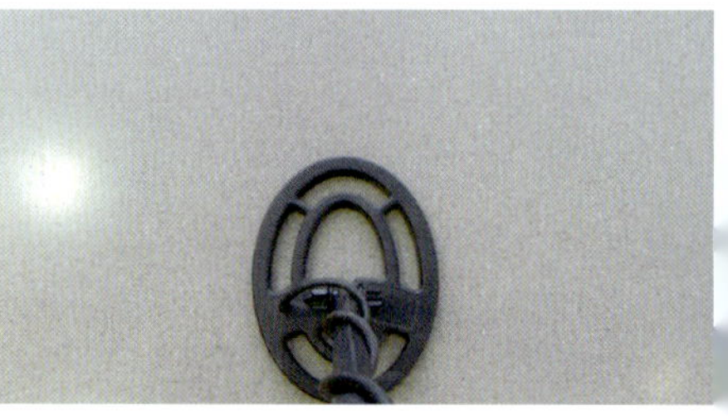

Silent Movie, 2014

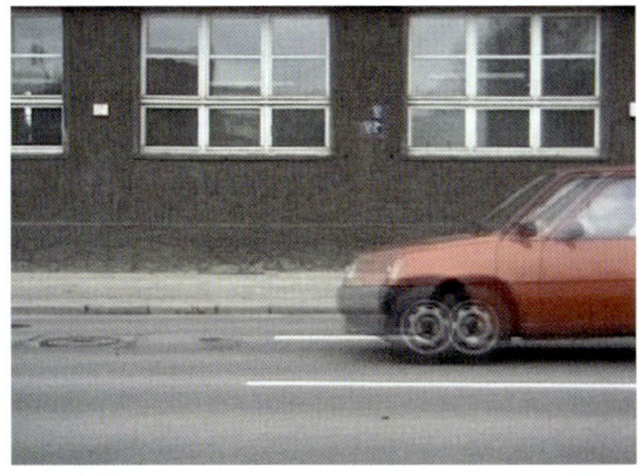
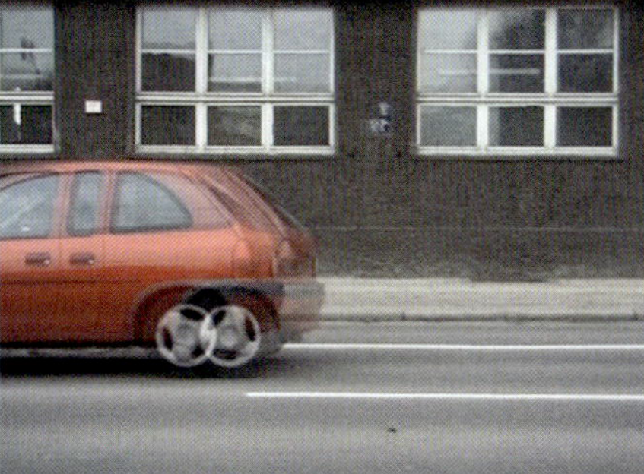
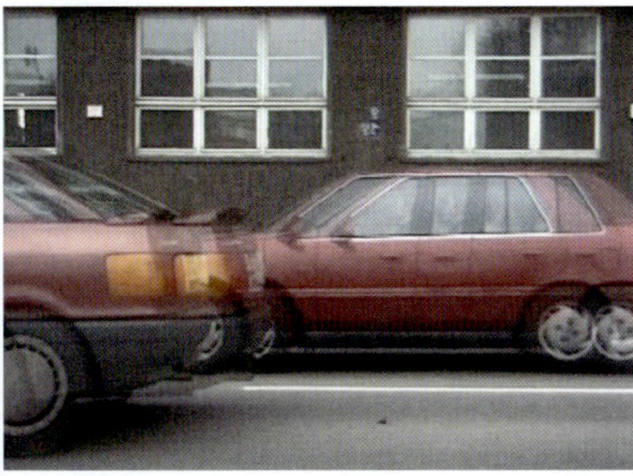
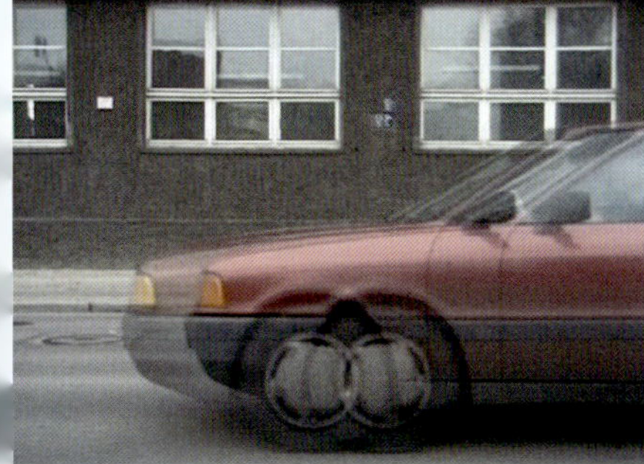
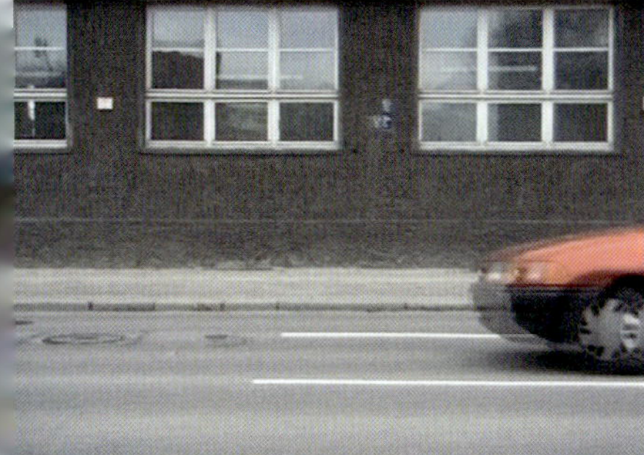

Monochrome Edit (Red), 1998

These incursions into cinematic languages and techniques have nothing heroic about them, nor do they seek to raise common objects above their mundanity—on the contrary. As Deleuze wrote of the Italian Neo-Realists, 'they turn the real into spectacle—and this fascinates for being the real thing . . . The everyday is identified with the spectacular . . . .'

Back in the white box, you re-encounter those objects that just a few minutes ago puzzled you—only now as old friends. As your understanding of Floyer's strategies grows, you will want to engage more boldly in their interpretation and
86 the mapping out of new connections. Seeing again that drill lying on the floor of the gallery, for instance: it is indeed the most commonplace tool you could possibly find at the local hardware store—and was actually purchased locally. The power cord meanders towards the wall and the plug is inserted . . . directly into the wall; there is no trace of an electricity outlet. In fact, the attentive viewer will understand that the drill itself, with the specific drill bit it sports, was used to drill the holes in the wall.

In works like this one, Floyer addresses the essence of the Readymade by linking it to the individual viewer's cultural perception of it as a truly vernacular object, something that is often overlooked. Thinking about Readymades readily brings to mind the name of Marcel Duchamp. But think again: Which non-French, or even 'urban' French person of the twenty-first century would identify Duchamp's *Bottle Rack* as a Readymade? Who has ever seen one of these objects just lying around, except in a museum? Unless you are a French farmer, you will have to concede that this object looks rather like a sculpture, and that there is nothing about it that resembles a found object, let alone a truly commonplace object—it is at most an archaeological artefact. By contrast, Floyer's precise method of finding and 'recreating' every possible work *in situ* ensures that the Readymade effect is maintained to its fullest extent, everywhere and always, acknowledging that the essence of a Readymade is time and place specific, and never ever universal. In fact, Ceal Floyer's readymades must be acquired on site; they have to be local brands and models—nothing unusual that could have the aura of an artwork, not even an imported piece of hardware. In downplaying any particularity the objects might have, Floyer pushes the viewer to invest extra effort in understanding the concept of the work.

By now, it should be clear that the works mentioned so far adhere to an uncompromising 'place specificity'—where it is 'place', more than the gallery space, that constitutes the context of the installation, with all its indigenous
86 cultural, vernacular, and even technical aspects. *Drill*, for example, will not be shown in a country where the holes in the wall cannot be drilled with the exhibited machine itself (that is, in countries with square or rectangular components in their plugs, such as the US and the UK). The aforementioned video
66 *1–25* changes according to the region in which it is screened. In an NTSC zone like the US, its title will be *1–24*, and the language in which the numbers will be written will always be the local one. The appliance seen in the slide
12 projection of *Light Switch* will be always the one common to the country where it is shown—which is why the list at the beginning of this book contains several versions and reproductions, as these were made specifically for different places and cannot be shown in any place other than the ones whose conventional switch matches the projection.

56 The video *Ongoing Projection* is a fine example of this kind of hyper-specificity with respect to context. The projection shows the blank pages of a notebook

turning slowly—turning, that is, in the 'normal' direction: from right to left. But when the work is shown in Israel, the direction of the pages is reversed. This would have been 'noteworthy' to viewers elsewhere in the world, but in a country where the language is read from right to left, it went unnoticed. Likewise, an iconic work like *Monochrome Till Receipt (White)* has to be recreated 34
for each venue at which it is shown, with local products freshly purchased from normal local supermarkets at current prices. Everything has to be up to date so as not to raise any suspicion of manipulation or give the impression that something extraordinary is being exhibited. Only then, after relinquishing the search for unusual or eccentric elements, can the viewer settle down to understanding the meaning of the piece of paper attached to the gallery wall.

At this stage, in order to understand further, you must turn to the crucial element in all of Floyer's works: the title. Yes, it is indeed a 'till receipt'—but the '(white)' provides the key to zooming in on the actual articles on the slip—all of which are pristine white. This means that in her quest for white products, the artist had to open boxes and packages to make sure the contents were white (you never see 'white wine' on the list, for instance, as wine is not actually 'white'). The 'white on white on white' take (white products on white paper on a white wall) might raise Malevichian or Rymanesque associations—and rightly so. Attentive viewers will find in the order of the items (which vary from version to version) a story that typically starts with a lot of (white) food products and ends with bicarbonate, paracetamol, and of course toilet paper; sometimes the list even includes cosmetic items like toothpaste, shoe polish, or Tic Tacs. Like a Baroque still-life painting, the products displayed according to the order in which they were entered in the till inevitably tell a tale of relentless gluttony and consumerism with occasional overtones of narcissism and social awkwardness. The story develops like a movie as we read the list of products from top to bottom. The deliberate process of the work's creation shows us a significant line separating the orthodox Readymade from a created or manipulated vernacular object like this one. Floyer's practice fluctuates freely between these parameters.

As we have seen, 'cinematic space' is space that goes beyond the frame and exceeds the focus of vision to encompass other spatial and cultural dimensions. It is the knowledge that important developments in the work might be happening beyond our visual frame, or that what we see is merely an indicator, a fragment of the work in question. It also means that, though triggered by a plastic object, the work of art is understood and grasped over time and along wider cultural lines. As Deleuze writes in his analysis of the way cinema operates, 'The essence of things never appears at the outset, but in the middle, in the course of its development, when its strength is assured.' Whether time-based or not, all of Floyer's works are apprehended along this axis of time, maintaining the essence of a medium in which duration is inherent to narrative.

As suggested earlier, apprehension of the work's title constitutes a pivotal
moment along this axis. The title of the work *Drill* denotes not only the machine, 86
but also the activity necessary to exhibit it—the drilling of holes in the wall.
The meanings of nouns and verbs often overlap, as they do in the video *Drop*, 130
where the imminent drip of a drop is the film's main character (unless it is an
allusion to the viewer's nerves). The same goes for *Scale*, the title of which turns 104
it into an identifiable object and an invitation to interpret the sound it emits.

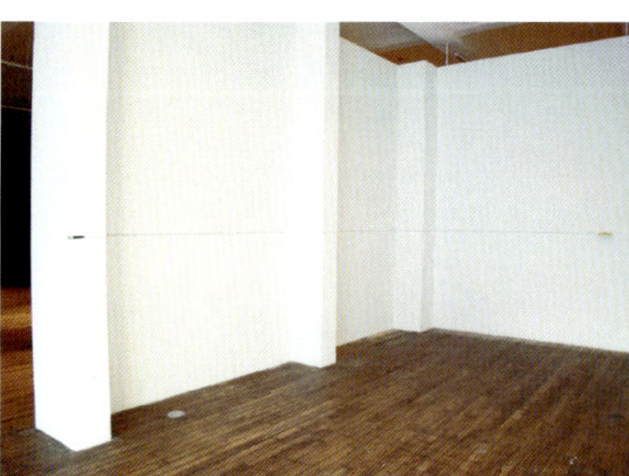

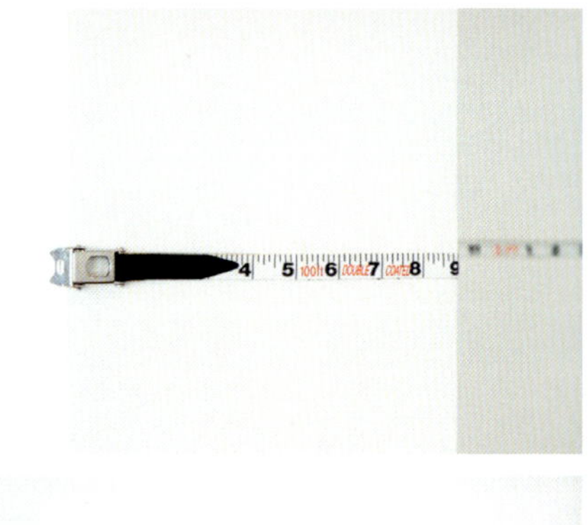

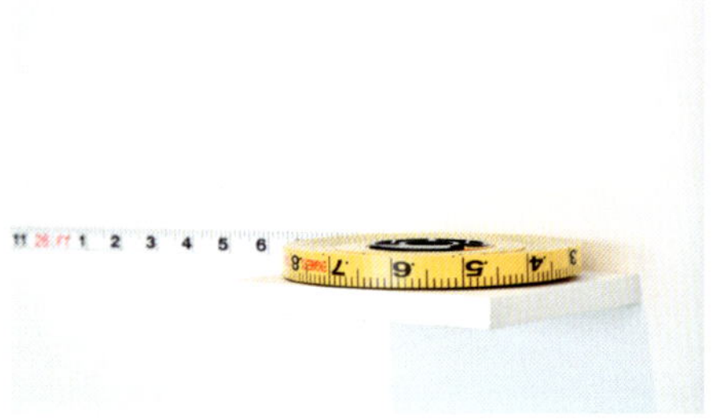

Nine Yards, 2006

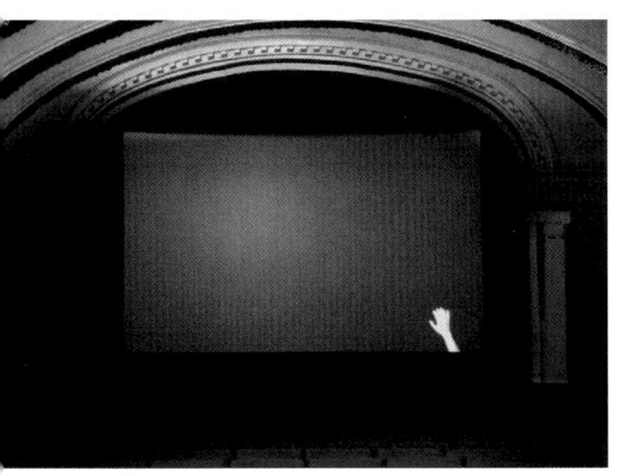

Minute, 1996

Minute, with its monotonously drumming fingers, should also be read as 'minute'—as in 'tiny'—a huge understatement when applied to a simple film projected onto a large cinema screen. Works will never be shown in places where the linguistic context of its title does not allow for the right set of associations. Similarly, *Nine Yards* alludes to a typically American idiom of uncertain etymology meaning 'everything, the whole lot', and will not make sense anywhere else.

As part of this projection in space and culture, Ceal Floyer's usual strategy is
80 to make 'empty' space an integral part of the work. *Trash*, for instance, projects the icon of a Macintosh computer trash bin on the lower-right corner of a
large, empty wall roughly resembling the proportions of a computer screen.
68 *Overgrowth*, the notional bonsai mentioned earlier, demands a space larger
than the one needed to contain the projector and the image. The viewer is
encouraged to imagine the tree growing larger and larger as the projector
14 recedes into the available space. *Long Distance (Diptych)* likewise covers an
enormous amount of space, although it is quite modest in size. The piece consists of two slide projectors that cast two small, converging circles on a far wall.
The distance between them is part of the work and the viewer cannot step
96 through. A work like *100%* is composed of ten round red stickers scattered
across the walls in the space, each one showing '10%' of the work; in this way,
it defines the entire space (or portion thereof selected by the artist) as a single
work of art.

70 *Plumb Line* helps us understand Floyer's definition of space and public sphere.
It consists of a regular plumb line used in construction to build perfectly vertical walls, a weight and a string hung from the ceiling in a non-utilitarian way—that is, not necessarily close to a wall. The plumb is more likely to be hanging in the middle of the space, or—as happened at the Hayward Gallery in London—suspended in a stairwell. The function of a plumb line in this work—as opposed to its usual function—is to establish the centre of the space, but Floyer assigns this marking device a very specific location based on variable parameters. The plumb is hung at the intersection of two diagonals, each one connecting two points in space that are calculated by Floyer to indicate the quantification of the spatial footprint of a given setting. Typically, this could include space outside the gallery itself—which is what accounts for the odd positions of the line.

Under the pressure of Floyer's disorienting strategies—from that first, disconcerting entry to the observation of the works and their connections to language, the vernacular, and each other—the viewer's understanding of the gallery space as a consecrated 'art space' is pushed towards the category of *any space whatsoever*. This anthropological term—loosely associated with Marc Augé's notion of *non-lieu*, or 'non-place'—normally denotes transit space, such as a metro stop, doctor's waiting room, or airport terminal: anonymous spaces people pass through between places of 'importance'. For Deleuze, though, this *espace quelconque* is a condition for the emergence of uniqueness and singularities. It functions in much the same manner that time-image cinema does: it places the identity of characters, the plot—and in our case, the artworks—in a state of crisis. 'Any-space-whatever is not an abstract universal, in all times, in all places,' writes Deleuze, 'It is a perfectly singular space, which has merely lost its homogeneity, that is, the principle of its metric relations or the connection of its own parts, so that the linkages can be made in an infinite number of ways. It is a space of virtual conjunction, grasped as pure locus of the possible.'

Still, before overwriting the anthropological definition of *any space whatsoever* with Deleuze's, it is worth noting that in such spaces individuals become depersonalized. No one notices or concerns themselves with others. Even if *any space whatsoever* is crowded, everyone in it is alone. It is for this reason that 'any space whatsoever' is a homogenous, de-singularizing space. It might be worth thinking of the gallery space in this way: as a space in which we move and behave, silently, ritually. Certainly, when we are involved in appreciating a Ceal Floyer exhibition, we somehow lose our individuality and become an integral part of the installation and the conceptual process her works demand.

A work that perhaps best defines Floyer's relation to the gallery as a transit space for objects and viewers alike is *Untitled Installation (Dotted Line).* *16*
Comprising a stencilled, dotted line, it takes in the entire perimeter of the walls, stairs, and architectural features of the gallery. The viewer knows these dotted lines as yet another archetypical signifier of play, meaning, 'cut or fold along the dotted line'. In our case, however, it defines the gallery space as an arena, an all-defining environment. This line stresses the unity of the installation—though it includes various works—while at the same time defining the exhibition as a 'playground' related to the language of play. The dotted line turns the walls into paper, space into a concept, and the whole world into a playground. Somewhere 'along the line' of the installation, nestled between the other works, the viewer will notice a plinth with a slide viewer showing an enlarged image of a pair of scissors. It will probably take some time before the viewer realises that it is part of the dotted line. The latter may already have been forgotten, or overlooked while the viewer was focussing on other works. But then, as usual, comes the title—in this case near the scissors—and by alluding to the dotted line, it inevitably explains that strange component running throughout the gallery. This DIY indicator, which unifies the whole space by prompting you to imagine the walls of the gallery (which after all is just another 'space whatsoever'), collapses and reinstates the works of art in their original dwelling place—the street.

At the end of the visit, you have the feeling that what 'disconcerted' you at the outset was actually a carefully orchestrated 'concert' of works, their connections, spaces, and meanings.

SERGIO EDELSZTEIN: RAUM, BELIEBIGER

Betritt man zum ersten Mal eine der Ausstellungen von Ceal Floyer, wird man vermutlich verdutzt sein, es sei denn, man ist ein erfahrener Betrachter ihres Werks. Neben identifizierbaren Kunstwerken (also Arbeiten auf Papier und Videos auf Bildschirmen) findet man eine Reihe der unterschiedlichsten Gegenstände in einem ansonsten eher leeren Raum. Das können Schilder und Aufkleber sein, gewöhnliche Alltagsgegenstände und alle möglichen Arten von Projektoren. Man mag sich dann durchaus fragen: »Was passiert hier eigentlich?« Das hat vor allem mit der Diskrepanz zwischen dem Raum, den man betreten hat – und der angeblich der Kunst geweiht ist –, und der Heterogenität und Unscheinbarkeit der Präsentation zu tun.

Verstärkt wird dieses Gefühl durch die »Provenienz« dieser unspektakulären
Objekte, von denen die meisten offensichtlich zu einem anderen Bereich als
einem Ausstellungsraum gehören: nämlich auf die Straße und zum Alltäglichen.
Unter diesen gewöhnlichen Dingen finden sich beispielsweise ein Müllsack, ein *28*
Eimer, eine auf dem Boden liegende Bohrmaschine, ein hängendes Senkblei, *38, 86, 70*
ein leerer Postkartenständer, eine doppelseitige Tafel, wie man sie in einer *110*
Kneipe oder einem Lokal finden würde und auf der das Tagesgericht ange-
zeigt wird, ein Ausgangsschild und weiteres mehr. *118, 88*

Nicht nur die Objekte im Raum, sondern auch auffällig platzierte Projektoren
unterschiedlicher Art ziehen sofort unsere Aufmerksamkeit auf sich. In Räumen für zeitgenössische Kunst sind diese Geräte gewöhnlich isoliert, dem
Blickfeld entzogen, sie hängen von der Decke oder sind in perfekt getarnten
Boxen (üblich sind weiße Boxen) installiert. In Floyers Installationen sind die
Projektoren allerdings nicht nur aufgrund ihrer Funktion wichtig, vielmehr tritt
ihre skulpturale Präsenz in einen Dialog mit den anderen Objekten. Zu einer
Projektion gehört beides: der Projektor und das Projizierte. *Overgrowth*, eine *68*
übergroße Projektion eines winzigen Baumes (gewöhnlich Bonsai genannt),
ist ein gutes Beispiel: Für diese Arbeit ist der Abstand des Projektors zur
Bildfläche ausschlaggebend, der Baum dient nur als Deleuze'sches »Opto-
zeichen«. Die meisten dieser Projektoren werfen ein einzelnes Bild auf die
Wand – selten sind es bewegte Bilder –, einen Lichtschalter *(Light Switch)*, *12*
einen Lichtspalt unter einer vorhandenen Tür *(Door)*, den Mülleimer eines *22*
Computers *(Trash)*; vier Diaprojektoren bringen eine mattweiße Glühbirne *80*
zum Leuchten *(Light)*, oder ein einziger Projektor versucht sisyphosmäßig, *18*
sich scharf zu stellen *(Auto Focus)*. Ein anderes, besonders sperriges Gerät *58*
wirft das riesige Bild einer Glühbirne hoch oben an die Wand *(Overhead*
Projection). Diese Projektoren projizieren Licht, und viele von ihnen setzen *94*
sich mit dem Licht und seinen Mechanismen auseinander und kehren dabei Ursache und Wirkung des Apparats und des dargestellten Objekts um. Der Lichtschalter und die Glühbirne werden beleuchtet, anstatt für Beleuchtung zu sorgen. Bei diesen Projektionen beeinträchtigt die Künstlerin die visuelle Qualität der Bilder, indem sie sie in einem hell erleuchteten Raum projiziert und ihnen so eine eher phantasmagorische Qualität verleiht. Video- und Diaprojektionen, die so gezeigt werden, verlieren an Schärfe, aber in Floyers Werk gewinnen sie an Bedeutung, indem der Projektor deutlich gezeigt wird und im Raum eine skulpturale Präsenz erhält – und auch indem die Wahrnehmungskonventionen des Kunstraums neu definiert und seine Grenzen ausgelotet werden. Wir gehen davon aus, dass ein Raum für zeitgenössische Kunst entweder gut ausgeleuchtet ist und die an den Wänden hängenden oder auf dem Boden stehenden Kunstwerke gleichmäßig beleuchtet werden, oder dass er stockdunkel ist und uns darauf vorbereitet, dass wir einen

Projektionsraum für Videos oder Filme, für Werke mit bewegten Bildern
betreten.
Tatsächlich lassen sich diese »Black Box«-Bestandteile auch in Floyers
Installationen finden, und man betritt sie ebenso empfänglich für eine bestimmte Form der Narration wie vorher den weißen Raum (»white box«).
Unsere Erwartung, ein Werk mit bewegten Bildern zu sehen, gibt Floyer den
Raum, genau damit zu spielen. In diesem Repräsentationskontext kommen-
tieren und entfalten ihre Arbeiten die Sprache des Kinos – angefangen beim
Mechanismus der Kamera und unserer Empfindung der Magie, die das Kino
76 hat. *Apollinaris* beispielsweise verwendet eine statische Bildeinstellung, es
werden Blasen gezeigt, die über einem Glas Sprudelwasser zerspringen.
Das Bild ist monumental vergrößert, es reicht vom Boden bis zur Decke und
von einer Wand zur anderen, sodass die Sprudelblasen eine astrale Qualität
erhalten. Der Titel verweist auf kohlensäurehaltiges Mineralwasser, aber auch
auf die Apollo-Raumschiffe. Es kann durchaus eine oder zwei Minuten dauern,
bis man versteht, was man sieht – aber die (durch den Titel unterstützte)
plötzliche Erkenntnis, dass diese erhabene Landschaft eigentlich ein Glas
Mineralwasser ist, ist zweifellos einer jener Floyer'schen Momente, die man
als »Epiphanie des Alltäglichen« bezeichnen kann.
134 Auch *Untitled Credit Roll* bedient sich eines Bestandteils des Films: Hier ist
es der Abspann (»credit roll«) am Ende des Films. Die Form des Abspanns
ist sehr typisch: Der Text ist zentriert und an den Rändern ungleichmäßig.
Floyers Abspann ist unscharf aufgenommen, dadurch wird er unlesbar, behält
aber dennoch den Charakter eines gekonnt gestalteten Zeichens, das das
gesamte narrative Medium des Kinos umfasst. Dabei wird die Narration zwar
preisgegeben, doch in den Vordergrund rücken unsere assoziativen Kräfte
und unser Wissens um das Medium. Unsere Assoziationen führen uns auch
ins Reich der abstrakten Malerei: Beim zweiten Betrachten mutet *Untitled
Credit Roll* eher wie ein endloses Gemälde von Rothko an als wie ein filmi-
sches Mittel.
Das Hinterfragen der Wahrnehmung des »bewegten Bildes« ist das Thema
130 von *Drop*. Wir sehen eine verschwommene Landschaft durch ein Fenster.
An dem Rahmen, den man im Anschnitt sieht, hängen zarte Regentropfen;
nichts scheint sich zu bewegen. Ihren Höhepunkt erreicht die Arbeit mit dem
Bruchteil einer Sekunde, in dem einer der Tropfen endlich fällt. Die Möglichkeit, »die ganze Geschichte« zu verpassen, während man selbstbezogen
überlegt, warum sich in dieser Arbeit mit bewegten Bildern nichts bewegt,
ist ziemlich hoch. Tatsächlich ist das Spiel mit der Ausdauer des Betrachters
eine der Strategien von Floyer, um uns einzubinden. Ein weiteres Beispiel
filmischer Ausdauer – wobei der Begriff »zeitbasiert« ad absurdum geführt
wird – ist die Arbeit *Minute*, eine 60 Sekunden lange 35-Millimeter-Sequenz,
die zwischen Trailern und einem Hauptfilm eingefügt werden soll. Die Arbeit
zeigt in Großaufnahme 60 Sekunden unablässigen Fingertrommelns, als ob
der Besitzer der Hand ungeduldig darauf wartet, dass der Film beginnt. Es
handelt sich tatsächlich um einen Ausdauertest.
Eine weitere konzeptuelle »Zeitarbeit«, die sich mit den technischen Details
66 von Video als Medium auseinandersetzt, ist *1–25*. Diese Arbeit spielt mit der
unterschiedlichen Bildfrequenz von Videosystemen (24 Bilder pro Sekunde
bei PAL, 25 bei NTSC). Das Bild zeigt die ausgeschriebenen Zahlen eins bis
vierundzwanzig oder fünfundzwanzig (je nach der Region, in der die Arbeit
gezeigt wird); jede Zahl wird so viele Sekunden lang gezeigt, wie im Bild

angegeben. Der Betrachter – dem die Bildfrequenzen eigentlich eher egal sind – ist gezwungen, mehrere Minuten vor dem Bildschirm auszuharren, um den konzeptuellen Subtext der Arbeit zu verstehen.
In anderen Videos zieht es Floyer vor, mit dem Bild selbst zu spielen. Je nach vorher festgelegten konzeptuellen Parametern schneidet sie Elemente heraus oder fügt sie ein. Einige Arbeiten spielen mit dem Herausschneiden von Klängen und Bildern. *Monochrome Edit (White)* und *Monochrome Edit (Red)* zeigen eine Straße, aus der alle entlangfahrenden Autos, die nicht die festgelegte Farbe haben, herausgeschnitten wurden. In einem weiteren Video, *Spectrum Edit*, wartete die Künstlerin in Echtzeit darauf, dass Autos in den Farben und der Sequenz des Regenbogens vorbeifuhren, um sie zu filmen. *Silent Movie* zeigt einen Metalldetektor, der sich auf der Suche nach Metall im Boden von links nach rechts bewegt. Floyer hat all die Pieptöne herausgeschnitten, mit denen Metall angezeigt wird, und so den Nutzen der Maschine untergraben.
Diese filmischen Arbeiten reflektieren das, was Gilles Deleuze das Prinzip des »Zeit-Bildes« nennt, sie beziehen einen Bildtypus ein, der die logische Aufeinanderfolge von Aktion und Reaktion zerstört und die Einheit des filmischen Raums zerschlägt. So entsteht ein vollkommen neuer Filmaufbau, der den Prozess der Wahrnehmung und des menschlichen Denkens ins Zentrum der filmischen Aktivitäten stellt.
Vor Jahren bin ich öfter mit meiner kleinen Tochter ins Kino gegangen. Das war gar nicht so einfach. Immer wenn im Film eine Figur aus dem Bild ging – durch eine Tür beispielsweise – lehnte sich meine Tochter, die damals ungefähr acht war, zu mir hinüber und flüsterte: »Wo ist sie (oder er) hingegangen?«
Es half gar nichts, ihr zu sagen, sie sollte der Entwicklung auf der Leinwand folgen. »Das ist nicht so wichtig«, sagte ich, »wichtig ist, was wir jetzt sehen, diese Figur kommt später wieder …« Aber sie bestand darauf: »Ja, ich weiß, das stimmt – aber wohin ist sie (oder er) gegangen?«
Ich habe Jahre gebraucht, bis ich diese Art des Denkens würdigen und verstehen konnte, dass im Kino – wie im Leben – das, was außerhalb des Bildes geschieht, genauso wichtig ist wie das, was wir tatsächlich sehen. Die Moderne hat den »negativen Raum« als ein zusätzliches Reich der Bedeutung entdeckt und entwickelt, einen Wahrnehmungsraum, in dem die Quantentheorien und andere wissenschaftliche Entdeckungen des frühen 20. Jahrhunderts ein Echo fanden. Der Kinofilm allerdings, für den der Schnitt ein entscheidendes Element ist, konnte alle möglichen Erzählstränge gleichzeitig präsentieren; er zeigt, was in einem Moment an unterschiedlichen Orten geschieht, oder präsentiert diese Stränge entsprechend dem Spannungsbogen, den der Regisseur aufbauen möchte. Der geschnittene kommerzielle Film hat die Möglichkeiten dessen, »was nicht gesehen wird«, aber »gewusst« werden muss, um eine Erzählung zu verstehen, nie ganz ausgenutzt.
Wie meine kleine Tochter das filmische Bild wahrgenommen hat, kommt mir immer dann in den Sinn, wenn ich darüber nachdenke, wie Ceal Floyers Arbeit als eine Erzählung sowohl im Raum als auch in der Zeit funktioniert, wo der Gegenstand den »Rahmen« repräsentiert, aber ein Großteil der Bedeutung auf anderen Gebieten liegt – kulturellen, linguistischen, geografischen oder auf die Kunstwelt bezogenen Feldern. Oder in der die »dargestellten« Objekte einfach außerhalb des Bildes existieren oder diese rahmenden Eigenschaften verwenden – wie dies die Hand, die die Kinoleinwand ausfüllt, in *Minute* tut –, um den größeren Raum dahinter anzudeuten.

Der filmische Aspekt von Floyers Werk ist auch die Grundlage ihrer Klangarbeiten, die vor allem auf synchretischem Klang basieren, das heißt »eine Konvergenz von Bedeutung, die nach Gestaltgesetzten und kontextuellen Festlegungen«, Klang und Gegenstand vereinen, ein von Michel Chion in seinem Buch *Audio-Vision* entwickeltes Konzept. »In Situationen, welche klare Erwartungen an den Klang erwecken – eine gehende Figur beispielsweise – kann man Synchrèse gar nicht vermeiden. Sie erlaubt, eine Geräuschsynchronität für diese Schritte mit so gut wie allem herzustellen – in *Mon oncle* vertonte Tati menschliche Schritte mit allen möglichen Gegenständen, darunter Tischtennisbälle und gläserne Objekte.« Floyers Klangarbeiten spielen fast immer mit diesen »Pawlow'schen« Effekten. Die undeutlichen aufsteigenden und absteigenden Klopfgeräusche, die man aus den Lautsprechern hört, aus
104 denen *Scale* besteht, lassen uns glauben, dass tatsächlich aufgenommen wurde, wie jemand eine Treppe hinaufsteigt. Die Lautsprecher klingen ganz unvermeidlich so, wie sie aussehen – wie Stufen, oder auch wie Tonleiterstufen.
38 Ein ähnlich willkürlicher Klang, der aus einem Eimer kommt *(Bucket)*, erweckt den Eindruck, dass Wasser hineintropft, obwohl das Geräusch keinerlei Verbindung zu Wasser hat. Das Geräusch des Grabens und von herunterfallender
26 Erde in *Working Title (Digging)*, abwechselnd aus zwei in einem bestimmten Abstand platzierten Lautsprechern zu hören, lässt uns glauben, jemand wäre tatsächlich beim Graben aufgenommen worden. In den oben erwähnten Videos *Monochrome Edit (White)* und *Monochrome Edit (Red)* wurden Autos mit nicht entsprechenden Farben herausgeschnitten, während der Klang ihres Heran- und Vorbeifahrens im Film zu hören ist und somit die akustischen Spuren der vorbeifahrenden Autos erhalten bleiben.

Diese Exkursionen in filmische Sprachen und Techniken sind keineswegs heroisch, und sie versuchen auch nicht, gewöhnliche Gegenstände über ihre Alltäglichkeit hinaus zu erheben – ganz im Gegenteil. Über die italienischen Neorealisten schreibt Deleuze: »Das Reale wird zum Schauspiel oder wird spektakulär, es geht eine wirkliche Faszination von ihm aus […]. Das Alltägliche wird mit dem Spektakulären identifiziert […]«.

Zurück in der »white box« begegnen wir diesen Objekten, die uns vor ein paar Minuten noch verwirrt haben – aber jetzt sind es alte Freunde. Während wir Floyers Strategien immer besser verstehen, werden wir mutiger, sie zu interpretieren und Verbindungen herzustellen. So beispielsweise bei der Bohr-
86 maschine, die wir erneut auf dem Boden der Galerie liegen sehen: Es ist in der Tat die gewöhnlichste Maschine, die man im lokalen Baumarkt kaufen kann – und sie wurde tatsächlich genau dort erworben. Das Stromkabel schlängelt sich Richtung Wand, und der Stecker ist eingesteckt, allerdings direkt in die Wand – von einer Steckdose keine Spur. Der aufmerksame Betrachter wird verstehen, dass genau diese Bohrmaschine, mit genau dem Bohreinsatz, der jetzt darauf ist, verwendet wurde, um die Löcher in die Wand zu bohren.

In Arbeiten wie dieser befasst sich Floyer mit dem eigentlichen Wesen des Readymade, indem sie es mit seiner kulturellen Wahrnehmung verbindet – der jeweilige Betrachter sieht es als in seinem Lebensbereich wirklich gewöhnliches Objekt an, was oft übersehen wird. Wenn man über Readymades nachdenkt, kommt einem schnell Marcel Duchamp in den Sinn. Doch betrachten wir das noch einmal genauer: Welcher Nicht-Franzose, oder selbst welcher »urbane« Franzose des 21. Jahrhunderts, würde Duchamps *Flaschenständer* als ein Readymade erkennen? Wer hat denn je eines dieser Objekte herumstehen sehen, außer vielleicht im Museum? Wenn man nicht gerade ein französischer

Bauer ist, muss man zugeben, dass dieses Objekt ganz wie eine Skulptur aussieht und dass es nichts hat, was einem gefundenen Objekt ähnelt, ganz zu schweigen einem wirklich allgemein üblichen, ganz gewöhnlichen Objekt – es ist bestenfalls ein archäologisches Artefakt. Floyers präzise Methode, jede nur erdenkliche Arbeit *vor Ort* zu finden und wiederzuerschaffen, stellt hingegen sicher, dass der Readymade-Effekt vollkommen erhalten bleibt, und zwar überall und immer, weil sie versteht, dass das Wesen eines Readymade zeit- und ortsspezifisch ist und nie und nimmer universell. Tatsächlich müssen Ceal Floyers Readymades vor Ort gekauft werden; es müssen lokale Marken und Modelle sein – nichts Ungewöhnliches, was die Aura eines Kunstwerks haben könnte, nicht einmal ein importiertes Stück Hardware. Indem jegliche mögliche Besonderheit der Objekte heruntergespielt wird, drängt Floyer den Betrachter dazu, sich besondere Mühe zu geben, das Konzept der Arbeit zu verstehen.

Inzwischen sollte klar sein, dass die erwähnten Arbeiten an einer kompromisslosen Ortsspezifizität festhalten – und der Ort, der den Kontext der Installation
ausmacht, geht weit über den Ausstellungsraum hinaus und umfasst eben
alle lokalen kulturellen und auch technischen Aspekte. *Drill* beispielsweise *86*
wird nicht in einem Land gezeigt, in dem die Löcher in der Wand nicht mit der
ausgestellten Maschine gebohrt werden können (also in Ländern mit recht-
eckigen oder quadratischen Steckerkontakten wie den USA oder Großbritannien). Das bereits erwähnte Video *1–25* ändert sich je nach dem Land, in *66*
dem es gezeigt wird. In einer NTSC-Zone wie den USA lautet der Titel *1–24*,
und die Zahlen sind immer in der Landessprache ausgeschrieben. Die in der
Diaprojektion von *Light Switch* gezeigte Vorrichtung wird immer die sein, die *12*
in dem Land üblich ist, in dem die Arbeit gezeigt wird – deshalb enthält die
Werkliste zu Anfang dieses Buches mehrere Versionen und Reproduktionen,
denn diese wurden jeweils für spezifische Orte gemacht und können nirgend-
wo gezeigt werden, wo die üblichen Schalter nicht der Projektion ent-
sprechen.

Das Video *Ongoing Projection* ist ein gutes Beispiel für diese Art von kontex- *56*
tueller Hyperspezifizität. Die Aufnahme zeigt die leeren Seiten eines Notiz-
buchs, die langsam umblättern – in der »normalen« Richtung, also von rechts
nach links. Aber wenn die Arbeit in Israel gezeigt wird, ist es umgekehrt. Dies
wäre für Betrachter an anderen Orten der Welt »bemerkenswert«, aber in
einem Land, wo man von rechts nach links liest, fällt es gar nicht auf. Ebenso
muss eine so zentrale Arbeit wie *Monochrome Till Receipt (White)* für jeden *34*
Ort, an dem sie gezeigt wird, neu ausgeführt werden, lokale Produkte werden
neu in normalen lokalen Supermärkten zu aktuellen Preisen gekauft. Alles muss
auf dem neuesten Stand sein, sodass gar nicht erst der Verdacht aufkommen
kann, etwas könnte manipuliert sein oder etwas Außergewöhnliches würde ausgestellt. Erst wenn man die Suche nach außergewöhnlichen oder exzentrischen
Elementen aufgegeben hat, kann man als Betrachter in Ruhe versuchen, die
Bedeutung des Stücks Papier an der Wand zu verstehen.

Um das noch besser zu verstehen, müssen wir uns jetzt dem entscheidenden Element in allen Werken von Floyer zuwenden: dem Titel. Ja, es ist in der Tat ein »Kassenzettel« (»till receipt«) – aber das »(white)« ist der entscheidende Hinweis, dass wir genauer betrachten, was auf dem Zettel steht, und dann entdecken, dass alle gekauften Produkte makellos weiß sind. Dies bedeutet, die Künstlerin musste auf der Suche nach weißen Produkten Schachteln und Packungen öffnen, um sicherzustellen, dass der Inhalt weiß ist (man sieht beispielsweise nie Weißwein auf der Liste, denn der ist ja nicht wirklich weiß). Der »Weiß-auf-Weiß-auf-Weiß«-Ansatz (weiße Produkte auf weißem Papier an einer weißen Wand) könnte zu Assoziationen mit Malewitsch oder Ryman führen – und das ganz zu Recht. Aufmerksame Betrachter entdecken in der Reihenfolge der Waren (die sich von Version zu Version unterscheiden) eine Geschichte, die üblicherweise mit vielen (weißen) Nahrungsmitteln beginnt und mit Natron, Paracetamol und natürlich Toilettenpapier endet; manchmal stehen auf der Liste sogar Pflegeprodukte wie Zahnpasta und auch Schuhcreme und Tic Tacs. Wie ein Stillleben des Barock erzählen die Produkte, ausgestellt in der Reihenfolge, in der sie in die Kasse eingegeben wurden, unweigerlich eine Geschichte von unablässiger Völlerei und Konsum mit einem gelegentlichem Beiklang von Narzissmus und sozialer Unbeholfenheit. Die Geschichte entwickelt sich, während wir die Liste von oben nach unten lesen, wie ein Film. Der wohldurchdachte Prozess der Entstehung dieses Werks zeigt uns die wichtige Grenzlinie, die das orthodoxe Readymade von einem eigens geschaffenen oder manipulierten ortsbezogenen Objekt wie diesem trennt. Floyers künstlerische Vorgehensweise fluktuiert frei zwischen diesen Parametern.

Wie wir gesehen haben, ist der »filmische Raum« im Werk von Floyer ein Raum, der über den Bildrahmen hinausgeht, der unser Blickfeld verlässt, um weitere räumliche und kulturelle Dimensionen zu umfassen. Es ist das Wissen, dass wichtige Entwicklungen in der Arbeit außerhalb unseres visuellen Rahmens geschehen könnten, oder dass das, was wir sehen, nur ein Indikator, ein Fragment des Werkes ist, über das wir nachdenken. Obwohl wir von dem dreidimensionalen Objekt den Anstoß bekommen, verstehen und erfassen wir das eigentliche Kunstwerk doch erst im Laufe der Zeit und im Zusammenhang breiter gefasster kultureller Einflüsse. Wie Deleuze in seiner Analyse der Funktionsweise des Kinos schreibt: »Das Wesen einer Sache erscheint niemals zu Anfang, sondern im Verlauf ihrer Entwicklung, sobald ihre Kräfte sich gefestigt haben.« Ob zeitbasiert oder nicht, alle Werke von Floyer werden erst mit der Zeit erfasst, und so wird das Wesen eines Mediums beibehalten, bei dem die Dauer der Erzählung inhärent ist.

Wie schon zuvor angedeutet, stellt das Verständnis des Werktitels ein Schlüs-
86 selmoment dar. Der Titel der Arbeit *Drill* bezeichnet nicht nur die Maschine,
sondern auch die Aktivität, die zum Ausstellen notwendig ist – das Bohren
von Löchern in die Wand. Die Bedeutungen von Hauptwörtern und Verben
130 überschneiden sich oft, wie beispielsweise in dem Video *Drop*, wo das be-
vorstehende Tropfen eines Tropfens die Hauptfigur des Films ist (wenn es
104 nicht auf die Nerven des Betrachters anspielt). Dasselbe gilt für *Scale*, hier
verwandelt der Titel die Arbeit in ein identifizierbares Objekt und eine Einladung, den von ihm ausgehenden Klang zu interpretieren. *Minute* mit seinen monoton trommelnden Fingern sollte auch als »minute« (engl. für winzig) gelesen werden – ein riesiges Understatement, wenn es einen einfachen Film bezeichnet, der auf eine große Kinoleinwand projiziert wird. Wie *Drill* wird auch diese Arbeit nie an Orten gezeigt, wo der sprachliche Kontext ihres Titels nicht die richtigen Assoziationen zulässt. *Nine Yards* verweist auf eine typisch amerikanische Redensart mit ungewisser Etymologie, die so viel wie »alles, das Ganze« bedeutet, was an einem anderen Ort nicht zu verstehen ist.

Es gehört mit zu dieser Projektion auf Raum und Kultur im umfassenden Sinn, dass Ceal Floyers übliche Strategie ist, »leeren« Raum zu einem festen

Bestandteil der Arbeit zu machen. *Trash* beispielsweise projiziert das Symbol 80
eines Macintosh-Computer-Mülleimers in die untere rechte Ecke einer großen
leeren Wand, deren Proportion ungefähr der eines Computerbildschirms entspricht. *Overgrowth*, der bereits erwähnte theoretische Bonsai, erfordert einen 68
größeren Raum als den, der für den Projektor und das Bild benötigt wird. Der
Betrachter wird ermuntert, sich vorzustellen, der Baum werde immer größer,
während der Projektor im zur Verfügung stehenden Raum zurückfährt. *Long* 14
Distance (Diptych) benötigt ebenfalls einen enormen Raum, obwohl die Arbeit
von bescheidener Größe ist. Sie besteht aus zwei Diaprojektoren, die zwei
aneinanderstoßende Kreise auf eine entfernte Wand werfen. Der Abstand
zwischen Projektoren und Projektion ist Teil der Arbeit, und der Betrachter
kann nicht dazwischentreten. Eine Arbeit wie *100%* besteht aus zehn runden 96
Aufklebern, die auf die Wände im Raum verteilt sind; jeder von ihnen zeigt
»10%« des Werks; auf diese Weise wird der ganze Raum (oder der von der
Künstlerin ausgesuchte Teil davon) zum Kunstwerk erklärt.

Plumb Line hilft uns, Floyers Definition von Raum und Öffentlichkeit zu ver- 70
stehen. Die Arbeit besteht aus einem regulären Senkblei, das beim Bau dazu verwendet wird, völlig vertikale Wände zu errichten, also aus einem Gewicht und einer Schnur, die zweckfrei von der Decke hängen und nicht unbedingt in der Nähe einer Wand. Das Senkblei hängt eher in der Mitte eines Raums, oder, wie in der Hayward Gallery in London, in einem Treppenhaus. Die Funktion eines Senkbleis ist es, das Zentrum eines Raums zu markieren, aber in Floyers Version wird dieses Markierinstrument einem ganz spezifischen Ort zugewiesen, der nach variablen Parametern ausgesucht wird. So ist das Senkblei an der Kreuzung von zwei Diagonalen aufgehängt, die jeweils zwei Punkte im Raum verbinden, die von Floyer berechnet wurden, um die Größe der räumlichen Erstreckung einer vorgefundenen Situation anzugeben. Üblicherweise gehören dazu auch Bereiche außerhalb des Ausstellungsraums, was die merkwürdigen Positionen des Senkbleis erklärt.

Vom ersten, verwirrenden Eindruck beim Betreten des Ausstellungsraumes und durch die Betrachtung der Arbeiten und ihrer Verbindungen zur Sprache, zum Alltäglichen im jeweiligen kulturellen Kontext und zueinander gerät die Definition des Ausstellungsraumes als geweihter »Kunstraum« unter Druck und lässt ihn in die Kategorie des »espace quelconque« (des beliebigen Raums) fallen. Dieser vom Anthropologen Pascal Auger geprägte Begriff bezeichnet normalerweise Durchgangsorte wie eine U-Bahnstation, ein Wartezimmer beim Arzt oder ein Flughafenterminal: Zwischen den »wichtigen« Orten sind dies die anonymen Orte, die Menschen passieren. Für Deleuze ist dieser »espace quelconque« allerdings gerade eine Bedingung für das Entstehen von Einzigartigkeit und Besonderheiten. Er funktioniert auf ganz ähnliche Weise wie der Zeit-Bild-Film: Er versetzt die Identität der Figuren, die Handlung – und in unserem Falle die Kunstwerke – in einen Zustand der Krise. »Ein beliebiger Raum ist keine abstrakte Universalie jenseits von Zeit und Raum«, schreibt Deleuze. »Es ist ein einzelner, einzigartiger Raum, der nur die Homogenität eingebüßt hat, das heißt das Prinzip seiner metrischen Verhältnisse oder des Zusammenhalts seiner Teile, so dass eine unendliche Vielfalt von Anschlüssen möglich wird. Es ist ein Raum virtueller Verbindung, der als ein bloßer Ort des Möglichen gefasst wird.«

Bevor wir allerdings Pascal Augers Definition des beliebigen Raums mit der Deleuzes überschreiben, wäre Augers Beobachtung zu erwähnen, dass in solchen Räumen Individuen entpersönlicht werden. Niemand beachtet oder interessiert sich für andere. Selbst wenn ein beliebiger Raum überfüllt ist, ist doch jeder darin allein. Aus diesem Grund argumentiert Auger, ein »beliebiger Raum« sei ein homogener, entindividualisierender Raum. Es könnte sich als lohnend erweisen, auch den Ausstellungsraum auf diese Weise neu zu denken: Als einen Raum, in dem wir uns schweigend und rituell bewegen und benehmen. Wenn wir eine Ausstellung von Ceal Floyer betrachten, sind wir involviert und verlieren irgendwie unsere Individualität, denn wir werden ein integraler Teil der Installation und der konzeptuellen Prozesse, die ihre Arbeiten verlangen.

Eine Arbeit, die Floyers Beziehung zum Ausstellungsraum als Transitraum für Objekte und auch Betrachter vielleicht am besten definiert, ist *Untitled*
16 *Installation (Dotted Line)*. Eine mit einer Schablone aufgetragene gestrichelte Linie verläuft entlang aller Wände, Stufen und anderer Bestandteile der Architektur des Ausstellungsraums. Wir kennen diese gestrichelten Linie als ein weiteres archetypisches Zeichen aus Spielen, es besagt, »entlang der gestrichelten Linie schneiden oder falten«. In unserem Fall allerdings definiert sie den Ausstellungsraum als eine Arena, als eine alles definierende Umgebung. Diese Linie unterstreicht die Einheit der Installation – obgleich sie unterschiedliche Arbeiten umfasst –, während sie gleichzeitig die Ausstellung mit der Sprache des Spiels verbindet. Die gestrichelte Linie verwandelt die Wände in Papier, den Raum in ein Konzept, und die ganze Welt in einen Spielplatz. Irgendwo »entlang der Linie« der Installation werden Betrachter zwischen den anderen Werken einen Sockel mit einem Diabetrachter entdecken, der eine vergrößerte Schere zeigt. Es wird wahrscheinlich eine Weile dauern, bis dem Betrachter klar wird, dass dieses Objekt zur gestrichelten Linie gehört. Letztere könnte man schon wieder vergessen oder gar nicht wahrgenommen haben, während man sich auf andere Arbeiten konzentrierte. Aber dann kommt wie üblich der Titel – in diesem Falle in der Nähe der Schere –, und indem er auf die gestrichelte Linie verweist, erklärt er dieses merkwürdige Detail, das sich durch den gesamten Ausstellungsraum zieht. Der Verweis »Mach es selbst« verbindet den gesamten Raum, indem er uns veranlasst, uns vorzustellen, dass die Wände des Ausstellungsraums (der ja schließlich auch nur ein weiterer »beliebiger Raum« ist) zusammenbrechen, und versetzt die Kunstwerke wieder an ihren ursprünglichen Ort – die Straße.

Am Ende des Ausstellungsbesuchs hat man das Gefühl, dass das, was einen zu Beginn verdutzt oder irritiert hat, tatsächlich ein sorgfältig orchestriertes »Konzert« von Werken, ihrer Beziehungen untereinander und ihrer Beziehungen zu Räumen und Bedeutungen ist.

Einige Zitate in diesem Essay wurden deutschen Übersetzungen entnommen:
Michel Chion, *Audio-Vision. Ton und Bild im Kino*, übers. von Alexandra Fuchs, Berlin: Schiene und Schoen, 2012, S. 58; Gilles Deleuze, *Das Zeit-Bild. Kino 2*, übers. von Klaus Englert, 2. Aufl., Frankfurt am Main: Suhrkamp 1999, S. 16 (über die italienischen Neorealisten); Gilles Deleuze, *Das Bewegungs-Bild. Kino 1*, übers. von Ulrike Bokelman, Frankfurt am Main: Suhrkamp 1996, S. 15 (zur Funktionsweise des Kinos) und S. 153 (zum beliebigen Raum).

BIOGRAPHY
BIOGRAFIE

Ceal Floyer was born in 1968. From 1991 until 1994 she studied at Goldsmiths, University of London. Floyer lives and works in Berlin. / Ceal Floyer wurde 1968 geboren. Von 1991 bis 1994 studierte sie am Goldsmiths, University of London. Floyer lebt und arbeitet in Berlin.

AWARDS AND NOMINATIONS
PREISE UND NOMINIERUNGEN

1997
Philip Morris scholarship, Künstlerhaus Bethanien, Berlin

2002
The Paul Hamlyn Award

2005
Bremerhaven-Stipendium, a working grant sponsored by the association Kunst und Nutzen in Bremerhaven, Germany

2007
Preis der Nationalgalerie für junge Kunst, Berlin

2009
Nam June Paik Art Center Prize, Nam June Paik Art Center, Gyeonggi-do, South Korea

The exhibition history and bibliography are based on archival information gathered by Esther Schipper, Berlin, Lisson Gallery, London, and 303 Gallery, New York. / Ausstellungsgeschichte und Bibliografie basieren auf Archivinformationen, zusammengestellt von Esther Schipper, Berlin, Lisson Gallery, London und 303 Gallery, New York.

EXHIBITIONS
AUSSTELLUNGEN

SOLO EXHIBITIONS
EINZELAUSSTELLUNGEN

1995
Picture Gallery, Science Museum, London

1996
Gavin Brown's Enterprise, New York
Anthony Wilkinson Fine Art, London
Tramway Project Room, Glasgow
Galleria Primo Piano, Rome (part of *Artisti Britannici a Roma*)

1997
Galleria Primo Piano, Rome
Lisson Gallery, London
Herzliya Museum of Art, Tel Aviv
City Racing, London
Galleria Gianluca Collica, Catania, Sicily

1998
Künstlerhaus Bethanien, Berlin (cat.)

1999
Kunsthalle Bern (cat.)
Casey Kaplan, New York

2000
Pinksummer, Genoa

2001
Ceal Floyer / Matrix 192: 37´ 4´´, UC Berkeley Art Museum and Pacific Film Archive, Berkeley
Massive Reduction, PEER, Shoreditch Town Hall, London
Inova (Institute of Visual Arts), Milwaukee
Ikon Gallery, Birmingham (cat.)

2002
Pinksummer, Genoa
Index, The Swedish Contemporary Art Foundation, Stockholm
X-rummet, Statens Museum for Kunst, Copenhagen (cat.)
Lisson Gallery, London

2003
Peel, Portikus, Frankfurt am Main
Again, Casey Kaplan, New York

2004
Waterline, Art Unlimited, Basel
Kabinett für aktuelle Kunst, Bremerhaven

2005
Pinksummer, Genoa
Contemporary Art Gallery, Vancouver
Esther Schipper, Berlin

2006
Safn, Reykjavik
Swiss Institute, New York
Lisson Gallery, London
303 Gallery, New York

2007
Kabinett für aktuelle Kunst, Bremerhaven
'Til I Get it Right, Rochester Art Center, New York
Museum Haus Esters, Krefeld (cat.)
Domaine de Kerguéhennec, Bignan
Centre d'Art Santa Monica, Barcelona

2008
Madre · Museo d'arte contemporanea Donnaregina, Naples
Esther Schipper, Berlin

2009
Billboard for Edinburgh, Ingleby Gallery, Edinburgh
Gakona, Palais de Tokyo, Paris
303 Gallery, New York
show, KW Institute for Contemporary Art, Berlin

2010
Auto Focus, Museum of Contemporary Art North Miami
Lisson Gallery, London

2011
303 Gallery, New York
Esther Schipper, Berlin
DHC / ART Foundation for Contemporary Art, Montreal
Works on Paper, Center for Contemporary Art, Tel Aviv
Things, Project Arts Centre, Dublin

2013
Kölnischer Kunstverein, Cologne
Darkning, Art Unlimited, Basel
Kabinett für aktuelle Kunst, Bremerhaven

2014
Lisson Gallery, Milan
Museion, Bolzano
Paper Work (with Karin Sander), Esther Schipper, Berlin

GROUP EXHIBITIONS
GRUPPENAUSSTELLUNGEN

1992
Hit & Run, Tufton Street, London

1993
Fast Surface, Chisenhale Gallery, London
Good Work, Bonington Gallery, Nottingham
Eye Witness, Endeavour House, London
Infanta of Castile, Goldhawk Road, London

1994
The City of Dreadful Night, Atlantis Lower Gallery, London
Making Mischief, St. James' Street, London
Fast Forward, Institute of Contemporary Art, London

1995
Five Artists, Frith Street Gallery, London
British Art Show 4, Manchester / Edinburgh / Cardiff (cat.)
4th Istanbul Biennale, Istanbul (cat.)
Just Do It, Cubitt Gallery, London
General Release: Young British Artists at Scuola di San Pasquale, Venice Biennale
Freddy Contreras / Ceal Floyer, The Showroom, London

1996
Viper, Bank TV, London & Manchester
A4 Favours, Three Month Gallery, Liverpool
Version 2.2, Saint-Gervais Genève, Geneva
Oporto Festival of Contemporary Art, Portugal
Kiss This, Focal Point Gallery, Southend
Life / Live, Musée d'Art Moderne de la Ville de Paris / Centro Cultural de Belém, Lisbon (cat.)

1997
Not Yet Titled, 7 Alexandra Mansions, Norwich
Pictura Britannica, Museum of Contemporary Art, Sydney / Art Gallery of South Australia, Adelaide / City Gallery, Wellington
Projects, Irish Museum of Modern Art, Dublin
Material Culture: The Object in British Art in the 80s and 90s, Hayward Gallery, London
I Luoghi Ritrovati, Centro Civico Per L'Arte Contemporanea La Grancia, Serre di Rapolano
You Are Here, Royal College of Art, London
Belladonna: A Selection, The Minories, Colchester
Urban Legends – London, Staatliche Kunsthalle Baden-Baden (cat.)
Sentimental Education, Cabinet Gallery, London
Treasure Island, Centro de Arte Moderna – Calouste Gulbenkian Foundation, Lisbon
Belladonna, Institute of Contemporary Art, London
Snowflakes Falling on the International Dateline, Casco, Utrecht
Light, Richard Salmon Fine Art, London / Spacex, Exeter

1998
Richard Wentworth & Ceal Floyer, Galería Carlos Poy, Barcelona
Minimalismus, Akademie der Künste, Berlin
Thinking Aloud, South Bank Centre touring exhibition: Kettles Yard, Cambridge / Cornerhouse, Manchester / Camden Arts Centre, London
Triennale der Kleinplastik, Stuttgart (cat.)
Malos Habitos, Soledad Lorenzo, Madrid (cat.)
Every Day, 11th Biennale of Sydney
New Art from Britain, Kunstraum Innsbruck, Innsbruck
In the Meantime, Galería Estrany-De la Mota, Barcelona
Then and Now, Lisson Gallery, London
Recent British Art at Kunstraum, Kunstraum Innsbruck
Drawing Itself, London Institute Gallery, London
Real / Life – New British Art 1998–1999, Japanese touring exhibition: Tochigi / Fukuoka / Hiroshima / Tokyo / Ashiya
Seamless, De Appel Foundation, Amsterdam (cat.)
Sunday, Cabinet Gallery, London
Dimensions Variable, British Council touring exhibition: Museum Ludwig, Cologne / Museum of Contemporary Art, Budapest (cat.)
Martin Creed, Ceal Floyer, John Frankland, Delfina Studios, London
Genius Loci, Kunsthalle Bern

1999
From Where to Here: Art from London, Göteborgs Konsthall
Trace, International Exhibition, Tate Gallery, Liverpool Biennial
Peace, Museum fur Gegenwartskunst, Zurich
Castello di Rivoli, Turin / Tramway, Glasgow (cat.)
Mirror's Edge, Bild Museet, Umeå / Vancouver Art Gallery
Luminous Mischief, Yokohama Portside Gallery, Kanagawa
This Other World of Ours, TV Gallery, Moscow
On Your Own Time, P.S.1 Contemporary Art Center, New York
Inside Out, Overgaden – Kulturministeriets Udstillingshus for Nutidig Kunst, Copenhagen
Richard Wentworth & Ceal Floyer, Galería Rafael Ortiz, Seville
Looking at Ourselves: Works by Women Artists from the Logan Collection, San Francisco Museum of Modern Art

2000
A Shot in the Head, Lisson Gallery, London
Film / Video Works, Lisson Gallery, London
Extra Ordinary, James Cohan Gallery, New York
Point of View – Works from a Private Collection, Richard Salmon Gallery, London
La répétition, la tête dans les nuages, Villa Arson, Nice
Making Time: Considering Time as a Material in Contemporary Video & Film, Palm Beach Institute of Contemporary Art, Florida
Drive, Govett-Brewster Art Gallery, New Plymouth
Pompeiorama, Casina Pompeiana, Naples
Quotidiana, Castello di Rivoli, Turin
Crossroads: Artists in Berlin, Communidad de Madrid
Edit, Badischer Kunstverein, Karlsruhe (cat.)
Action: We're Filming, Villa Arson, Nice (cat.)

2001
Loop – Alles auf Anfang, Kunsthalle der Hypo-Kulturstiftung, Munich (cat.)
Ingenting, Rooseum Center for Contemporary Art, Malmö
Passion, Galerie Ascan Crone, Hamburg & Berlin
Out of Bounds: Working Off Paper, Luckman Gallery, California State University, Los Angeles
Media Connection, Palazzo delle Esposizioni, Rome
Squatters #1, Witte de With Center for Contemporary Art, Rotterdam / Museu de Serralves, Porto
Nothing, Northern Gallery for Contemporary Art, Sunderland / Contemporary Arts Centre, Vilnius / Rooseum Center for Contemporary Art, Malmö
City Racing 1988–1998: A Partial Account, Institute of Contemporary Art, London

2002
Summer Cinema, Casey Kaplan Gallery, New York
40 Jahre: Fluxus und die Folgen, Kunstsommer Wiesbaden, Wiesbaden 2002
Loop: Back to the Beginning, Contemporary Arts Center, Cincinnati
Pot, The Liverpool Biennial of Contemporary Art, Liverpool (cat.) / Galeria Fortes Vilaça, São Paulo
Invitation, Museum für Moderne Kunst, Frankfurt am Main
Four Women and One Pregnant Man, Galleri MGM, Oslo
Tempo, The Museum of Modern Art, New York (cat.)
Liminal Space, Center for Curatorial Studies, Bard College, New York
Colour White, De La Warr Pavilion, Bexhill-on-Sea (cat.)
Sunday Afternoon, 303 Gallery, New York

2003
Centre Culturel Suisse, Paris / Museum am Ostwall, Dortmund
Lapdissolve, Casey Kaplan Gallery, New York
Band Wagon Jumping, Norwich Gallery, Norwich
Perfect Timeless Repetition, c/o Atle Gerhardsen, Berlin
Spiritus, Magasin 3, Stockholm

2004
Around The Corner, Cristina Guerra Contemporary Art, Lisbon (cat.)
The Stars Are So Big, the Earth Is So Small . . . Stay as You Are, Esther Schipper, Berlin
Umedalen Skulptur 2004, curated by Galleri Stefan Anderson, Umeå
(Dys)Function, Lunds Konsthall, Lund
9th Triennale Kleinplastik Fellbach, Fellbach
Schöner Wohnen, Be-Part, Platform voor actuele kunst, Waregem (cat.)
Five Billion Years, Swiss Institute, New York
Densité Plus ou Moins 0, Ecole Nationale Supérieure des Beaux-Arts, Paris / Fri-Art, Fribourg
Was ist in meiner Wohnung wenn ich nicht da bin?, Chodowieckistr 34, Berlin (cat.)

2005
Slide Show, Baltimore Museum of Art / Contemporary Arts Center Cincinnati / Brooklyn Museum of Art, New York (cat.)
Daumenkino: The Flip Book Show, Kunsthalle Düsseldorf (cat.)
Snow White and the Seven Dwarfs, Fundación Marcelino Botin, Santander (cat.)
What's New, Pussycat? Neuerwerbungen und Sammlung Ströher, Museum für Moderne Kunst, Frankfurt am Main (cat.)
The Stars Are So Big, the Earth Is So Small . . . Stay as You Are, Studio Manuela Klerkx, Milan
Light LAB: Alltägliche Kurzschlüsse, Museion, Bolzano (cat.)
Beauty So Difficult, Fondazione Stelline, Milan (cat.)
Material Matters, Herbert F. Johnson Museum of Art, Ithaca, New York
Eindhovenistanbul, Van Abbemuseum, Eindhoven
Not a Drop But the Fall, Künstlerhaus Bremen, Bremen (cat.)
Radio Kills The Video Stars / Side A, FRAC Champagne-Ardenne, Reims
36 x 27 x 10, White Cube, London / Palast der Republik, Berlin

2006
Lichtkunst aus Kunstlicht, Museum für Neue Kunst, Karlsruhe (cat.)
Reykjavik Arts Festival, Reykjavik
Wrong, Klosterfelde Linienstraße, Berlin
If It Didn't Exist You'd Have To Invent It: A Partial Showroom History, The Showroom, London
La Monnaie Vivante, CAC Brétigny, Brétigny-sur-Orge
Nothing, Schirn Kunsthalle Frankfurt, Frankfurt am Main (cat.)
Group Show, Galleri MGM, Oslo
The Known and The Unknown, Galleri Nicolai Wallner, Copenhagen
Just Another Kind Of Rendezvous, Künstlerhaus Bremen
Shanghai Biennial (cat.)
As If By Magic, Bethlehem Peace Centre
Nam June Paik Award 2006, Museum für Angewandte Kunst, Cologne (cat.)
5 Milliards d'Années, Palais de Tokyo, Paris
Artificial Light, Virginia Museum of Fine Arts, Richmond / Museum of Contemporary Art at the Goldman Warehouse, Miami
The Secret Theory Of Drawing, The Drawing Room, London
The Shadow, Palazzo delle Papesse Centro Arte Contemporanea, Siena
Seeing Double, Ramapo College of New Jersey, Mahwah
ON/OFF, FRAC Lorraine, Metz (cat.)
The Invisible Shadow, Museo de Arte Contemporánea, Vigo (cat.)

2007
Brave New Year, 303 Gallery, New York
Gb Agency, Paris
Landschaft (Entfernung), Württembergischer Kunstverein, Stuttgart
Design by Accident, Dover Publications, Inc., NY, 1968, Croy Nielsen, Berlin
New Acquisitions Show, Tate Modern, London
Draw, mima, Middlesbrough (cat.)
Half Square, Half Crazy, Villa Arson, Nice
The Art of Failure, Kunsthaus Baselland, Muttenz/Basel
Das Kapital: Blue Chips & Masterpieces, Museum für Moderne Kunst, Frankfurt am Main
The Invisible Show, Centro José Guerrero, Granada (cat.)
Made In Germany, Kestnergesellschaft, Hannover (cat.)
Silenzio: una Mostra da Ascoltare, Fondazione Sandretto Re Rebaudengo, Turin
13. International Project Space, Birmingham
Perspektive 07, Lenbachhaus, Munich
Preis der Nationalgalerie für Junge Kunst 2007, Hamburger Bahnhof – Museum für Gegenwart, Berlin (cat.)
For Sale, Cristina Guerra Contemporary Art, Lisbon
Artificial Light, Virginia Commonwealth University, Richmond, Virginia
Winter Palace, De Ateliers, Amsterdam
What You See Is What You Guess, FRAC Champagne-Ardenne, Reims
Ceal Floyer & Dan Flavin, Ingleby Gallery, Edinburgh
Twice Told Tales, Galerie Michel Rein, Paris
The Invisible Show, Center for Contemporary Art, Tel Aviv (cat.)

2008
Can Art Do More?, Art Focus5, Jerusalem
50 Moons of Saturn, Turin Triennial
Five Minutes Later, KW Institute for Contemporary Art, Berlin
Point of Origin, Artspace, Sydney
Reality Check, Statens Museum for Kunst, Copenhagen
Museum as Medium, Museo de Arte Contemporánea, Vigo
Above the Fold, Kunstmuseum Basel – Museum für Gegenwartskunst
Zweimal hat ihn niemand gesehen, Künstlerhaus Bremen
Now You See It, Aspen Art Museum

2009
I Repeat Myself When Under Stress, Museum of Contemporary Art Detroit
Desire Acquire, Galerie Bob van Orsouw, Zurich
Time Code, Dundee Contemporary Art
The Quick and the Dead, Walker Arts Center, Minneapolis
Nam June Paik Award, Nam June Paik Center, Gyeonggi-do, South Korea
STILL / MOVING / STILL, Cultuurcentrum Knokke-Heist

2010
Triumphant Carrot: The Persistence of Still Life, Contemporary Art Gallery, Vancouver
Shut Your Eyes in Order to See, Praz-Delavallade, Paris
Curious?, Kunst- und Ausstellungshalle der BRD, Bonn
Don't Look Now, Kunstmuseum Bern
High Ideals & Crazy Dreams, Galerie Vera Munro, Hamburg
Sphères 2010, Galleria Continua / Les Moulins, Paris

2011
Continuum – the Perception Zone, Tallinn Art Hall
Conceptual Tendencies 1960s to Today – Works from the Daimler Art Collection, Daimler Contemporary, Berlin
Color in Flux, Museum Weserburg, Bremen
About Painting, abc – art berlin contemporary
Wunder, Deichtorhallen, Hamburg
Humid But Cool, I Think, Taro Nasu Gallery, Tokyo
Void if Removed, Le Plateau, Paris
Mystics or Rationalists?, Ingleby Gallery, Edinburgh
Höhenrausch.2, Offenes Kulturhaus Oberösterreich, Linz
Open House, Singapore Biennale 2011

2012
The Same Thing But Different – On the Impossibility of Repetition, Andrae Kaufmann, Berlin
Au Lait!, La Maison de La vache qui rit, Lons-le-Saunier
La Nuit Blanche: Bodies and Buildings, Christina Ritchie, Toronto
Guangzhou Triennial, Guangdong Museum of Art
Wunder, Kunsthalle Krems
Kabinettstücke / Cabinet Pieces, Museum Weserburg, Bremen
Invisible: Art about the Unseen, 1957–2012, Hayward Gallery, London
A Drawing Show (curated by Dan Graham), Galerie Micheline Szwajcer
Explosion! Painting as Action, Moderna Museet, Stockholm
Manifesto Collage: About Change Collection Visits the Berlinische Galerie, Berlinische Galerie, Berlin
documenta 13, Kassel

2013
Whitechapel Gallery, London
Collection Sandretto Re Rebaudengo: Have You Seen Me Before?, Whitechapel Gallery, London
Reframing the Ordinary, Lothringer13_halle, Munich
Fail Better: Moving Images / Besser Scheitern: Film + Video, Hamburger Kunsthalle, Hamburg
The Light Show, Hayward Gallery, London

Fragile?, Isola di San Giorgio Maggiore, Venice
Open Spaces / Secret Places: Works From the Sammlung Verbund, Vertikale Galerie, Vienna
Rineke Dijkstra: The Krazy House, Museum für Moderne Kunst, Frankfurt am Main
Wall Works, Hamburger Bahnhof – Museum für Gegenwart, Berlin

2014
Light Show, Auckland Art Gallery
Visual Deception: Into the Future, The Bunkamura Museum of Art, Tokyo
Reinventing the Wheel: The Readymade Century, Monash University Museum of Art, Melbourne
The Event Sculpture, Henry Moore Institute, Leeds
Unendlicher Spass / Infinite Jest, Schirn Kunsthalle Frankfurt, Frankfurt am Main
I Don't Know Dem: Ceal Floyer, Halvor Rønning, Joakim Martinussen, Andy Boot, Spreez, Munich
The Part in the Story Where a Part Becomes a Part of Something Else, Witte de With Center for Contemporary Art, Rotterdam
Summer Exhibition, Royal Academy of Arts, London

2015
IN/VISIBLE, ikop, Eupen
Four Floors (part of the show *The Retraction of Things*, curated by Lukas Töpfer), KW Institute for Contemporary Art, Berlin
Dealing with Surfaces, Gesellschaft für aktuelle Kunst, Bremen
More Konzeption / Conception Now, Museum Morsbroich, Leverkusen
Visual Deception: Into the Future, Nagoya City Art Museum, Nagoya
Light Show, Hyogo Prefectural Museum of Art, Kobe
Light Show, Museum of Contemporary Art, Sydney
Poetic Minimalism, Salon Dahlmann, Berlin
So ein Ding muss ich auch haben: Neupräsentation der Sammlung, Lenbachhaus, Munich
Pequod: Esther Schipper and Johnen Galerie at 11 Columbia, 11 Columbia, Monaco
'Til I Get It Right, LABOR, Mexico City
Imaterialidade, SESC Belenzinho, São Paolo
Double Take, Nature Morte, New Delhi
Zehn Räume, drei Loggien und ein Saal, Sprengel Museum, Hannover (upcoming)

BIBLIOGRAPHY
BIBLIOGRAFIE

MONOGRAPHS
MONOGRAFIEN

Ceal Floyer, exh. cat. Künstlerhaus Bethanien, Berlin, 1997 (Floyer 1997).
Ceal Floyer, exh. cat. Kunsthalle Bern,1999 (Floyer 1999).
Ceal Floyer, exh. cat. Ikon Gallery, Birmingham, 2001 (Floyer 2001).
Ceal Floyer, exh. cat. X-rummet, Statens Museum for Kunst, Copenhagen, 2002 (Floyer 2002).
Ceal Floyer, exh. cat. The Contemporary Art Gallery, Vancouver, 2005 (Floyer 2005).
Ceal Floyer: Construction, exh. cat. Kunstmuseen Krefeld, 2007 (Floyer 2007).
Ceal Floyer, exh. cat. Madre · Museo d'arte contemporanea Donnaregina, Naples 2008 (Floyer 2008).
Ceal Floyer: Auto Focus, exh. cat. Museum of Contemporary Art, North Miami, 2010 (Floyer 2010).
Works on Paper, exh. cat. Center for Contemporary Art, Tel Aviv, 2011 (Floyer 2011).
Ceal Floyer, exh. cat. Kölnischer Kunstverein, 2013 (Floyer 2013).
Ceal Floyer, exh. cat. Museion Bolzano, 2014 (Floyer 2014).

SELECTED ARTICLES, ESSAYS, AND REVIEWS
ARTIKEL, AUFSÄTZE UND KRITIKEN (AUSWAHL)

Kyriacou, Sotiris, 'Ceal Floyer/Freddy Contreras', *Art Monthly* 187 (June 1995).
Barrett, David, 'Playing Dumb: David Barrett on Ceal Floyer', *Art Monthly* 193 (February 1996).
Muller, Brian, 'Ceal Floyer', *Flash Art* 194 (May–June 1997), p. 116.
Archer, Michael, 'Ceal Floyer, City Racing', *Art Monthly* 207 (June 1997), pp. 32–33.
Worsdale, Godfrey, 'Soundings: Ceal Floyer', *Artist's Newsletter* (June 1997), p. 25.
Muller, Brian, 'Ceal Floyer: Seeing the light', *Contemporary Visual Arts* 16 (1997), pp. 48–53.
Archer, Michael, 'Ceal Floyer', in: Floyer 1997, n.p.
Gohlke, Gerrit, 'Compression', in Floyer 1997, n.p.
Maite Lorés, 'Ceal Floyer: Contact Print 1–24', artist collaboration commissioned for *Contemporary Visual Arts* 21 (1998), pp. 66–68.
Fortnum, Rebecca, 'A Slight Intervention on the Work of Elizabeth Wright and Ceal Floyer', *Make* 83 (March 1999), pp. 26–27.
Ammann, René, 'Ceal Floyer', *Artforum International*, vol. 38, no. 1 (September 1999), p. 62.
Halle, Howard, 'Ceal Floyer', *Time Out New York* 210 (September 30–October 7, 1999).
Mac Giolla Leith, Caoimhin, 'Liverpool Biennal Of Contemporary Art', in: 'Best of the 90s', special issue, *Artforum International*, vol. 38, no. 4 (December 1999), p. 158.
Fibicher, Bernhard, 'Figures of Speech', in: Floyer 1999, n.p.
Blazwick, Iwona, 'Ceal Floyer', in: Floyer 1999, n.p.
Israel, Nico, 'Ceal Floyer – Casey Kaplan', *Artforum International*, vol. 38, no. 6 (February 2000), pp. 119–20.
Mathonnet, Phillipe, 'Avec trois fois rien, Ceal Floyer cherche à suggérer infiniment plus', *Le Temps*, November 3, 2000.
R.C., 'Ceal Floyer', *The Guardian Guide*, February 3, 2001.
Safe, Emma, 'Ceal Floyer', *Metro* (West Midlands), February 7, 2001.
Clark, Robert, 'Ceal Floyer', *The Guardian*, February 12, 2001.
McLaren, Duncan, 'How I Became a Mouse for a Moment and Joined an Artwork', *Independent on Sunday*, March 4, 2001.
Musgrave, David, 'Ceal Floyer', *Art Monthly* 244 (March 2001), pp. 45–46.
Lewisohn, Cedar, 'Ceal Floyer Ikon Gallery', *Flash Art* 217 (March–April 2001), pp. 116–17.
Mac Giolla Léith, Caoimhín, 'Ceal Floyer', *Artforum International*, vol. 39, no. 8 (April 2001), p. 150.
Esche, Charles, and Mark Lewis, *Afterall* 3 (2001), pp. 5–7.
Floyer, Ceal, 'Three Pages 2000', *Afterall* 3 (2001), pp. 104–06.
Safe, Emma, 'Ceal Floyer', *Contemporary Visual Arts* 34 (2001), p. 64.
Pollack, Maika, 'Ceal Floyer's Symbolic Loops – The Opposite of Sublime', in: 'The Magazine', special issue, *Loop* 3 (2001), p. 150.
Rosenberg, Angela, 'Ceal Floyer', *artist Kunstmagazin* 49 (2001), n.p.
Millar, Jeremy, 'Just Like That', in: Floyer 2001, pp. 17–33.
Lubbock, Tom, 'Ceal Floyer', *The Independent*, May 11, 2002.
Jones, Jonathan, 'Ceal Floyer', *The Guardian*, May 18, 2002.
Herbert, Martin, 'Ceal Floyer', *Time Out*, June 12, 2002.
Sumpter, Helen, 'Commercial Spaces: Ceal Floyer', *Hot Tickets*, June 14, 2002.
Chapman, Peter, 'Ceal Floyer', *The Independent*, June 15, 2002, p. 16.
Malvern, Jack, 'Empty Bin Bag Wins £30,000 Art Prize', *The Times*, October 18, 2002, p. 8.
Reynolds, Nigel, 'Art or rubbish? Bin Creator Scoops £30,000', *Daily Telegraph*, October 18, 2002, p. 10.
Stange, Raimar, 'Art Light – Über die ästhetischen Strategien von Ceal Floyer', *Kunst-Bulletin*, October 2002, pp. 34–39.
Torp, Marianne, 'Slapstick Semiotics: On Ceal Floyer's Work', in: Floyer 2002, pp. 4–25.
Rosenberg, Angela, 'Nocebo of Rationality', in: Floyer 2002, pp. 34–43.
Psibilskis, Liutauras, 'Ceal Floyer', *Artforum International*, vol. 41, no. 9 (May 2003), p. 181.
Hartlieb, Carola, 'Ceal Floyer und Spencer Finch im Frankfurter Portikus (08.11.–04.12.03)', http://www.art-in.de/incmu2.php?id=517, November 5, 2003.
Leach, Christin, 'Ceal Floyer and Darren Almond', *The Times*, January 25, 2004.
Scharrer, Eva, 'Ceal Floyer' (review), *Artforum International*, vol. 44, no. 2 (October 2005).
De Ruyter, Thibaut, 'Ceal Floyer – Galerie Esther Schipper', *artpress* 317 (November 2005).
Ritchie, Christina, 'Perfectly Logical', in: Floyer 2005, n.p.
Cambell-Johnston, Rachel, 'Ceal Floyer', *The Times*, January 3, 2006.
Eichler, Dominic, 'Ceal Floyer – Esther Schipper, Berlin, Germany', *Frieze* 96 (January–February 2006), p. 155.
Godfrey, Mark, 'Ceal Floyer', *Art Monthly* 296 (May 2006), p. 296.
Colin, Anna, 'Ceal Floyer, Récurrence et répétition', *art press 2*, no 2 (August–September –October 2006), pp. 95–97
Demos, T. J., 'Ceal Floyer – Lisson Gallery', *Artforum International*, vol. 45, no. 1 (September 2006), p. 393.
Hall, Emily, 'Ceal Floyer', *Artforum International*, vol. 45, no. 1 (September 2006).
Diaz, Eva, 'Ceal Floyer', *Modern Painters* (December 2006–January 2007).
Boucher, Brian, 'Ceal Floyer at the Swiss Institute', *Art in America* (January 2007).
Heydebreck, Amélie, 'Ceal Floyer', *Monopol* 1 (2007), p. 92.
Tilmann, Christina, 'Ceal Floyer', *Der Tagesspiegel*, September 14, 2007, p. 31.
Richter, Peter, 'Willkommen in dieser unbefriedigenden Situation' (review), *Frankfurter Allgemeine Zeitung*, September 14, 2007, p. 37.
'Ceal Floyer' (artist's statement), *Süddeutsche Zeitung Primetime*, September 26, 2007, p. 14.
Kuhn, Nicola, 'Klack, klack, klack', *Der Tagesspiegel*, September 29, 2007, p. 28.
'Sisyphos, verfremdet – Preis der Nationalgalerie an Ceal Floyer', *Frankfurter Allgemeine Zeitung*, September 29, 2007, p. 35.
Liebs, Holger, 'Gefühlige Schachtel – Preis der Nationalgalerie an Ceal Floyer verliehen', *Süddeutsche Zeitung*, September 29–30, 2007, p. 20.
Ruthe, Ingeborg, 'Ceal Floyer hoch oben auf ihrer Tonleiter', *Berliner Zeitung*, September 29–30, 2007, p. 31.
Lamm, April Elisabeth, 'Ceal Floyer', in: 'Im Auge des Betrachters', *Vanity Fair* (German edition) (September 2007), pp. 116–18.
Hilgenstock, Andrea, 'Magierin des Verborgenen', in: 'Preis der Nationalgalerie für junge Kunst', supplement, *Die Welt*, September 2007, p. WR3.

Weiss, Christina, 'Neue Sicht auf die Welt', in: 'Preis der Nationalgalerie für junge Kunst', *Die Welt*, supplement, September 2007, p. WR1.
Robecchi, Michele, 'National Galerie Prize for Young Art 2007', *Flash Art*, vol. 40, no. 257 (November–December 2007), p. 61.
Graham, Dan, 'Ceal Floyer', in: Catherine Sullivan, 'The Artists' Artists', *Artforum International*, vol. 46, no. 4 (December 2007), p. 122.
Bellenbaum, Rainer, 'Unter Preisverdacht: Über den "Preis der Freunde der Nationalgalerie" im Hamburger Bahnhof, Berlin', *Texte zur Kunst* (December 2007), pp. 229–32.
Martin, Sylvia, 'Ceal Floyer: Construction', in: Floyer 2007, pp. 10–41.
Blom, Ina, 'Ceal Floyers Kino ohne Film', in: Floyer 2007, pp. 42–55.
Basting, Barbara, 'Wenn der Lichtspalt unter einer Tür schon Kunst ist', *Tages-Anzeiger*, July 31, 2008, p. 43.
sba, 'Minimale Eingriffe', *Neue Zürcher Zeitung*, August 2, 2008, p. 46.
Schlaegel, Andreas, 'Ceal Floyer – Esther Schipper – Berlin', *Flash Art*, vol. 41, no. 263 (November–December 2008), p. 87.
Godfrey, Mark, 'Drain', in: Floyer 2008, pp. 11–43.
'Portfolio par / by Ceal Floyer', in: *Palais / 08* (Palais de Tokyo, spring 2009), pp. 28–41.
Buhr, Elke, 'Preview: Ein erster Blick auf Ceal Floyers Installationen', *Monopol* (August 2009), pp. 104–05.
Meixner, Christiane, 'Eine Frage der Anschauung – So simpel und dabei doch so komplex: Ceal Floyers minimalistische Arbeiten in den Berliner Kunstwerken', *Der Tagesspiegel*, August 24, 2009, http://www.tagesspiegel.de/kultur/ausstellungen-alt/minimalismus-eine-frage-der-anschauung/1586730.html, (accessed August 31, 2015).
Quin, John, 'Ceal Floyer – Show', *Art Review* (October 2009), p. 135.
Haase, Amine, 'Ceal Floyer: Show – In der Endlosschleife der Kunst', *Kunstforum* 199 (October–December 2009), pp. 264–67.
Pestana, Claudia, 'Ceal Floyer: Nothing to Look At . . . But Witnessing Works', in: *Nam June Paik Art Center Prize 2009*, exh. cat. Nam June Paik Art Center, Gyeonggi-do (South Korea), 2009, pp. 105–08.
Clearwater, Bonnie, 'Ceal Floyer: Auto Focus', in: Floyer 2010, n.p.
Pohl, John, 'Looking beyond real life', *The Gazette*, February 25, 2011.
Lévy, Bernard, 'Ceal Floyer – Un peu d'attention, s'il vous plaît', *Vie des Arts* (Spring 2011), n.p.
Redgrave, Veronica, 'Ceal Floyer – A Look at Things', *Vie des Arts* (Spring 2011), n.p.
Prince, Mark, 'Ceal Floyer - Lisson', *Art in America* (April 2011), pp. 134ff.
Roubert, Chloé, 'Ceal Floyer – Montreal DHC / ART Foundation for Contemporary Art', *Canadian Art* (Summer 2011), n.p.
Valcourt, Tracy, 'Ceal Floyer', *Border-Crossings* (June–August 2011), n.p.
Ackermann, Tim, 'Kein Fehler im System', *Welt am Sonntag*, August 14, 2011, p. 46.
Campbell, James D., 'Ceal Floyer – DHC / ART, Montreal, Canada', *Frieze* 141 (September 2011).
Stange, Raimar, 'Ceal Floyer', *Art Review* 53 (October 2011), p. 148.
Edelsztein, Sergio, 'Ceal Floyer: The Prosaics and Poetics of Paper', in: Floyer 2011, pp. 26–22.
Kohler, Michael, 'Doppelter Boden des Offensichtlichen', *Kölner Stadt-Anzeiger*, September 5, 2013, p. 25.
Wirth, Heidrun, 'Urenkelin des Dada', *Kölner Kultur*, September 5, 2013, p. 10.
Wessler, Moritz, 'Ceal Floyer im Kölnischen Kunstverein', in: Floyer 2013, pp. 4–12.
Mac Giolla Léith, Caoimhin, 'Warnzeichen', in: Floyer 2013, pp. 16–28.
'Überfluss an Licht', *Die neue Südtiroler Tageszeitung*, http://www.tageszeitung.it/2014/01/31/ueberfluss-an-licht/ January 31, 2014.
Schwarzer, Heinrich, 'Belichtetes Licht', *Die neue Südtiroler Tageszeitung*, February 14, 2014, http://www.tageszeitung.it/2014/02/14/belichtetes-licht/ (accessed August 31, 2015).
Crasemann, Lena, 'Ceal Floyer: Was es scheint und was es ist', in: *Künstler, Kritisches Lexikon der Gegenwartskunst*, vol. 2, 2014.
Ragalia, Letizia, 'The "gaze" of Ceal Floyer at Museion', in: Floyer 2014, pp. 10–21.
Edelsztein, Sergio, 'Ceal Floyer's Works at an Exhibition', in: Floyer 2014, pp. 36–59.
Ritchie, Christina, 'How To Be Ceal Floyer', in: Floyer 2014, pp. 76–93.

INTERVIEWS

Watkins, Jonathan, 'Have Trojan Horse, Will Travel: A Conversation with Ceal Floyer', in: Floyer 2001, pp. 7–11.
Schreiber, Anne, 'Ohne Schnickschnack', Preis für Junge Kunst 07 – Künstlerinterview Ceal Floyer, www.artnet.de, September 20, 2007.
Codognato, Mario, 'Talking About Language: Interview with Ceal Floyer', in: Floyer 2008, pp. 47–57.
Lack, Jessica, 'Ceal Floyer – Genuine Reductionist', *Art World* 9 (February–March 2009), pp. 132–36.
Pestana Claudia, 'Ceal Floyer's Response: Reconstructed from an Interview Held on November 24, 2009', in: *Nam June Paik Art Center Prize 2009*, exh. cat. Nam June Paik Art Center, Gyeonggi-do (South Korea), 2009, pp. 101–04.

PREFACE

A Handbook on the work of an artist no longer unknown is long overdue. Until now there has not been a satisfactorily systematic investigation of her work. Since her graduation from Goldsmiths, University of London, in 1994, Ceal Floyer's intelligent and humorous works have enriched numerous large-scale exhibitions, including the Venice Biennale and Documenta. Her precise, bare-bones method of working, reminiscent of minimal and conceptual approaches, embraces the entire spectrum of media. In many cases, she merges the artistic with everyday themes and motifs—though essentially her work is about making detours towards the perception of apparent irrelevancies, which, in her hands, unfold an undetected force.

For the Kunstmuseum Bonn and the Aargauer Kunsthaus, Ceal Floyer conceived two individual exhibitions: each was realised in consideration of its particular location and with the help of Volker Adolphs and Stefan Gronert in Bonn, and Madeleine Schuppli and Nicole Rampa in Aarau. While the selection sometimes overlaps, the different context of each place informs our perception of the work. For both museums, which have previously collaborated on various projects, engagement with Ceal Floyer's work is a natural extension of having worked with artists who present new possibilities of seeing and thinking.

The publication at hand fulfils the need for a broad overview sparked by these site-specific exhibitions. It highlights sixty-three works selected by the artist herself and was produced in close collaboration with the artist, her studio team, the publication's editor, Susanne Küper, the Kunstmuseum Bonn, and the Aargauer Kunsthaus along with the galleries Esther Schipper, Berlin, Lisson Gallery, London, and 303 Gallery, New York.

Stephan Berg
Kunstmuseum Bonn

Madeleine Schuppli
Aargauer Kunsthaus, Aarau

VORWORT

A Handbook zu einer Künstlerin, die längst keine Unbekannte mehr ist, über deren Werk aber bislang kaum eine befriedigende, umfassende Untersuchung vorliegt, war überfällig. Seit ihrem Abschluss am Goldsmiths, University of London, 1994 hat Ceal Floyer zahlreiche große Ausstellungen – darunter die Biennale von Venedig oder die documenta – mit ihren intelligenten und humorvollen Arbeiten bereichert. Ihre präzise, auf das Notwendigste reduzierte, sowohl an minimalistische wie auch konzeptuelle Ansätze erinnernde Arbeitsweise umfasst das gesamte Spektrum der Medien. In vielen Fällen verschmilzt sie künstlerische und alltägliche Themen und Motive, wobei es wesentlich darum geht, die Wahrnehmung auf scheinbare Nebensächlichkeiten zu lenken, die unter ihrem Zugriff eine ungeahnte Brisanz entfalten.
Ceal Floyer hat für das Kunstmuseum Bonn und das Aargauer Kunsthaus jeweils eigene, auf die unterschiedliche räumliche Situation bezogene Ausstellungen konzipiert, die sie in Bonn mit Volker Adolphs und Stefan Gronert und in Aarau mit Madeleine Schuppli und Nicole Rampa realisiert hat. Es gibt zwar Überschneidungen bei der Auswahl der Werke, doch werden diese an einem anderen Ort und in einem anderen Zusammenhang anders wahrgenommen. Für beide Museen, die schon bei früheren Projekten kooperierten, steht das Engagement für das Werk von Ceal Floyer im Rahmen einer konsequenten Auseinandersetzung mit Künstlerinnen und Künstlern, die neue Möglichkeiten des Sehens und Denkens eröffnen.
Der sich gerade an der ortspezifischen Präsentation entzündende Wunsch nach einem breiteren Überblick wird durch die vorliegende Publikation nun erstmals befriedigt. Sie umfasst 63 von Ceal Floyer selbst ausgewählte Arbeiten und ist in enger Zusammenarbeit zwischen der Künstlerin, ihrem Atelierteam, der Herausgeberin Susanne Küper, dem Kunstmuseum Bonn und dem Aargauer Kunsthaus sowie den Galerien Esther Schipper, Berlin, Lisson Gallery, London, und 303 Gallery, New York entstanden.

Stephan Berg
Kunstmuseum Bonn

Madeleine Schuppli
Aargauer Kunsthaus, Aarau

SUSANNE KÜPER: HOW *CEAL FLOYER, A HANDBOOK* CAME INTO BEING, AND HOW TO USE IT

A Handbook documents sixty-three works selected by Ceal Floyer herself. Organised chronologically, it begins in 1992 with *Light Switch** and ends with *The Answer** from 2015. Floyer makes notable distinctions between media, whether projections, audio, video, or light installations, sculptures, audio sculptures, or works hung on the wall. Her selection covers all these categories, which are important to her, but the transition between them is made all the more fluid once these categories are propelled to the margins.

For Floyer, language is an important medium. English is her mother tongue—specifically British English. In her view, all other biographical details are marginal. Floyer takes nothing as it seems: instead, she turns meaning on its head, relegating the most obvious content to the wings.

The book begins with a comprehensive list of titles organised alphabetically. This list provides one with an idea of the scope of her oeuvre and moreover *12, 142
reveals just how many different versions there are of same works. Examples of this include *Light Switch* and *Monochrome Till Receipt (White)*: her works 12, 34
are never static but dependent on their respective linguistic and cultural contexts. The list itself reads like a poetic language-game.

The documentation of the sixty-three works is based on a targeted selection of installation views in conjunction with explanatory descriptions in English and German where needed. The explanatory texts concentrate on the facts, keeping the linguistic possibilities and differences of each language in mind. There are no literal translations. When no further explanation is needed—in either language—none is given.

Mark Godfrey (Senior Curator of International Art at Tate Modern, London) and Sergio Edelsztein (Director of the Center for Contemporary Art, Tel Aviv) have followed Ceal Floyer's work for many years. While Godfrey's text focuses on characteristics such as light, principles, and time, Edelsztein addresses the relationship between objects and space in Floyer's installations and exhibitions specifically. We learn that a *Tautological Circular Dot* is a 'tcd', and artist Tacita Dean explains exactly what that is in her thoughtful, humorous portrait of her friend. Dean underscores the precision of Floyer's work without neglecting its reverse, describing the artist's extremely simple yet highly accurate artistic transformation of complex ideas as a continual balancing act.

Indeed, Floyer works very precisely. However, her concepts are never rigid: they are in constant flux. Titles vary, for example, according to the length of wall on which the work is installed: Title *Variable (. . .)*. If one sees notebook 48
pages flipping by in the video *Ongoing Projection*, the direction of the turning 56
pages reverses as soon as the work is shown in a cultural setting where one reads from right to left, as Edelsztein points out in his essay. This way of working does not make documentation easy or easily systematic. For this reason, the *A Handbook* makes no claim to being definitive. It is rather a proposal, a means of documentation, a manual that invites entry into Floyer's way of working on any given page. Yvonne Quirmbach's clear layout and cover design speak for themselves.

As the book's editor, I visited Floyer's studio regularly and was able to experience her way of working and thinking at first hand. The book is the product of teamwork and grew out of a deep respect for the artist. I would like to thank Ceal for her trust in me, and for allowing me such an in-depth look into her practice. Mihaela Chiriac, Matti Isan Blind, and Luise Nagel have worked with the artist for a long time and are intimately familiar with her methods, enabling Ceal Floyer to tread an uncompromising path with a team that unfailingly supports her. *A Handbook* came about thanks to constructive cooperation with this team.

SUSANNE KÜPER: WIE *CEAL FLOYER, A HANDBOOK* ENTSTANDEN IST UND WIE MAN ES NUTZEN KANN

A Handbook dokumentiert 63 Werke von Ceal Floyer, die die Künstlerin selbst ausgewählt hat. Chronologisch geordnet, beginnt die Dokumentation 1992 mit *Light Switch** und endet mit *The Answer** von 2015. Floyer selbst unterscheidet im Wesentlichen zwischen Medien – seien es Projektionen, Installationen, installative Projektionen, Audio-, Video- oder Lichtinstallationen, Skulpturen, Audioskulpturen und Wandarbeiten. Ihre Werkauswahl deckt diese für sie wichtigen Kategorien repräsentativ ab, doch sobald die Kategorien an den Rand treten, werden die Übergänge zwischen den Werken fließend.

Für Floyer ist die Sprache ein wichtiges Medium. Englisch ist für sie »Muttersprache«, das britische Englisch ist ihr am nächsten. Weitere Informationen zu ihrer Biografie erscheinen ihr marginal. Floyer nimmt nichts, wie es zu sein
scheint, sondern arbeitet daran, Bedeutungen auf den Kopf zu stellen und
**12, 142* scheinbar eindeutige Inhalte zu verschieben.

Das Buch beginnt mit einer alphabetisch geordneten Liste der Titel aller
Arbeiten von Ceal Floyer. Sie vermittelt eine Vorstellung vom Umfang des
Gesamtwerks und zeigt gleichzeitig an, wie viele verschiedene Fassungen
12 es von einigen Arbeiten gibt. *Light Switch* oder *Monochrome Till Receipt*
34 *(White)* sind beispielhaft dafür, dass die von Floyer konzipierten Werke nie
statisch sind, sondern sich an ihren jeweiligen sprachlichen und kulturellen
Kontext anpassen. Die alphabetische Titelliste liest sich wie ein poetisches
Sprachspiel.

Die Dokumentation der 63 Werke stützt sich auf eine gezielte Auswahl von Abbildungen und Installationsansichten im Zusammenspiel mit den Werkinformationen und erläuternden englischen und deutschen Beschreibungen. Bei den auf Faktisches konzentrierten erläuternden Texten wurden die Möglichkeiten der jeweiligen Sprache genutzt und sprachliche Besonderheiten und Unterschiede beachtet, weshalb sich englische und deutsche Texte in vielen Fällen unterscheiden. Informationen in der jeweiligen Sprache werden nur dann gegeben, wenn sie notwendig erschienen, in einigen Fällen wurde bewusst ganz darauf verzichtet.

Mark Godfrey (Senior Curator International Art an der Tate Modern, London) und Sergio Edelsztein (Direktor des Center for Contemporary Art, Tel Aviv) verfolgen die Arbeit von Ceal Floyer schon seit vielen Jahren. Während Godfrey sich in seinem Text für dieses Handbuch auf solche Wesensmerkmale der Werke wie Licht, Zeit oder bestimmte Ordnungsprinzipien konzentriert, behandelt Edelsztein vor allem das Verhältnis von Werk und Raum in Floyers Installationen und Ausstellungen. »Tautological circular dot« ist ein »tcd«, und was das ist, beschreibt die Künstlerin Tacita Dean in dem feinfühligen und humorvollen Porträt ihrer Freundin. Dean unterstreicht die Präzision von Floyers künstlerischer Arbeit und lässt auch die Kehrseite davon nicht außer Acht, indem sie die möglichst einfache und präzise künstlerische Umsetzung von hochkomplexem Denken als permanente Gratwanderung beschreibt.

Floyer arbeitet sehr präzise, doch sind ihre Konzepte nie starr, sondern
ändern sich permanent. Beispielsweise variieren Titel abhängig von der Länge
48 einer Wand, auf der die Arbeit installiert ist: *Title Variable (…)*. Beim Blättern
56 eines Notizbuches in *Ongoing Projection* wechselt – wie Sergio Edelsztein in
seinem Essay anmerkt – die Richtung, in der sich die Seiten bewegen, sobald
die Arbeit in einem Kulturkreis gezeigt wird, in dem von rechts nach links
gelesen wird. Diese Arbeitsweise macht es nicht leicht, Floyers Werk systematisch zu ordnen und zu dokumentieren. Deshalb legt *A Handbook* auch

nichts endgültig fest und erhebt keinen Anspruch auf Vollständigkeit. Es ist im wörtlichen Sinn ein Handbuch, das zum Einstieg in das Werk an jeder beliebigen Stelle einlädt. Yvonne Quirmbachs klares Layout und das Buchcover sprechen für sich selbst.

Als Herausgeberin dieses Buchs war ich für ein Jahr regelmäßiger Gast in Floyers Atelier und konnte ihre Arbeitsweise und ihr Denken unmittelbar erleben. Das Buch ist das Ergebnis von Teamarbeit und einem tiefen Respekt für diese Künstlerin. Ich möchte mich an dieser Stelle bei Ceal für ihr Vertrauen bedanken und für die Möglichkeit, einen so tiefen Einblick in ihre Arbeitsweise zu bekommen. Mihaela Chiriac, Matti Isan Blind und Luise Nagel arbeiten seit langem mit der Künstlerin zusammen und sind mit ihrem Werk eng vertraut. Ceal Floyer geht einen kompromisslosen Weg in der Kunst – zusammen mit einem Team, das sie dabei zuverlässig unterstützt. *A Handbook* ist das Resultat der konstruktiven Zusammenarbeit mit diesem Team.

PHOTO CREDITS
FOTONACHWEIS

Augustin Ochsenreiter, courtesy: Museion, Bolzano *15, 19, 89, 103, 135 (top / oben), 137*
Andrea Rossetti, courtesy: Hamburger Bahnhof – Museum für Gegenwart, Berlin *17 (bottom right / unten rechts)*
Uwe Walther, courtesy: KW Institute for Contemporary Art, Berlin *17 (top and bottom left / oben und unten links), 73, 107 (top / oben), 113, 117*
Stefan Altenburger, courtesy: Kunstmuseum Basel – Museum für Gegenwartskunst *23, 39*
Dominic Uldry, courtesy: Kunsthalle Bern *25*
Daniel Malhão / Rosário Sousa, courtesy: Cristina Guerra Contemporary Art, Lisbon *27*
Courtesy: Lisson Gallery, London *29, 154 (bottom / unten)*
Axel Schneider, courtesy: MMK – Museum für Moderne Kunst, Frankfurt am Main *31*
Peppe Avallone, courtesy: Fondazione Donnaregina per le arti contemporanee, Naples *33, 49, 71*
© Tate, London 2015 *35*
Courtesy: Astrup Fearnley Museet and Collection Erling Kagge, Oslo *36*
Ilona Ripke, courtesy: Städtische Galerie im Lenbachhaus München – Dauerleihgabe Sammlung KiCo *37*
Gary Kirkham, Hugo Glendinning, courtesy: Ikon Gallery, Birmingham *41, 43, 150 (top / oben), 157 (bottom / unten)*
Steven Brooke, courtesy: Museum of Contemporary Art North Miami *45, 69*
John Berens, courtesy: 303 Gallery, New York *51, 119, 127 (bottom / unten)*
Courtesy: Esther Schipper, Berlin *52*
Sebastiano Pellion di Persano, courtesy: Esther Schipper, Berlin *53*
Uwe Zucchi, courtesy: picture alliance / dpa *55*
Courtesy: CCA – Center for Contemporary Art, Tel Aviv *57*
Andrea Rossetti, courtesy: Esther Schipper, Berlin *59, 125, 127 (top / oben), 129*
Ken Adlard, courtesy: Lisson Gallery, London *61, 91, 107 (bottom left and right / unten links und rechts), 121, 123, 133, 139, 141*
Amelie Proché, courtesy: Kölnischer Kunstverein, Cologne *63*
Courtesy: Index – The Swedish Contemporary Art Foundation, Stockholm *65*
Richard-Max Tremblay, courtesy: DHC/ART Foundation for Contemporary Art, Montreal *67, 95*
Roman März, courtesy: documenta 13, Kassel *75*
Carsten Eisfeld, courtesy: Esther Schipper, Berlin *79, 87, 99, 101, 109, 111*
Scott Massey, courtesy: CAG – Contemporary Art Gallery, Vancouver *81*
Courtesy: Esther Schipper, Berlin; Lisson Gallery, London; 303 Gallery, New York *83*
Dave Morgan, courtesy: Lisson Gallery, London *85, 156*
Courtesy: Humboldt Universität zu Berlin *93*
Moritz Wesseler, courtesy: Kabinett für aktuelle Kunst, Bremerhaven *97*
Jens Ziehe, courtesy: Hamburger Bahnhof – Museum für Gegenwart, Berlin *105*
André Morin, courtesy: Palais de Tokyo, Paris *115*
Courtesy: Gavin Brown's Enterprise, New York *151 (bottom / unten)*
Richard Salmon Fine Art, London *153 (bottom / unten)*
Jakob Skou-Hansen und Riccardo Buccarella, courtesy: X-Rummet, Copenhagen *157 (top / oben)*
Courtesy: Swiss Institute, New York *172*
Hugo Glendinning, courtesy: The Arts Council of England *173*

All others: / Alle anderen: copyright Ceal Floyer

THANKS
DANK

Ceal Floyer would like to thank her studio team for their longstanding and unfailing support of her work, in the first place: / Ceal Floyer möchte an erster Stelle ihrem Studioteam danken, das ihre Arbeit seit langem zuverlässig unterstützt:

Matti Isan Blind
Mihaela Chiriac
Luise Nagel

Ceal Floyer and Susanne Küper would like to extend a word of thanks to the people who participated in the development of this book: / Ceal Floyer und Susanne Küper danken allen, die an der Entstehung dieses Buches beteiligt waren:

Tacita Dean
Sergio Edelsztein
Mark Godfrey
for their thoughtful and insightful contributions / für ihre kenntnisreichen und einfühlsamen Beiträge

April Lamm
for her support with the documentation of works / für Ihre Unterstützung bei der Werkdokumentation

Yvonne Quirmbach
for the clear and convincing book design / für die klare und überzeugende Buchgestaltung

and / und
Hatje Cantz Verlag
for the constructive collaboration and for the thorough execution of the book / für die konstruktive Zusammenarbeit und die sorgfältige Produktion des Buchs

Ceal Floyer thanks especially the galleries that have represented her work for many years, Esther Schipper, Berlin, Lisson Gallery, London, and 303 Gallery, New York, and also initiated and supported the book project. By name she would like to thank: / Ceal Floyer dankt vor allem auch den Galerien Esther Schipper, Berlin, Lisson Gallery, London und 303 Gallery, New York, die sie seit langem vertreten und dieses Buchprojekt angestoßen und unterstützt haben. Sie möchte sich namentlich bedanken bei:

Kathryn Erdmann
Ruth Hogan
Kim Klehmet
Florian Lüdde
Esther Schipper
Erika Weiss
Florian Wojnar

Kunstmuseum Bonn and Aargauer Kunsthaus encouraged and supported the publication from the beginning. They will introduce *A Handbook* on the occasion of a solo exhibition. Ceal Floyer thanks the teams of both museums. Her special thanks go to: / Das Kunstmuseum Bonn und das Aargauer Kunsthaus haben die Publikation von Anfang an unterstützt und mitgetragen. Sie werden *A Handbook* im Rahmen einer Einzelausstellung vorstellen. Ceal Floyer dankt dem Team beider Museen. Vor allem gilt Ihr Dank:

Volker Adolphs
Stefan Gronert
Nicole Rampa
Madeleine Schuppli

Particular thanks go to / Besonderer Dank geht an:

René Arnold
Thomas Demand
James Floyer

This publication is the result of a collaboration between the Kunstmuseum Bonn, the Aargauer Kunsthaus, Aarau, Esther Schipper, Berlin, Lisson Gallery, London, and 303 Gallery, New York, in conjunction with the exhibition / Diese Publikation erscheint auf gemeinsame Initiative des Kunstmuseum Bonn, des Aargauer Kunsthauses, Aarau, Esther Schipper, Berlin, Lisson Gallery, London und 303 Gallery, New York anlässlich der Ausstellung

CEAL FLOYER

Kunstmuseum Bonn
October 29, 2015 – January 10, 2016 /
29. Oktober 2015 – 10. Januar 2016

Aargauer Kunsthaus, Aarau
January 30 – April 10, 2016 /
30. Januar – 10. April 2016

Editor / Herausgeberin:
Susanne Küper

Concept / Konzept:
Ceal Floyer, Susanne Küper

Documentation of works /
Werkdokumentationen:
Matti Isan Blind
Mihaela Chiriac
Ceal Floyer
Susanne Küper
April Lamm

Translations / Übersetzungen:
April Lamm
(German–English / Deutsch–Englisch)
Wilhelm Werthern
(English–German / Englisch–Deutsch)

Copyediting / Lektorat:
Nikki Columbus (Mark Godfrey, 'Drain')
Uta Hasekamp (German / Deutsch)
Irene Schaudies (English / Englisch)

Graphic design / Grafische Gestaltung:
Yvonne Quirmbach, Berlin

Typeface / Schrift:
Neue Helvetica

Project management / Projektmanagement:
Cassandra Edlefsen Lasch, Hatje Cantz

Production / Herstellung:
Anja Wolsfeld, Hatje Cantz

Reproductions / Reproduktionen:
perfect image, Ostfildern

Printing / Druck:
F&W Druck- und Mediencenter, Kienberg

Paper / Papier:
Symbol matt plus, 170 g/m²

Binding / Buchbinderei:
Verlagsbuchbinderei Karl Dieringer, Gerlingen

Published by / Erschienen im
Hatje Cantz Verlag
Zeppelinstrasse 32
73760 Ostfildern
Germany / Deutschland
Tel. +49 711 4405-200
Fax +49 711 4405-220
www.hatjecantz.com
A Ganske Publishing Group company
Ein Unternehmen der Ganske Verlagsgruppe

Hatje Cantz books are available internationally at selected bookstores. For more information about our distribution partners, please visit our website at www.hatjecantz.com.

ISBN 978-3-7757-4077-7

Printed in Germany

Kunstmuseum Bonn
Friedrich-Ebert-Allee 2
D-53113 Bonn
www.kunstmuseum-bonn.de

Director / Intendant:
Stephan Berg

Exhibition / Ausstellung:
Volker Adolphs, Stefan Gronert

Administration / Verwaltung:
Gabriele Kuhn, Vera Scheel

Registrar:
Barbara Weber

Press and public relations /
Presse- und Öffentlichkeitsarbeit:
Anne Fischer

Education / Bildung und Vermittlung:
Sabina Leßmann

Conservation / Restauratorische Betreuung:
Antje Janssen, Nicole Nowak

Heads of workshops / Leitung der Werkstätten:
Reinhard Behrenbeck, Martin Wolter

Exhibition technology / Ausstellungstechnik:
Josef Breuer, Eberhard Wagner

Aargauer Kunsthaus, Aarau
Aargauerplatz
CH-5001 Aarau
www.aargauerkunsthaus.ch

Director / Direktorin:
Madeleine Schuppli

Exhibition / Ausstellung:
Madeleine Schuppli

Curatorial assistant / Kuratorische Assistenz:
Nicole Rampa

Administration / Ausstellungssekretariat:
Verena Reisinger (Head / Leitung)
Deborah Müller

Communication, press, marketing /
Kommunikation, Medien, Marketing:
Filomena Colecchia, Saskia Werdmüller

Guided tours and events /
Führungen und Veranstaltungen:
Doris Huber

Education department / Kunstvermittlung:
Christin Bugarski (Head / Leitung)
Silja Burch (Deputy head / Stellv. Leitung)
Simone Flüeler (Assistant / Volontärin)
Lukas Veraguth (Trainee / Praktikant)

Exhibition installation / Ausstellungsaufbau:
David Blazquez (Head / Leitung)
Matthias Berger

Installation team / Aufbauteam:
Daniel Desborough, Tom Heinzer, Stefan Lenz,
Brigitte Plüss, Markus Scherer, Lukas Steiner

Building services / Haustechnik:
Arnold Glatthard

Visitor services /
Besucherdienst, Kasse, Empfang:
Daniela Stäuble (Head / Leitung),
Jeannette Hofmann, Ursula Hostettler,
Martina Nyffeler, Barbara Müller

Bookshop / Buchhandlung:
Helen Moser